"This book is a gem! With amazing intellectual erudition, practical insight, and wisdom, Henry Spaulding has shown himself to be one of our most able young theologians and ethicists. *Iconoclastic Sex is* timely, important, and deeply insightful."

—Andrew Root
Professor of youth and family ministry, Luther Seminary

"While Christian sexual ethics has occupied the attention of many Christian ethicists, the moral issue of human sex trafficking only recently has begun to be addressed by theologians. With Iconoclastic Sex, Henry Spaulding offers an imaginative and creative treatment of not only trafficking but sexual ethics itself. His genuine concern for the lived experiences of vulnerable persons is evident throughout its pages. I hope this book is read widely and stimulates further thought and action."

—Tobias Winright
Professor of moral theology, St. Patrick's Pontifical University

"Henry Spaulding's argument that sex is the same for both trafficking and purity culture is shockingly convincing. He sensitively and creatively shows the profound harm inflicted by rigid 'code ethics' while presenting an alternative that is at once moving, empowering, and life-giving."

—Craig Hovey
Professor of religion, Ashland University

"Tearing down cherished beliefs about purity, Henry Spaulding sets forth an unusual but compelling sexual ethic. Read this book and you will weep for what is lost and hope for what can yet be found. It is a fully human book, and no greater endorsement than that can be given."

—D. Stephen Long
Professor of ethics, Perkins School of Theology, Southern Methodist University

"There is an assumption at work in much of the anti-trafficking movement that our faith has adequately prepared us to engage in work with and in service of the sexually exploited and vulnerable. That assumption has led to a host of unintended consequences and has undermined much of our efforts. In *Iconoclastic Sex*, Henry Spaulding lays out a profound and transformative sexual ethic that is desperately needed for this work. I highly and passionately recommend it as a resource for the church."

—Greg Arthur
Co-director, Free The Girls

"Examining the failings of evangelical sexual ethics in light of sex trafficking is a bold and urgent need. Henry Spaulding reframes ethics appropriate to how purity codes map unhealthy patterns onto women and open further damage for survivors of trafficking. Through participation in God's reconciliation and entry into Christ's love, he opens new possibilities for mutuality and flourishing through practices of testimony and witness, as well as covenant, in Christian community."

—Nell Becker Sweeden
Associate professor of Christian theology, Nazarene Theological Seminary

"A strikingly original treatment of sexual ethics which uses as its points of departure what the author rather shockingly describes as the interrelated problems of sex trafficking and purity culture. The book engages and is haunted by dominant evangelicalism's failures while retrieving and creating a richer, distinctively Christian theological vision. Those who understand this book will be either outraged or appreciative. Count me in the latter camp."

—David P. Gushee
Distinguished university professor of Christian ethics, Mercer University

Iconoclastic Sex

Iconoclastic Sex

Christian Sexual Ethics and Human Trafficking

Henry Walter Spaulding III

CASCADE *Books* • Eugene, Oregon

ICONOCLASTIC SEX
Christian Sexual Ethics and Human Trafficking

Copyright © 2024 Henry Walter Spaulding III. All rights reserved. Except for brief quotations in critical publications or reviews, no part of this book may be reproduced in any manner without prior written permission from the publisher. Write: Permissions, Wipf and Stock Publishers, 199 W. 8th Ave., Suite 3, Eugene, OR 97401.

Cascade Books
An Imprint of Wipf and Stock Publishers
199 W. 8th Ave., Suite 3
Eugene, OR 97401

www.wipfandstock.com

PAPERBACK ISBN: 978-1-7252-8720-4
HARDCOVER ISBN: 978-1-7252-8721-1
EBOOK ISBN: 978-1-7252-8722-8

Cataloguing-in-Publication data:

Names: Spaulding, Henry Walter, III, author.

Title: Iconoclastic sex : Christian sexual ethics and human trafficking / Henry Walter Spaulding III.

Description: Eugene, OR: Cascade Books, 2024 | Includes bibliographical references and index.

Identifiers: ISBN 978-1-7252-8720-4 (paperback) | ISBN 978-1-7252-8721-1 (hardcover) | ISBN 978-1-7252-8722-8 (ebook)

Subjects: LCSH: Sexual ethics—Religious aspects—Christianity. | Human trafficking—United States. | Purity, Ritual—Christianity.

Classification: BT708 .S655 2024 (print) | BT708 (ebook)

To

Bobo, Darla, Stacy, and Tracy

Regina, Terry, Phoebe, and Twyla

Your stories matter and your voices matter.
Thank you for trusting me with them.

Table of Contents

Acknowledgments ix

Introduction: Christian Sexual Ethics and Human Trafficking 1

Chapter 1: On Trafficking and Purity 19

Chapter 2: Hearing from Survivors: Trafficking and Purity Codes 58

Chapter 3: Iconoclastic Bodies: Karl Barth and the Indicative of Reconciliation 80

Chapter 4: Iconoclastic Sex: Sexual Ethics from the Margins 103

Chapter 5: Love Never Fails: Provisional Sexual Ethics 148

Conclusion: Eschatology and Sexual Ethics 210

Bibliography 221

Name/Subject Index 231

Acknowledgments

As I write these words, the majority of the Western church enters the season of Lent, which is a time for reflection and confession. I admit that at the beginning of this text, I must do both. The first seeds of this book emerged from a lecture on sexual ethics in an introductory course on Christian ethics for master's students. The conversation that ensued led me to develop thoughts that I only intended to use in a lecture for that course. However, after much encouragement, I presented a few papers that became the proposal for the present work. To be clear, human trafficking did not feature prominently in the papers and presentations. However, due to the work of many excellent students (specifically, I would like to name Bailey Phillips and Micayla Wilson for their encouragement) and my sister Megan Burden, I became interested in how Christian ethics could best serve this population. Ethics never occurs in abstraction, but only in response to the lived experiences of people.

A book is not the labor of a single author, even if the book is written by one. I have many people to thank. First and foremost, I want to thank my parents Henry and Sharon Spaulding. My father is a theologian and before I entered grade school wrote a text on sexuality, his first, but not last, book. The words in that text were my first conversation partners on this topic. These are the first words of theology I remember reading: "The clear teaching of the Scriptures is that human sexuality is a gift from God."[1] I marked this passage, and it has guided my approach to this subject ever since. My father's scholarship and commitment to the Christian community has been and will always be a light to my path. At the time of submission of this text, he entered retirement, which is not an end of his vocation, but merely the next step. He and my mother's love has sustained me throughout my life. As in all things, thank you.

Second, I want to thank my wife, Michaela. My father dedicated his book on sexual ethics to my mother, and I intended to do the same. However,

---

1. Spaulding II, *Untangling the Sexual Revolution*, 38.

she graciously suggested that I dedicate the book to the study participants. This act illustrates her overwhelming kindness and selflessness and is one of the many reasons why I love her. The next one is for you, dear.

This book only exists because of the study contained within. I felt that anyone who writes about the issues covered here (e.g., trafficking, purity culture) should speak directly with those impacted by trafficking and purity culture. Therefore, when crafting the argument of this book for the proposal, I knew that I needed to interview survivors of trafficking and those who grew up under purity culture teachings. The pseudonyms of these participants appear in the dedication page of this book. I want to thank them again for participating in this study and pray that I represented their voices faithfully.

In addition to the direct participants, I cannot express my gratitude enough for the individuals who helped me craft the study. I am not an expert at qualitative research. However, my dear friend Dr. Brenita Nicholas-Edwards helped me every step of the way. Without her, there would be no book. In addition, I need to give a special thanks to Bailey Phillips, who conducted all of the interviews and recruited some of the participants, along with Emmalyn Jerome. I also want to give a special thank you to Aubrey Shaffer and Ben Slater for helping me code the research data.

The final group of people I want to thank for their help in the study are the individuals who financially contributed to my campaign that covered the costs of the money given to participants in the study as well as funding costs related to the study and the book. Many of these names are current or former students. This is a small gratitude for such a great gift. I want to thank: Matt and Miranda Musick, Henry and Sharon Spaulding, Mary Kate Corcoran, Taylor Hutchins, Martha Lowe, Brody Swisher, Allie Cacciola, Amanda Ballmer, Diana Champion, Alex McGilvery, Jon and Shannon Gerlach, Nathan Figueroa, Stephanie Lobdell, Rachel Conner, Michelle Leighty, Ben Brown, Josh Snook, Hunter Winey, Nathan Lahr, Scott Sharp, Grayson George, Brenita Nicholas-Edwards, Lauren Lain, Larry Ritterbeck, Elizabeth Heimbach and Joe Witosky, Macyn Siegenthaler, Joe Hurst, Savannah Sparks, Jackson Moody, and Michaela Bruce.

In addition to the study, I want to thank all of those individuals who offered valuable feedback on drafts of this book and the proposal chapters. Specifically, I want to thank Craig Hovey, a dear mentor and friend, and Henry Spaulding II, for reading the book in its entirety and giving me valuable feedback. I would like to thank Rodney Clapp as well for his hours on the text. There is no better editor to partner with on such a project. Special thanks also goes to Erin Dufault-Hunter, Amanda Montgomery, Greg Arthur, Stephanie Lobdell, Michaela Bruce, Bailey Phillips, Micayla Wilson,

Gavin Gortner, and Michael Rodden. I also thank my many students who endured my lectures on this topic and challenged me to articulate it well. I am, also, an ordained elder of the Church. Though in the pages of this text, I find myself somewhat critical of her, I nonetheless am committed to serving her. My love for the Church is evident in this work. I long only to call her to her best self and name her unique place in serving and solidarity among those caught in the web. It can be a place of healing or condemnation. I pray she chooses the former.

Finally, I want to thank the team at Cascade Books for their encouragement and help along the way. Specifically, I want to thank Rodney Clapp to whom I first pitched the book as well as Michael Thomson and Charlie Collier, who gave guidance and encouragement along the way. Lastly, I want to thank Heather Carraher, my typesetter, for her patience with me as I asked for edits.

I wrote this book over the course of several years and a great deal during the COVID-19 pandemic, political turmoil, and the continued legacy of racial injustice. I struggled writing this text for many reasons and the folder filled with unused materials, rewritten drafts, and even alternate versions of the book attest to my torment. The following pages represent, to the best of my ability, an honest look at the issues contained. Ultimately, I only hope the reader receives the book in the spirit I intend, as a search for a new way.

Hank Spaulding
Lent 2023

Introduction

Christian Sexual Ethics and Human Trafficking

INTRODUCTION: CHRISTIAN SEXUAL ETHICS IN A WORLD OF TRAFFICKING

WHEN ONE OPENS A book on Christian sexual ethics, one traditionally finds a detailed analysis of sexual relationships and their varying degrees of moral appropriateness. These books provide theological justifications for certain moral norms pulling from various sources such as Catholic moral teaching, Scripture, philosophical sources, scientific inquiry, and personal experience. These books' strengths lie in their certainty about the positions they propose and the trajectory upon which they send their readers.

The present work shares similarities with this approach but also departs significantly. Like these books, the present volume considers a variety of theological and philosophical sources to discuss various moral issues in sexual ethics. However, it is different because it starts from a particular place, human trafficking. Though this phenomenon is now in the mainstream of theological writing, especially among the activism of evangelical Christians, there does not yet exist a book-length treatment that attempts to reconfigure sexual ethics in light of the contemporary prevalence of trafficking in many communities today. That is because, for the most part, especially in the US domestic context, sexual ethics textbooks do not center the voices of those at the margins. Some books on sexual ethics address the correct ordering of the family and marriage but do not touch on the domestic and sexual abuse that cultivate atmospheres of violence toward women. Other books will talk about the joys of married sex or virginity but will leave out the rage this cultivates against women who have sex before marriage, leading to their expulsion from durable networks and possible reliance on survival sex. Still others will consider masturbation, contraceptive devices, and abortion but will not cover realities such as addiction and racism as significant indicators of trafficking.

To be clear, one still should reflect on the moral significance of marriage and contraceptives along with the other features of sexual ethics previously described. A lack of attention to trafficking does not disqualify one's work. However, a theme of *this* text is that sexual ethics operates under a profound privilege, namely that many authors *do not have to* consider the realities of trafficking as a central concern in *their* lives or the lives of their readers. The gap exists because trafficking lives behind a veil of invisibility due partially to its appearance as something else (i.e., a bad romantic relationship), a caricature (i.e., the addict, the "prostitute"), or the failure of the community to take responsibility for trafficking's presence.[1] Trafficking does not occur in a vacuum but rather requires group complicity in a system that keeps it invisible and pushes those trapped in its web further to the margin. The sexual ethics proposed here provides a theological lens through specific accompanying virtues and practices to defame the idols of sexual ethics that support that complicity. There are many aspects to anti-trafficking work, but communities must not forget the daily formations and moral codes that either position them to receive or reject people.

To combat the social exclusion of trafficking, the language of this book utilizes an ancient theological tradition of iconoclasm, though in a novel way to connect to other theological works. This use of iconoclasm reorients Christian sexual ethics back to the central indicatives of the gospel instead of privileged images and idols that hold it captive. Iconoclasm is the defamation of false images that present themselves as the fullness of the gospel story in order to open up creaturely realities to a transcendent source for transformation. Certain images hold us captive *disguised* as the presence of the holy. These images must be placed next to God in Christ so that the idols can fall. In the sexual ethics of the present work, iconoclasm proposes a rejection of achieved sanctity through purity codes in order to reclaim sexuality's sheer gift. As Natalie Carnes argues, the iconoclast dares to imagine themselves as a blasphemer and breaker of images.[2] I adopt this imagery because only through blaspheming the code fetish inherent in sex trafficking can a theologically rich practical reason serve Christian sexual ethics. Christian sexual ethics must expose the idols of code. Christ performs a breaking and blaspheming, as evidenced in the crucifixion and resurrection, which ushers in a profoundly new reality. As Carnes writes,

---

1. I do not use the term *prostitute* lightly, but rather only signify how the figure of the prostitute caricatures those caught in the web.

2. Carnes, *Image and Presence*, 10.

"The cross breaks brokenness by showing that brokenness—sin, violence, torture, death—cannot exclude God's presence."[3] The power of this revelation establishes a differing moral order, and it is noncompetitive and nonpossessive in that the cross represents the "ubiquity of the divine presence" in God's world.[4] No metric turns grace into a possession; thus, ethics cannot resemble a code that guarantees goodness. Grace appears to the believer, like the resurrection of Christ, as a stranger in the places where humanity neglects Christ, among the least of these (Matt 25:39–40) and is a free gift.[5] To be formed in the way of the cross involves entering this liminal space with the crucified Christ to take down those crucified from their crosses by freeing them from the vicious cycle of code fetishism and social exclusion. As such, *I argue for an iconoclastic sexual ethics that defames the sexual ethics based on codes and its accompanying images of purity and privilege to cultivate a new, just desire for the openness to receive the other (God and neighbor) from beyond themselves in all their sacredness, which contributes to their flourishing through solidarity and mutuality.*

An iconoclastic ethic gives a preferential option for those at the margin, not only those for whom sexual ethics occurs without coercive pressure. There is no perfect vessel imaged in the present account of ethics, but only the quest to live well within creation. Thus, there is grace in iconoclastic sex for each to know their dignity expressed in Christ's "being-for" each person, no matter their past or image. Iconoclasm empowers individuals to know this sacred thing to be true: Jesus loves me this I know, for the Bible tells me so. Sexual ethics, in its iconoclastic mood, cultivates and enacts a deep appreciation of Christ's love for creation and healthy outlets for sexuality. Iconoclasm, thus, defames all that stands in the way of this deep and abiding truth. Specifically, it is the work that defames images that too long sit unchecked and unquestioned as to their place in Christian teaching, to rob them of their power. Only when this is done can new ideas and ethical norms arise. When preparing a book on sexual ethics considering the reality of trafficking, such defaming must occur.

NAMING TRAFFICKING: THE DARK SIDE OF SEXUAL ETHICS

The first defamation comes by way of the treasured image of trafficking. For many individuals, the word *trafficking* summons images of the blockbuster

---

3. Carnes, *Image and Presence*, 88.
4. Carnes, *Image and Presence*, 88.
5. Carnes, *Image and Presence*, 137.

film *Taken,* starring Liam Neeson, who plays a former US government spy named Bryan Mills. In retirement, Mills attempts to reconnect with his daughter and estranged wife. After reluctantly agreeing to allow his daughter to attend a series of concerts with her friend (and roommate) in Europe, Mills receives a distressing call. While Mills helplessly listens, his daughter describes how several men have broken into their apartment. They abduct both young women, which leads Mills on an action-adventure trip of retribution culminating in the rescue of his daughter. This film brought the reality of trafficking once again into the mainstream consciousness, causing Christian and non-Christian anti-trafficking organizations to emerge in its wake. The abduction of white women by men of color for the purpose of sexual exploitation galvanized people into action, even if this was not the face of trafficking either globally or domestically.

The reality of trafficking emerges from a matrix of exclusion, poverty, racism, abuse, and addiction, not from abduction primarily. The leading cause of trafficking is vulnerability, but that vulnerability takes shape in various ways. No single story captures the fullness of the reality of trafficking, and it is shameful to perpetuate the story of *Taken* as the main or even primary structure of trafficking. In order to correct this, I provide three examples of trafficking that illuminate its true face.

Allison

Kimberly Mehlman-Orozco tells the story of a young girl named Allison. Allison was economically vulnerable and a runaway from the start.[6] Allison was not sold or given to someone to make money; she was alone and without a home. James, her trafficker, pulled up next to her in a blue Lincoln late one night with promises of clothes, food, water, and shelter.[7] Allison reluctantly got into the car and received a fast-food meal and some new clothes as James drove Allison to a nearby motel to attend a party.[8] Once they arrived, James introduced Allison to two older female sex workers whose feminine presence set Allison at ease.[9] As the night unfolded, James offered Allison drugs and alcohol to put her mind at ease. As Mehlman-Orozco recounts, Allison was encouraged to drink to feel included and assuage fears.[10] These events all occurred before the switch in the evening. Once Al-

---

6. Mehlman-Orozco, *Hidden in Plain Sight*, 5–6.
7. Mehlman-Orozco, *Hidden in Plain Sight*, 6.
8. Mehlman-Orozco, *Hidden in Plain Sight*, 6.
9. Mehlman-Orozco, *Hidden in Plain Sight*, 6.
10. Mehlman-Orozco, *Hidden in Plain Sight*, 6–7.

lison was intoxicated enough, with the aid of the two older sex workers, James sexually assaulted Allison to make her ready for sex work.[11] Though committing unspeakable violence, James would maintain the narrative that he loved Allison. Many women who experience trafficking in America are not abducted, as in *Taken*, but manipulated to believe their trafficker was their boyfriend.[12] This is the process of trauma bonding, where assault and addiction lead to a bond between the trafficker and the trafficked individual.[13] Even though this is trafficking, Allison understood her sex work as an act of love for her boyfriend and as her own choice.

Kelsey Collins

Like Allison, Seattle native Kelsey Collins provides another account of domestic trafficking arising from a romantic partnership. Unlike Allison, Kelsey was not a runaway and had a stable relationship with her mother. However, Kelsey's life begins with images of abuse and trauma. Kelsey's father was abusive to Kelsey, her mother, and her siblings. Kelsey's mom Susan was a geneticist at a local research hospital and ultimately fled with her children, but not before the environment of abuse left its mark.[14] Kelsey appeared unimpacted at first, with a high interest in school even though she struggled with a learning disability. When Kelsey reached puberty, she began acting out, and during this period, she began running into legal troubles. Eventually, at age sixteen Kelsey began dating an older man. Though hardened at this point due to criminal activity, Kelsey was still just a kid who would write her new boyfriend's name in "sparkly, blue glue" on posters to hang in her bedroom.[15] During this period, her boyfriend suggested she should sell her body for money. Though she was initially very resistant, something changed dramatically. The family noticed that in the time leading up to her sophomore year of high school, Kelsey would return home from her boyfriend with cuts and bruises.[16] At this point, family and experts think that Kelsey developed a trauma bond with her boyfriend. The abuse and violence from her boyfriend develop to such a degree that the victim of abuse adopts a warped understanding of protection and love when the abuser does *not* beat them. When abuse is withheld, the victim sees it

11. Mehlman-Orozco, *Hidden in Plain Sight*, 7.
12. Bernstein, *Brokered Subjects*, 115.
13. Mehlman-Orozco, *Hidden in Plain Sight*, 14.
14. Kelleher, "Teen Missing After Testimony Against Pimp."
15. Kelleher, "Teen Missing After Testimony Against Pimp."
16. Kelleher, "Teen Missing After Testimony Against Pimp."

as protection and a gift.[17] The complete trauma bond serves the end of the trafficker, who knows that if the victim loves him, she will not testify against him.

Through a long process, Kelsey eventually returns to her family and agrees to testify against her trafficker. However, the prosecutor fails to place Kelsey in witness protection, and ultimately she goes missing. Furthermore, when her mother places several missing person posters around her city, authorities ask her to take them down to not interfere with their investigation. Even more devastating for Susan is that the police refuse to search for Kelsey because, in their eyes, she is a criminal who ran from home. The failure is systemic and involves not just her father, law enforcement, and the men who bought her services, but an entire community.

The Sara Lawrence Dorm Dad

The last example is unique but illustrates another salient point about trafficking. The events described here occurred on the campus of Sarah Lawrence College in New York.[18] A group of students decided to rent a campus house to split the cost of living. One of the students, Talia Ray, tells many stories about her imprisoned father who heroically tried to save Talia from her abusive mother and received jail time because of her mother's lies. The father, Larry Ray, was abusive and manipulative to his family, convincing Talia from a young age that he was wrongfully accused. After his release from prison, Larry moved into his daughter's house with little to no protest from housemates or their parents. Larry began endearing himself to these students by making them expensive dinners and telling false stories about a long career working for the CIA. Larry became the confidant of the students in the house and, for many, like a second father.

Things took a turn for the worse when Larry offered to rent a condo closer to campus and let the students say there. During this period, Larry became more manipulative and coercive to the students. Larry already endeared himself to the students by serving as a "house dad" for the young women when they went through challenging coursework or break ups. However, he began controlling every aspect of each student's life, from eating to bedtimes. He even told Talia's boyfriend to stop taking his antipsychotic medication.[19] Slowly, Larry cultivated an atmosphere of control over every aspect of the environment. It was during this time that Larry began

---

17. Kelleher, "Teen Missing After Testimony Against Pimp."
18. For more on this story, see Marcus and Walsh, "Stolen Kids of Sarah Lawrence."
19. Marcus and Walsh, "Stolen Kids of Sarah Lawrence."

extorting the students for money. As Rob Frehse summarizes, "[Larry] extorted payments from victims after getting them to make false confessions about causing damages to him, his family, and associates, according to the indictment. Victims drained their parents' savings, opened credit lines, and sold real estate ownership to pay Ray."[20] However, this was not the only form of extortion and fraud. Larry began coercing all apartment members into forced labor and a few women into sex for sale. One woman, Claudia Drury, was told she contributed to damages at another of Larry's properties and owed him an exorbitant debt. Larry, threatening legal action, coerced Claudia into becoming an escort, selling herself for almost $10,000 an hour, with the profits going to Larry to cover her debt.

How did this happen? Larry slowly chipped away at the students' reality. He convinced them of false medical and psychological diagnoses and controlled every aspect of their lives, from food to sleep. However, Larry also was able to sever the relationship between these students and their families. Larry would often communicate on behalf of students to their parents about false reasons why the student would not be coming home for holidays or other get-togethers. This level of gaslighting, emotional manipulation, fraud, and social isolation led to the fraudulent coercion of Claudia and others into trafficking.

What, then, is trafficking?

These stories are all unique but present the different facets of trafficking. There is no single story of trafficking, but there is a matrix of themes. The themes that the reader needs to detect are domestic violence (sexual, emotional, and physical), social isolation, racism, addiction, failures of law enforcement, insecurity, and in many cases, the manipulation by a loved one. One should note the variety of people who find themselves in the web of trafficking (e.g., a runaway, a college student). This web names the constellation of issues that create conditions of trafficking in a way that accounts for the variety of experiences that lead to it. If there is a definition, we can appeal to the Trafficking Victims Violence Protection Act, which defines sex trafficking as a "commercial sex act induced by force, fraud, or coercion, or in which the person induced to perform such act has not attained 18 years of age."[21] These stories of trafficking help visualize the various manifestations of fraud, force, and coercion in two ways. First, the traditional approach to anti-trafficking work lies in law enforcement. Many assume better

20. Frehse, "Sarah Lawrence Father Trafficking Case."
21. "Trafficking Victims Violence Protection Act of 2000" (TVPA).

legislation and criminal prosecution will lead to a decrease in trafficking. As these stories illustrate, criminal approaches negatively impact the one who is trafficked and rarely traffickers. In addition, mistreatment at the hands of law enforcement, as indicated in the stories above, lead to a deep mistrust of law enforcement officials. Thus, a different approach should emerge in response to this failure that does not diminish the need for better laws but argues in favor of a more comprehensive approach.

Second, one should see the complete communal failure to support many of these women, including law enforcement and family. Ethics, especially sexual ethics, arise from relationality, so a relational breakdown is important to note in trafficking. Goodness is not an abstract concept, but the messy ways individuals orient toward one another. In these stories of trafficking, one witnesses a myriad of broken relationships. Kelsey's abuse caused immense trauma and pain that precedes her abuse, and the Sarah Lawrence students were defrauded into their own exploitation.

PURITY CULTURE: THE CREATION OF EXCLUSION AND VIOLENCE

How can Christian theology address this reality? More specifically, what role can Christian sexual ethics play in healing the brokenness of trafficking? A traditional teaching on purity culture, which at its heart asks young people to wait until marriage for sex, would seemingly solve trafficking according to its defenders if taken literally. However, as already articulated, trafficking does not occur in a vacuum but through a formation that occurs well before the instances of trafficking itself. To merely legislate, either morally or otherwise, against the manifestation of trafficking without looking at the undergirding moral factors that make it possible will not decrease its presence. In short, prescribing purity culture as an answer to human trafficking is the moral equivalent to shaming a gun shot victim for their wound. Thus, moral commands that merely legislate abstinence do not get at the cause. Sadly, like the law enforcement officials in Kelsey's story, the purity culture mentality only sees someone as unclean according to customs of sexual purity. Thus, a new moral imagination must emerge in response to the unique challenges raised by trafficking. Not only must this imagination continue an abolitionist strain in Christian moral thought, but it must also think critically about the small formations required to create communities that can resist the contributing factors of trafficking.

I argue that specific images of purity capture the imagination of much of popular Christian moral thinking, with some significant exceptions.[22] *By images, I mean ideal bodies and relationships that hijack the moral process by coding certain pre-moral assumptions into ethical practices that must exist before any moral discernment.* For example, the image of the "prostitute" sets certain permissions and responses before one ever hears the story of those caught in the web. These "code fetishes," as I will call them, turn ethics in general and sexual ethics in particular into practices of accumulation to gain access to acceptance into durable networks. Thus, purity culture and its accompanying images reveals itself to be implicated in the existence of trafficking.

Purity culture is an amalgamation of teachings originating in the evangelical church about sex that present a women's virginal body as possessing a "purity" that she must give to her husband on the night of their wedding. Purity codes, as a concept, originate theologically with the Levitical codes and in controversies such as the Donatist affair in the fourth and fifth centuries, but the purity code realism and purity culture of the twentieth century is unique. To be clear, other Christian traditions from mainline Protestants and even Roman Catholic churches utilize teachings similar to or duplicates of purity culture. However, the specific teaching around "purity" and sex emerge from a US Protestant, evangelical context and these images still dominate those communities.

Purity presents a gendered, theological base that creates a hierarchy between bodies that matter and bodies that do not. Female bodies without sexual experience far exceed those that possess sexual experience because purity is a possession lost with sexual activity. Men are not treated according to the same standard in purity culture but must "protect" women's purity, leading to a differing interaction with their sexual expression. In return, women hide their bodies and mind their personalities so as to not tempt men.

A recent manifesto by Linda Kay Klein explores the impact of purity culture teaching on families, especially young women. Klein's book, *Pure,* illustrates how purity culture participates in the same logic of trafficking that occurs within the church.[23] One woman's story, that of Rosemary, speaks directly to the themes raised in the stories of trafficking. At a young age, Rosemary discovered sexually explicit materials and quickly developed a porn addiction. During this period, her brother began making sexual advances on

---

22. For example, I highlight the work of Margret Farley, Karen Iyer-Peterson, Lisa Sowell Cahill, Lewis Smedes, and David Gushee as those searching for a better Christian sexual ethics. This work draws from and also depends on many of their insights.

23. Klein, *Pure*.

her. Upon her revealing her addiction and her brother's actions, Rosemary's parents sent her to counseling for porn addiction and told her brother to leave her alone. Like all communities of purity culture, Rosemary's family finds women's sexuality more dangerous than men's. Eventually, Rosemary's brother sexually assaulted her, and when her parents learned of the assault, they responded by blaming Rosemary without addressing her brother's behavior. Rosemary reflects on this in her purity culture context:

> The church views men as animals with no agency. The whole "as a girl it's your job to stop guys from doing stuff" line of thinking. So my parents treated my brother like he'd messed up but nothing more, and I felt really blamed. They acted like it was consensual, like it was sex. Sex is so penalized in evangelicalism, it's easier to chalk rape and abuse up to sex and be done with it. But I don't think what happened between me and my brother was sex at all. This was *abuse*.[24]

The way that the evangelical church presents sex impacts the broader church culture by declaring it dirty and bad. Rosemary's story illuminates that even in an instance of sexual assault, she was the one to blame. The abuse was not only permitted but encouraged by the permission given to her brother. Furthermore, Rosemary's sexuality was to blame, evidenced in her eventual expulsion from the home so as not to tempt her brother into further sexual activities.

The themes in Rosemary's story resemble those in the stories of trafficking. In her story, abuse and sexual violence were minimized and permitted in the context of a family relationship. Rosemary's parents gaslighted her into believing a different version of reality than the one that occurred. She was isolated and lacked stability in housing. A gendered hierarchy assumed that women's bodies were available to men. Lastly, the Christian community assumed the worst about Rosemary. The formation displayed in evangelicalism perpetuates trafficking. Thus, a sexual ethic formed around different patterns of behavior will address trafficking.

THE DEFAMING POWER OF THE GOSPEL

In order to focus the theological lens on the work that will emerge from this study, I appeal to a passage of Scripture (Acts 16:16–24) that speaks directly to the new kinds of postures necessary to confront trafficking and promote an ethical practice of sex. The passage comes near the middle of Acts as

---

24. Klein, *Pure*, 234.

Paul continues his mission to Greece and Macedonia. During this mission, Paul and Silas encounter a young slave woman who has a "spirit of divination." (vs. 16, NRSV) This woman shouted for many days that Paul and Silas were slaves, but of the Most High God (vs. 17). As the text indicates, Paul was very "annoyed" by this and rebuked the false spirit to come out of her (vs. 18, NRSV), then her owners immediately become enraged because their "hope of making money was gone" (vs. 19, NRSV). The owners then drag Paul and Silas into the marketplace, proclaiming that they are unlawful by advocating for false customs (vs. 20–21). As a result, Paul and Silas are thrown in prison and beaten for their disruption.

This passage can easily go unnoticed as it stands between the conversion of Lydia (Acts 16:11–15) and Paul's speech to the Athenians (Acts 17:16–34). However, Paul enlivens a new vision in this passage. The woman, identified as a slave girl, addresses Paul and Silas as fellow slaves, but as Willie James Jennings describes, she sees herself inside the apostles' speech.[25] She is enslaved, but she also understands herself to be spiritual. Her speech attempts to make the slaveries of herself and the apostles the same, but as Jennings argues, this "is a sick optic."[26] The religious understanding of her slavery is the authentication of her enslavement as a spiritual reality.

Too often, the church desires the spirituality of the slave girl, but Paul rejects it. In fact, he is annoyed by it. Paul's turning to the slave girl is a turning to her language of enslavement. In her proclamation of the disciple's work, she offers them a kind of praise. However, the disciples see through the praise to something else, namely a demonic spirit. The religion that arises from the demonic must be exorcised, and as such, Paul casts out the spirit that makes use of her agency.[27] The church must see beyond the pious talk of the slave girl because not all religious language leads to liberation. Similarly, the Christian community must become obsessed with hearing the voices of the free by challenging the voices that keep them oppressed.[28]

Exorcism and iconoclasm are the ways out for the slave girl. She needs freedom from the voices of oppression that use her agency and must find a new agency found in the testimony of the Spirit. Many women who experience trafficking and purity culture think of these voices as their own, uncoerced activity, but in this passage, Paul gives a language to untangle agency while still empowering agents. The way that events such as domestic violence are bound up in theological speech must be undone. Paul does

25. Jennings, *Acts*, 159.
26. Jennings, *Acts*, 159.
27. Jennings, *Acts*, 160.
28. Jennings, *Acts*, 160–61.

not merely subvert the demonic spirit posing as religious justification but defames it and the entire religiosity and piety that undergird it. The gospel respects no system of enslavement and frees the enslaved voices so that they might speak and join the voices of the community. As Jennings emphatically states, "Churches should long to hear freed voices and follow the Spirit in increasing their number."[29] Testimony, thus, is the response to the freedom that God gives. Each testimony expresses a new voice whose agency no longer serves the binding logic of an oppressive master. This freedom is the source of new moral activity and, thus the way out of the participation in trafficking articulated even inside Christian sexual ethics.

The shift in ethics does not come without a cost. Those who will not recognize the testimony of abolition remain under the old order of oppressive religion. Those caught under old religion will claim, as this young woman's former master, that this kind of sexual ethics represents a false custom. I assume that many will hear any deviation from purity culture in this way. Nonetheless, one must press into the defaming nature of the gospel that respects no treasured idol and no pseudo-sacred image. In short, Christian sexual ethics must learn to live in an *iconoclastic* mood.

ICONOCLASTIC SEX: AN ARGUMENT

To this end, the iconoclastic mood is the place to begin again in Christian sexual ethics. Much of sexual ethics, Christian or otherwise, remains possessed by specific images that *code* the mind with practices and forms of life that merely perpetuate the systems of trafficking in implicit and explicit ways. Thus, the argument of this book does not lie in merely describing a sexual ethic for or against trafficking. I assume that the reader does not need a theological rejection of trafficking any more than they need one to move out of the way of a speeding car. Furthermore, this book does not argue for cultivating a more just mode of human trafficking. Rather, this book will address how Christian sexual ethics, through the adherence to certain purity images that require social exclusion, create insecurity that shares similarities with the insecurities that lead to trafficking. In short, the family that kicks their sexually promiscuous daughter out of their house to maintain adherence to purity culture does not protect the gospel and only creates the conditions where she can be trafficked. Therefore, this book addresses the affections and virtues surrounding sexual ethics to reclaim the central theological convictions of the faith from idolatrous imagery.

29. Jennings, *Acts*, 160–61.

In addition, the constructive work of this book through Christ seeks the defamation of these codes and images, in order to open new encounters with God and new testimonies of God's people. The shift from code to divine encounter instills the centrality of God's indicative work among us rather than the code fetishes that hold our minds captive to a demonic spirit. Code ethics works in two ways, first as a technical ethics obsessed with following a specific technique rather than the cultivation of character, and second as an image that prefigures what a moral agent must look like as a precondition for moral activity. The obsession with purity coding malforms the mind and cultivates social exclusion for those who do not meet the code fetish, as Rosemary's parents illustrate. As such, an iconoclasm of the idols and images operative in purity culture's moral imagination sets ethical thinking and doing on new trajectories that uplift, affirm, and celebrate the sacred character of human bodies. Such an iconoclasm does not elevate certain forms of life or relationships as the beginning of sexual ethics but instead searches for the ultimate meaning of sex as a start. Furthermore, it denies any approach to sexual ethics that makes sexual capital (i.e., one's possessed sexual history, attractiveness, and experience) a prerequisite for communal life. Only the community capable of receiving and loving bodies from various places and pasts can genuinely embody the gospel in a world of trafficking. Such a formation leads to a noncompetitive moral agency of God's gracious giving and, thus, a sexual ethic of bodily meaning not tied to one's sexual capital.

Before progressing to the outline, I must define a central term, namely *sexual capital*. Used throughout this book, sexual capital, as R. T. Michael defines it, is "the value of the stock of the several skills and capabilities that constitute one's sexual resources, some of which are quintessential endowments but others of which are generated or altered through personal strategies, efforts and experiences."[30] Purity culture traffics in precisely this capital. The formal activity of exchange lies in disgust or pleasure at another's sexual capital. Disgust, as will be shown, is a powerful motivator for social exclusion. The repulsion that people feel at the site of immoral practices creates cultural conventions capable of killing and making alive. Many of conventions of disgust revolve around sexuality and sexual behavior. Sexual capital, thus, is merely the requisite sexuality required to avoid disgust. Even as Michael offers this definition, he rejects it because sexual capital does not have a formal market; however, I disagree. Trafficking and purity culture represent formal markets. In trafficking, an individual's skills and capabilities emerge as resources to convert nonfinancial assets into

---

30. Michael, "Sexual Capital," 645.

durable networks (i.e., the assurance of the trafficker). In purity culture, one converts the absence of experience into the durable network of the church. The point is simple: communities code sex in specific ways to cultivate an "entrance fee" into that community. The entrance fee occurs in implicit and explicit ways inside the human mind every day.

Thus, this book argues that Christian sexual ethics is blasphemous to the economy of sexual capital of social disgust and presents good news to those caught in systems of sex trafficking and purity culture by proclaiming that the goal of the body is not sex, sexual desire, or capital, but complete, noncompetitive participation in the life of God. The body is always a gift, not dependent on endowments or attributes; in short, it is free of capital's destructive capture. If sexuality is a part of our humanity as God's creatures, then any sexual practices encouraged by Christian theology must *contribute* to human flourishing. In short, Christian sexual ethics must reinforce the recognition of the beloved nature of bodies. Sexual practices and desires that either implicitly or explicitly encourage the perpetuation of trafficking and the commodification of bodies are not practices that lead to flourishing. Therefore, not only will this book speak to sexual ethics, but ethics in general.

THE LAYOUT OF THE ARGUMENT

The argument of this book, namely the defaming of codes and images to open a path to divine encounter and moral agency, proceeds as follows. In the first chapter, I will survey the literature on human trafficking to establish a grammar for the structure and causes of trafficking as it exists in the research. This survey will include sociological research and some theological musings about the images of purity operative in both Christian and non-Christian engagements with trafficking. In short, specific images emerge (i.e., the fallen woman, the Whore of Babylon) that code our understanding of trafficking that prevents the liberation of individuals from their bondage. I focus primarily on US domestic trafficking in this analysis to counteract the assumption that trafficking is only a global phenomenon.

After completing this portion, I turn to moral disgust as a fundamental impulse, which accounts for the mistreatment of individuals caught in the web of trafficking. Moral disgust revolves around images of pure and impure that utilize a sexual optic. These images find a certain home in evangelical ethics that provides the grammatical codex offered to survivors and the themes explored in the literature review. I use evangelical ethics because it represents much of the Christian faith today in the US and a sizeable demographic in the fight against trafficking. I explore the impact of social disgust and conclude with a brief account of how this codes the moral imagination according to a certain toxic form of goodness expressed as social exclusion.

In chapter 2, I measure how this "social exclusion" model impacts the survivors of trafficking and those who experienced evangelical purity codes firsthand. I utilize the testimonies of survivors through a qualitative study that guides the remainder of the engagement with the social exclusion model. I interview eight women, all of whom reside in the US domestic context. Half of the women interviewed are survivors of trafficking and the other half are survivors of evangelical purity codes. The testimonies of both groups illustrate that the codes of purity and impurity cultivate the insecurity of trafficking.

This study focuses on the US domestic context for two reasons. First, it challenges any exclusive narrative that trafficking is only an overseas phenomenon and one wherein white, Western women experience trafficking from the US into different countries. Second, I focus on domestic trafficking to show how the insecurities experienced in trafficking parallel the insecurities *created by* evangelical purity culture. In this way, domestic trafficking and evangelical teachings on sexuality overlap significantly by the latter grooming for the former. To be abundantly clear, there is no voice in evangelicalism, past or present, that states they want trafficking. However, purity ideologically participates in the same logic as trafficking and can prepare a subject to be trafficked. The tragedy undergirding this connection is that evangelicalism makes up the largest religious group interested in antitrafficking work and promotes a very popular sexual ethic. Still, they fail to see how the latter works against their efforts in the former.

In chapter 3, I turn to a new account of sexual ethics grounded in a shift to the indicative mood. A shift to the indicative mood from the imperative mood that challenges the specific moral images completely immanent to the imperative mood. Instead, it celebrates the reception of a new reality. I sharpen this account of the indicative mood with a brief exploration of iconoclasm so that the indicative mood "deconstructively" interacts with the code fetishes. I prioritize a thick description of this iconoclastically ordered indicative through Karl Barth's theology of reconciliation. Shifting to this indicative, which is not merely an image but reality itself, suggests that the most urgent moral task of the church is the ability to be together and not excluded. Thus, this prepares Christian sexual ethics to place intimacy and reception as core postures of moral living. The reality of reconciliation performs an iconoclasm on any sexual ethics that sees exclusion as a necessary task of its witness. In short, the indicative mood provides the exorcism of demonic spirits to liberate voices to share their testimony.

In chapter 4, I take the indicative mood shaped by iconoclasm through reconciliation to translate it into moral activity. Since the goal is to remain in the indicative mood, I use Karl Barth to maintain the connection. Barth's command ethics emerges as an encounter with the indicative. Rather than a naked command imperative the command of God is at once disruptive to our moral categories yet formative in that it shapes humans to act in specific ways and receive from God the necessary virtue that locates our humanity. Thus, Barth's ethics commands specific actions without falling prey to code fetishism while shaping particular virtues. I briefly compare Barth with American theologian Jonathan Edwards to illustrate this point.

With Barth's ethics of divine command in hand, I turn back to the survivors of trafficking and purity codes. Like Paul, this is the moment that exorcises the demonic spirits and liberates new speech. The command of God is an encounter that sets free, providentially, all to testify to God's activity. Thus, testimony or witness becomes a liturgical activity that forms the Christian community. Reconciliation means that certainty provided by testimony opens the community to hear the speech of others. Testimony empowers the agent to act in response to God and receive others into beloved community. As with commands in general, testimony will shape people around the theological bases discerned in stories of trafficking to prescribe orienting virtues that enact those bases in everyday life. These bases and virtues will form the content of iconoclastic sex.

In chapter 5, I will provide a provisional sketch of iconoclastic sex as a means to actively resist trafficking through the embodiment of a different moral life. I begin with an account of sex and its meaning. The errors of social exclusion begin when ethicists do not first seek to discern the moral meaning of sex. Using the theological bases and corresponding virtues, I counter this posture to affirm the dignity of another person, critique the structures that diminish humanity and the ability to enter covenants with people, in order to encourage their flourishing. From there, I move to sexual relationships proper such as marriage, family, and children, but also sex work and pornography. These relationships must serve the ends of iconoclastic sex rather than set its terms. To fully explain this, I contrast iconoclastic sex with traditional theological teaching in the *haustafeln* (Household Codes). Iconoclastic sex does not reinscribe orders of power onto relationships but instead liberates, like the slave girl in Acts 16, for participation in God's indicative of reconciliation.

In the second half of the chapter, I argue that iconoclastic sex must consider the implication of Christian sexual ethics and social exclusion in the high number of racial minorities and LGBTQ+ youth who suffer under the weight of the web of trafficking. Minority communities, both sexual and racial, are disproportionately overrepresented among those trafficked. Thus, I show how the social exclusion model manifests certain spirits that perpetuate trafficking. Social exclusion implicates Christian sexual ethics in social evils. One must address these persistent issues if iconoclastic sex proposes an alternative to trafficking.

I conclude the book with a reflection on eschatology and ethics. The reason the proposed sexual ethics are provisional arises from the eschatological posture one must adopt as a Christian. Our human categories do not yet possess the whole truth of the coming new creation. Though ethics can be faithful to the new creation, it must never think its code perfectly expresses it or possesses new creation. To do such would be to collapse back into code making. Instead, Christian sexual ethics must remain open to receive as the posture to judge moral activity in the present. Such moral discernment takes shape more as a testimonial taste that locates one's moral capacities within the ability to see and respond to God's beauty in the world.

In the end, I ask readers to follow the argument to its end. The problem with any sexual ethic today is that it places its hands on our idols. Tampering with idols always risks violence, as Paul and Silas illustrate. However, if Christians genuinely desire a world without trafficking, they must embrace new formations in the small, everyday moments that reorient their ability to receive others into the beloved community expressed in a mutual expression of agency. Sexual ethics does not cultivate goodness against another person's badness but instead listens to the testimonies of those liberated by God.

1

On Trafficking and Purity

INTRODUCTION

LUDWIG WITTGENSTEIN WRITES, A "*picture* held us captive. And we could not get outside it, for it lay in our language, and language seemed to repeat it to us inexorably."[1] Wittgenstein, making a claim on modern philosophy, speaks also to our present state of sexuality. Sexual ethics, I argue, does not merely consider the commands or virtues necessary for sexual ethics but proposes certain images, specifically purity images, that guides its work. Such an approach moves disgust and contamination into the center of Christian ethics as the means to regulate moral behavior. One must learn, in short, to be disgusted by the right things. This approach creates certain privileges among those who do not experience the realities of human trafficking. The suffering of those who experience trafficking slips behind one of these images of purity. When the agent no longer resembles the image, nothing else matters. Sexual ethics thus becomes a zero-sum game, an all-or-nothing measure where transgressing purity leads to contamination and expulsion from the community to keep it moral. The ends of ethics in this mood consider the moral uniformity and purity of the community as a direct result of individuals within the community.

In this chapter, I will address this privilege. I begin with a literature review of sociological and theological accounts of human trafficking. For clarity, I focus primarily on the US domestic context to show how the privilege of Christian sexual ethics misses the majority type of trafficking experienced here. Through this process, I note specific Christian responses

1. Wittgenstein, *Philosophical Investigations*, 41e (§115), emphasis original.

to trafficking and theological images (i.e., the fallen woman, the Whore of Babylon) that undergird and perpetuate trafficking through images of purity and impurity, illustrating Christian theology's implication in its reality. From this review, I articulate a web of trafficking couched not merely in bad choices but circumstances that funnel people into systems of trafficking. I use the psychological insights of disgust as a means to illustrate how images of purity cultivate social insecurity through the exclusion of the impure. To this end, I illustrate the complicity of Christian theology in this reality of disgust through purity code realism. I choose evangelical ethics as they are the primary religious voice in the US domestic context and a prominent religious voice in the anti-trafficking movement. The discrepancy between the ethics and survivors will further drive the need for new sexual ethics to address survivors' needs.

PART I: A FRAMEWORK FOR DOMESTIC TRAFFICKING IN THE UNITED STATES

Trafficking is not a new institution when considered historically, and the central definition utilized by practitioners and experts in the field emerges from legislation in the Trafficking Victims Protection Act (TVPA). It defines sex trafficking as a "commercial sex act induced by force, fraud, or coercion, *or* in which the person induced to perform such act has not attained 18 years of age."[2] However, this definition is by no means standard or universal, but individuals believe they know the image of a person in trafficking when they see it. As Elizabeth Bernstein writes, "the image of the trafficking victim has been durable as well as malleable."[3] As such, Yvonne Zimmerman offers another definition of trafficking, which "refers to the wide variety of processes by which individuals become enslaved ... [and are] unable to leave a situation without fear of violence and is paid nothing or next to nothing for any duration of time."[4] When deploying the language of slavery, one must avoid constructing ill-fitting metaphors. When the average American hears the word *slavery*, they commonly imagine chattel slavery in the United States. However, for most cases of domestic trafficking, such an account of slavery does not quite fit. Mostly, individuals who experience domestic trafficking are not stolen from another country and placed in chains. Instead, they are vulnerable people who, through processes of emotional, psychological,

---

2. "Trafficking Victims Violence Protection Act of 2000" (TVPA).
3. Bernstein, *Brokered Subjects*, 6.
4. Zimmerman, *Other Dreams of Freedom*, 4.

and violent coercion, fraud, or force, participate in sex for sale to maintain subsistence.

The ill-fitting picture of trafficking emerges at the turn of the twentieth century through the changing nature of media. Print media journalists like William Stead and George Turner, according to Gretchen Soderlund, created a narrative around which the modern understanding of sex trafficking emerged. As Soderlund argues, how one communicates a new story impacts public opinion.[5] The reporting on sex trafficking arose dramatically in light of a 1907 story run by the *Chicago Tribune*, which detailed cases of forced labor in the United States. This story famously coined the phrase "white slavery" because the individuals involved were Caucasian.[6] The story became sensationalized by applying the language of chattel slavery to this new image of white slavery. As already noted, the word *slave* possesses grave connotations, and most scholars attempt to avoid the term. However, this scandal created institutional knowledge about trafficking that led to the association of trafficking with white persecution.[7] Curiously enough, as the story spread, so did the popularity of the newspapers.[8] The firestorm of this sensationalism in reporting drove political platforms and created an elitism at the center of trafficking that survives to the present day.[9] This kind of reporting relied more heavily on issues that transcended facts so much so that sensational stories won over national audiences while ignoring racial and socioeconomic realities that undergird the facts of trafficking. Though this would also begin a push in the media to shift from objectivity to sensation, it would also shape the modern image of trafficking. The ideological culture wars created by trafficking disrupted efforts to understand trafficking on its own terms.[10]

Statistics on Trafficking in the US Domestic Context

Against the sensationalized picture of trafficking, statistics help clarify the truth amid competing narratives. For example, there are cases of human trafficking *into* the United States, numbering anywhere from 14,500 to 17,500 every year.[11] This number comprises individuals from other coun-

5. Soderlund, *Sex Trafficking*, xiii.
6. Soderlund, *Sex Trafficking*, 3.
7. Soderlund, *Sex Trafficking*, 14, 25.
8. Soderlund, *Sex Trafficking*, 86–87.
9. Soderlund, *Sex Trafficking*, 133.
10. Soderlund, *Sex Trafficking*, 173.
11. Bales and Soodalter, *Slave Next Door*, 6.

tries such as "Africa, Asia, India, China, Latin America, and the former Soviet states." It consists of the most "desperate, the uneducated, and ... impoverished immigrants seeking a better life."[12] These cases are distinct from migrant smuggling, which were not for labor or sexual exploitation. However, this number does not include those individuals trafficked already *within* the United States. Thus, the actual number of those experiencing trafficking is unknown. However, in a study conducted in 2004, the number who experience trafficking in the US could be as high as 200,000.[13]

Though labor trafficking comprises a significant portion of these numbers, the largest percentage is for sexual exploitation. Close to 80 percent, both globally and locally, of all trafficking, involves sexual exploitation for profit.[14] The number of individuals trafficked *from* the United States to other countries is relatively small relative to the number of citizens of the United States trafficked within its borders. This number is significant and the fastest growing crime in the nation.[15] Less than 1 percent of cases among those trafficked into the United States find a legal resolution.[16] In terms of domestic traffickers, an even smaller number of individuals ever face charges.

Contributing Factors: The Web of Trafficking

Only a few traffickers face criminal charges because those who experience trafficking often do not recognize their traffickers as traffickers.[17] As Elizabeth Bernstein writes, in criminal proceedings, "the first-person accounts suggested that the women typically entered into prostitution of their own accord."[18] Furthermore, the traffickers train women in a grammar that disguises the violence inherent in the relationships. For example, experts acknowledge that traffickers often teach women under a single trafficker to refer to one another as "wife in-laws."[19] In this analysis, the traffickers hide their violence and coercion under a web of familial jargon that creates a sense of family among the sex workers and leads prosecutors to believe the

---

12. Bales and Soodalter, *Slave Next Door*, 6–7.

13. U.S. Department of Justice, *Report to Congress from Attorney General John Ashcroft on U.S. Government Efforts to Combat Trafficking in Persons in Fiscal Year 2003*.

14. United Nations, *Trafficking in Persons Report*.

15. Mehlman-Orozco, *Hidden in Plain Sight*, 23.

16. Bales and Soodalter, *Slave Next Door*, 7.

17. Bernstein, *Brokered Subjects*, 50–51.

18. Bernstein, *Brokered Subjects*, 51.

19. Bernstein, *Brokered Subjects*, 51.

workers participate in trafficking willingly. Thus, trafficking looks like other crimes such as domestic violence in the legal system rather than trafficking.

One cannot overstate the role that domestic violence plays in trafficking relationships. "Domestic violence relationships," as D. E. Roe-Sepowitz and company write, "occur between family or household members, and they are characterized by an unequal access to power wherein one member of the relationship maintains power and control over the other through the use of physical, verbal, and emotional abuse."[20] As these authors continue, such an understanding of domestic abuse highlights a significant overlap between the issues facing victims of domestic abuse and those in the web of trafficking. For example, power dynamics are a central feature of both sex trafficking and domestic violence. In many cases, women who overlap lack a strong social network, thus requiring that they find it in other places. As with Allison, the relationship she needed was one that enabled subsistence. Vulnerability leads to relationships where the power dynamics can be exploited and abused. Some relationships can become more violent as the relationship isolates women from their other social networks and even can go as so far as to push them into trafficking.[21] In this way, domestic violence is a significant contributing factor for trafficking that perpetuates a certain kind of grooming for sex for sale, imbalance of power, and abuse.[22]

Abuse, when coupled with access to resources and imbalance of power, begets another aspect of domestic violence, namely survival sex. Though the agent may not understand sex to be for survival, any relationship where sex is required for access to housing, food, safety, love, drugs, or any material need would meet that criterion. As defined by researchers, survival sex is the "exchange of sex for food, money, shelter, drugs, and other needs and wants."[23] According to researchers, the majority of survival sex occurs as a means to economic subsistence. These needs also include the perpetuation of addiction, which is a means to keep trafficked agents dependent upon traffickers and, therefore, in a cycle of survival sex.[24] The ones who engage in survival sex are, statistically, among the most vulnerable and marginalized in society. Thus, survival sex is need driven, not choice driven. Much

---

20. Roe-Sepowitz et al., "Victim or Whore," 884.

21. Roe-Sepowitz et al., "Victim or Whore," 884–86.

22. Roe-Sepowitz et al., "Victim or Whore," 888.

23. Walls and Bell, "Correlates of Engaging in Survival Sex among Homeless Youth and Young Adults," 424.

24. See Whyte IV, "Sexual Assertiveness in Low-Income African American Women." See also Greene, Ennett, and Ringwalt, "Prevalence and Correlates of Survival Sex Among Runaway and Homeless Youth."

of the confusion around sex work and trafficking exists on the hinge of this distinction.[25]

Researchers indicate that among the individuals who acknowledge their participation in survival sex, several economic factors contribute to their decisions. The main factor is houselessness. In a study of African American women in the US, a significant portion of sexual activity performed among this sample group occurred due to fear of becoming houseless.[26] Furthermore, the longer one remained houseless the greater the likelihood of survival sex.[27] Lacking material and social resources led many to trade sex for shelter, food, and connection.

The abusive features of trafficking are quite traumatic. When approaching the realities that individuals face, one must acknowledge the intense trauma suffered in these relationships. Trauma impacts the lives of those who experience trafficking and can lead to irregular activity. Trauma that influences activity is properly identified as moral injury, which creates a negative self-picture arising from certain experiences can further perpetuate the actions committed within trafficking. Moral injury, as a concept, recently emerged as a central topic of study in the ethics of war. As ethicists of war Tobias Winright and E. Ann Jeschke define it, "moral injury is a debilitating sense of shame and guilt that soldiers experience because of actions they have done or observed in war. Indeed, moral injury has been described as a 'bruise on the soul, akin to grief or sorrow.'"[28] In other words, moral injury is not PTSD, but rather a kind of guilt and sadness resulting from trauma. Even if the war or action in war is ultimately just, soldiers nonetheless feel a sense of cognitive dissonance in relation to war.

To this end, a comparison can be drawn between the soldier and the individual caught in the web of trafficking. Individuals who experience trafficking are often drugged, sexually assaulted, and abused. Child abuse, sexual assault, and the experience of such desperation that leads to survival sex all leave bruises on the soul. Depending on their background, as indicated above, the agent often transgresses deeply held religious or moral beliefs, which causes a pain unseen to the eye. Though the survivor can find healing, this hurt and trauma, though not permanent, nonetheless leaves a mark. This activity harms a self-image and tempts individuals to believe they are unworthy of human dignity.[29]

---

25. See Clingan et al., "Survival Sex Trading in Los Angeles County."
26. Whyte IV, "Sexual Assertiveness in Low-Income African American Women."
27. Caccamo, Kachur, and Williams, "Narrative Review."
28. Winright and Jeschke, "Combat and Confession," 170–71.
29. Ward, *Wealth, Virtue, and Moral Luck*, 89.

One such element of self-image is the trauma bonding that occurs in many relationships of trafficking. As already indicated, those caught in the web of trafficking often do not recognize their relationship to their trafficker as trafficking. Rather, many view their trafficker as a romantic partner who loves and cares for them even though they abuse them. According to researchers out of the Ohio State University, "trauma bonds are emotional attachments between victims and their abusers or captors that occur in a wide variety of exploitative relationships. These bonds are typically marked by paradoxical complexities of abuse, control and dependency, and deep feelings of love, admiration, and gratitude in the victim for the abuser."[30] The complex connection of love and affection not only make it difficult to prosecute the abuser or even for the abused to find a compelling reason to leave, but the bond also cultivates the internalized feeling of shame given by the abuser.[31] In short, the individual experiencing abuse stays because of a sense of guilt and self-hatred that assents to abuse due to the belief that it is warranted or deserved.

Trauma bonding also involves a great deal of domestic violence. Domestic abuse attempts to sever human relationships and sexuality from their sacred character. The result is not only physical harm, but emotional and spiritual harm. Victims of domestic violence often experience "depression, low self-esteem, and fear among other peripheral consequences such as isolation from positive support and complex economic instability."[32] The message often communicated to people in relationships of domestic violence is that another would not "want" to be with them other than their abuser. This prolonged exposure to abuse (physical, sexual, and emotional), trauma, and isolation often pushes those caught in the web "into sex trafficking by creating a highly exploitative situation in which victims have few financial or social supports."[33] The experience of such abuse against oneself or one's loved ones harms an internal self-understanding that perpetuates and pushes individuals into situations of trafficking.

Many of the women surveyed in the preceding analysis identify domestic violence as a central part of their journey. The moral injury that emerges from the context of domestic violence is a damage to the humanity within the victim. As Margret Farley writes, the crimes associated with domestic violence are "crimes against what makes humans, 'human.'"[34] The physical

---

30. Casassa, Knight, and Mengo, "Trauma Bonding Perspectives."
31. Casassa, Knight, and Mengo, "Trauma Bonding Perspectives," 2.
32. Roe-Sepowitz et al., "Victim or Whore," 884.
33. Roe-Sepowitz et al., "Victim or Whore," 884.
34. Farley, "Forgiveness in Service of Justice and Love," 326.

and psychological scars resulting from abuse leads to a hurt another cannot see with their eyes alone. While this hurt does not eliminate agency and the ability to make moral decisions, it does leave its mark because it aims to destroy that sacredness at the heart of the human.[35]

Agency: Choice

One issue worth exploring here is the ongoing discussion between proponents of sex work and those who want to hold survivors accountable for personal choices. The call to distinguish true agency from false agency arises from a modern emphasis on the freedom of the will, which in the West descends from the work of Immanuel Kant. I am suspicious of the ability for many to achieve the level of freedom theorized by Kant, only because his optic of freedom arose from certain privileged, gendered, and colonial assumptions necessary to the Kantian agent, but support the need for a robust account of agency. To be clear, Kant's position on subjectivity is nuanced and complex, but his philosophical work nonetheless structures agency toward a particular subjectivity under a presumption of universality. Therefore, he cultivates an ideal subjectivity that only certain agents can inhabit while also inhibiting the ability to think outside of a particular form of life coded into ethics as freedom.

Briefly, Kantian ethics holds universality and necessity as central to its moral philosophy. The dichotomy accords ethics the ability to operate from a rationally defensible position free of the constraint of empirical approaches while also taking the material world seriously. Thus, the task of ethics and moral philosophy lies in the legislation of moral law through the categorical imperative.[36] Moral philosophy, in this way, operates from a pure posture of *a priori* laws sharpened by human experience. In short, the performance of moral duties occurs through the broad acceptance of specific codes performed regardless of context and situation, thus obeying Kant's dictum, "act only in accordance with that maxim through which you can at the same time will that it become a universal law."[37] The formal acceptance of this betrays an essential feature in Kant's work, namely the importance of a free will. At the heart of Kant's philosophy is, thus, a social contract to which all must assent to be afforded the status of rational beings. The code one must perform in executing a duty is not imposed from the outside. Instead, it must arise as a feature of the will. If codes arise from the

---

35. Farley, "Forgiveness in Service of Justice and Love," 327.
36. Kant, *Grounding of a Metaphysics of Morals*, 45.
37. Kant, *Grounding of a Metaphysics of Morals*, 73.

will, they must not be externally imposed. The agent is autonomous in that they can legislate their own moral law. For the most part, the ones who wish to distinguish between sex work and sex trafficking would see this as the goal in the differentiation. Kant does not argue for fixed codes and actions but rather permissibility for moral action. The agent operates in a vein of subjective and objective evaluation to perform an action others would in similar circumstances. Performing in such a way is not absolute freedom but rather a universality of performance. This rejection is precisely why I remain suspicious of Kantian agency. Rather, only a certain kind of individual is truly capable of freedom and everyone else merely grasps at agency while idolizing it as the only true exercise of it.

The problem that the Kantian agent must recognize is that Kant did not think external factors should impact moral decisions. Kant directly critiques proponents of moral luck (i.e., that circumstances can shape our choices). In this way, ethics is a work of intellection, not sensibility, and thus unrelated to external circumstances. The neutrality of Kant's moral philosophy betrays the fact that he profoundly resonates with male and European subjectivity. Criticisms of Kant point out that this arises from a European colonial posture.[38] For example, Kant implicitly identifies "rational" as thinking in a "European" way.[39] Those who rely on sensibility are "irrational" and, thus, not moral. Kant presupposes a colonial posture that excludes women and eliminates all outside the narrow lenses through which he views agency.[40] Thus, Kant implicitly assumes a particular moral subject, male and European, not impacted by external circumstances. One must see that Kant's agent must possess a freedom that transcends external circumstances and this position finds its way into the criticisms of those who cannot see the survivor of trafficking and can only hold them accountable for individual choice. Kant does not merely offer a moral philosophy but a rubric for who can perform the moral life and who cannot.

Kant's account of agency also impacts the way that proponents of chosen sex work wish to distinguish between it and trafficking. The differences proposed by those who experience trafficking and those who *choose* sex work in an ideal sense may not exist as clearly as observers think. Yet, agency presents problems for women in trafficking. For example, many who find themselves trapped in a system of trafficking do not call the police for fear of violence at their hands.[41] As the U.S. State Department suggested in a

---

38. See Carter, *Race*, 101–2.
39. Carter, *Race*, 99, 102.
40. Kant, *Observations on the Feeling of the Beautiful and Sublime*, 81 (§3).
41. As Mehlman-Orozco observes in her study of a survivor named Francesca, she

2004 study, those who claim to engage in prostitution and related activities "fuel the growth of modern-day slavery by providing a façade behind which traffickers for sexual exploitation operate."[42] The façade articulated here is an essential feature in this comparison between sex work and sex trafficking. For many who experience trafficking it subjectively feels like a loving relationship between themselves and their trafficker. Agency in such a relationship lacks the clear freedom of Kantian agency. As such, to the one who experiences domestic violence and trafficking find a distorted view of love and sex. Even in violence, the one experiencing trafficking thinks of the situation as one's own choice, even if performed under coercion or duress.

The Kantian agent presents an ideal subjectivity that troubles an observer's ability to recognize trafficking. The difference between sex work as a chosen field and sex trafficking is no choice. There is a similar agency because those who experience trafficking do not lack agency. The sex worker's ideal agency is, according to advocates and sex workers, without coercion. However, economic factors trouble even the ideal account of agency which causes problems even for those who choose sex work. The ideal inherent in those that want to distinguish prostitution from trafficking is that one can choose to maximize the assets of one's body to make money. Highlighting the difference in choice is essential because the individuals in trafficking often *appear* to choose their plight but do so in light of constraints and pressures, but financial gain imposes itself on the free choice of the sex worker. In short, one can choose sex work, but one cannot choose the kind of market into which one sells their body. This imposition constrains the will. Bernstein states that the vast majority who experience trafficking and prostitution experience similar trauma that impacts what choices they make. She writes that most if not all the "victims" of trafficking have

> not only grown up in circumstances of extreme poverty, homelessness, and familial instability but also had been subjected to a great deal of violence throughout the course of their young lives. Experiences of child sexual abuse at the hands of stepfathers and brothers were mentioned frequently, as were multiple instances of brutal stranger rape.[43]

---

does not call the police though she has a phone and opportunity because of the fear of the violence at the hands of police. This failure to call ultimately set back her case. See Mehlman-Orozco, *Hidden in Plain Sight*, 77.

42. U.S. Department of State, "Link Between Prostitution and Sex Trafficking."
43. Bernstein, *Brokered Subjects*, 50.

Thus, choice alone does not determine the difference between prostitution and trafficking. Both can "choose," but the impact of manipulation, gaslighting, and trauma on choice must remain crucial elements to consider.

PART II: IMPLICATING CHRISTIANITY IN THE PERPETUATION OF TRAFFICKING

Trafficking is not an isolated occurrence but occurs at the intersections of innumerable interests and concepts that motivate certain means of encounter. Many factors, such as drug use, domestic violence, and trauma, contribute to trafficking. There also exists a great deal of social disgust that makes the suffering of victims in trafficking and survivors of trafficking invisible to the larger public. A central institution that cultivates this social disgust is evangelical Christianity. Evangelical interest in anti-trafficking activism has a strong political history. When President George W. Bush took office in 2001, the Trafficking Victims Protection Act was already signed into law by President Bill Clinton. President Bush oversaw this initiative and it formed a central piece of his domestic and international policy.[44] The result of the push toward anti-trafficking work led to broad bipartisan support of the administration not only in terms of the intentional anti-trafficking but also broad support for other policies, such as his incursion into Iraq.[45] Bush opened the possibility for Christian NGOs to advocate on behalf of the United States to expand this work across the world. Thus, evangelicalism became very involved in advocacy and anti-trafficking work.

Undergirding anti-trafficking work is the theological language of fallenness and evil. This rhetoric of evil arose first in a presidential speech of George W. Bush. In 2003 Bush took center stage in the United Nations to address the pandemic of trafficking. In so doing, he became the first world leader to make such an open declaration. Bush referenced the "perverse form of evil" in trafficking and referred to anti-trafficking work as a fight against it.[46] He continued, "life is a gift of our Creator—and it should never be for sale."[47] The clear theological language that characterizes sex trafficking as a fight against evil to protect the gift of the Creator mobilizes evangelicals to respond in unprecedented ways to this crisis both globally and locally.

44. Zimmerman, *Other Dreams of Freedom*, 52–53.

45. Bernstein, *Brokered Subjects*, 36.

46. Bush, "Remarks on Signing the Trafficking Victims Protection Reauthorization Act of 2005," quoted in Zimmerman, *Other Dreams of Freedom*, 53.

47. Bush, "Remarks at the National Training Conference on Human Trafficking in Tampa, Florida," quoted in Zimmerman, *Other Dreams of Freedom*, 53.

As Yvonne Zimmerman argues, this language of evil intentionally conveys that trafficking is "more than ordinary criminality" and a "violation of the moral order that stands over and above human affairs."[48] The evil found in the lapse in the moral order results in a need to punish and correct those who transgress.

Zimmerman argues that this tactic by the former president obscured the material references with spiritual platitudes.[49] Zimmerman helpfully illustrates that Bush's focus on evil underwrites a certain kind of violence that captures female bodies. Zimmerman terms this capture the "fallen woman" narrative that surrounds the introduction of evil into the discourse on sex trafficking.[50] The evangelical purity codes of sex impact the discourse on trafficking, namely, the moral order that breaks at the loss of virginal purity. This purity code qua code does not make room for exceptions, even in trafficking. It is a moral posture that "codes" perceptions about sex according to the logic of purity. For the evangelical, the purity movement that influences a cottage industry of purity code realism also impacts the optics under which the trafficked individual must exist. Even if a woman only has sex because of trafficking, they still lack purity and thus exist as a threat to purity through the introduction of impurity into the community. Such language impacts all their faculties and requires a condescending view of women in trafficking.

The disdain for the trafficked individual is nowhere more evident than in the "rescue" movements. One witnesses the continued disdain for survivors in rescue culture because they are still impure and they need to be "taught" how to be pure. The rescue and reintegration plan, for example, merely transitions those who experience sex trafficking into labor trafficking. Bernstein summarizes the stories of several women who returned to trafficking after being "rescued" by a Christian anti-trafficking organization in Thailand. The women commented that the harsh conditions of the work were finally too much to bear. The organization specializes in social entrepreneurship for women seeking an alternative means of income to trafficking. The women agreed to do what the organization called "prayer work" instead of sex work. Nevertheless, the conditions were like that of slavery of a different kind. As Bernstein summarizes, the women were "micromanaged by their new missionary-employers."[51] For example, their pay, which was not exorbitant, "would be docked for missing daily prayer sessions, for

---

48. Zimmerman, *Other Dreams of Freedom*, 55.
49. Zimmerman, *Other Dreams of Freedom*, 60.
50. Zimmerman, *Other Dreams of Freedom*, 117.
51. Bernstein, *Brokered Subjects*, 87.

being late to work, or for minor behavioral infractions [such as dress]."⁵²
The punishments in this system of goodness occur under the guise of training or rehabilitation of immorality, which illustrates the rescuers' belief in the impurity and immorality of the survivors. Furthermore, the workers were restricted in their travel and monitored, similar to their surveillance in sex work. Therefore, any account of anti-trafficking work must include anti-labor trafficking as well.

Impure Images: The Criminal, the Fallen Woman, and the Whore of Babylon⁵³

The language of impurity centralizes the images that marginalize and create social insecurity. The visual optics that evangelicals and other groups bring to trafficking begets an entire social imagination structured around images of life that grant permission to exist. The "fallen woman" language exists within evangelical anti-trafficking work and often perpetuates the kinds of abuse present in trafficking itself. One must look beyond merely the personal contributing factors (e.g., sexual abuse, trauma, domestic violence) to the social structures that make the suffering of those caught in the web invisible behind lenses of cultural evil. Certain cultural images serve the larger society as a means to caricature the people who experience trafficking and justify their mistreatment. All terms exist inside and outside of a theological rationale that merely perpetuates their existence and sets up a certain response to those caught in the web of trafficking.

The Criminal and the Addict

The first image is the criminal. Recalling Kelsey's story, those who exhibit delinquency in the eyes of the public primarily lose any social capital necessary to find a friendly hearing among law enforcement and other law-abiding

---

52. Bernstein, *Brokered Subjects*, 87.

53. The images of the Whore of Babylon and the fallen woman dominate the literature around sex work and trafficking in the Christian tradition. The Whore of Babylon is a specific instantiation of a long biblical tradition that focuses negative attention to sex workers of all kind. The prostitute, the figure of the Whore of Babylon, is a figure in Hebrew and Christian Scriptures that tempts not only sexual infidelity but also spiritual infidelity. One cannot overstate how important this image is for many people's imagination. This is also true for the fallen woman, who is the figure that represents a moral defect at the heart of the sex worker. Both prefigure the individual who might resemble their appearance. These images must be explored and analyzed.

citizens.⁵⁴ The criminal is such a binding figure in the culture. As Michel Foucault writes, "the condemned man represents the symmetrical, inverted figure of the king."⁵⁵ Crime binds certain bodies to immorality to marginalize a person from society. That Kelsey was "just a prostitute" in the eyes of the court, leading to her disappearance, illustrates Foucault's emphasis on punishment and criminality. In this kind of social imagination, delinquency is a mere labor pain of the criminal about to be born into the world. However, actual criminal conviction only confirms what the citizen suspects in fear of delinquency. Such is the case in Kelsey's story in Seattle. The presence of criminality creates a larger permission to mistreat and condemn those who suffer at the margin. As Mehlman-Orozco notes after observing the trial of another trafficked woman named Francesca, that she "didn't present herself as a particularly sympathetic victim. In addition to having received some of the money from her sexual exploitation, she had also engaged in other criminal activities, such as drug use and car theft."⁵⁶ Though sympathetic to Francesca, Mehlman-Orozco reifies the entire social imagination of those who gaze upon trafficking. Because Francesca received money or "participated" in the crime, then the trauma of trafficking was not a crime against her but deserved. Criminality, either appeared or indicted, is a death sentence for those with little to no social capital and prevents the attainment of any social capital beyond recidivism. Thus, as Foucault continues, "it is the certainty of being punished and not the horrifying spectacle of public punishment that must discourage crime."⁵⁷ Therefore, the one who experiences trafficking must remain on the margins in order to discourage it.

Criminality is not merely a judicial term, but theological as well. One can examine, for example, the rise of white evangelicalism in the Second Great Awakening and its interpretation of law and punishment. For example, Charles Finney, the leading voice of the Second Great Awakening, was a former lawyer turned revivalist that affirmed a very positive anthropology.⁵⁸ Undergirding this anthropology was the Americans' successful history of expelling the British and developing their constitutional order. In short, if God's revelation was naturalizable, Americans seized it. Finney gave American Christians an understanding of law as arising deeply from the world through a set of antinomies such as law and gospel, pure and impure. As Kate Bowler writes, this "orthodox rationalism" proposes a "seamless

---

54. Mehlman-Orozco, *Hidden in Plain Sight*, 88–90.
55. Foucault, *Discipline and Punish*, 29.
56. Mehlman-Orozco, *Hidden in Plain Sight*, 77.
57. Foucault, *Discipline and Punish*, 9.
58. See Bowler, "Legal Mind of American Christianity," 28–29.

integration of all knowledge, mundane and divine, as the fullest expression of God's revelation."[59] Such integration meant that the laws around, for example, sexuality fulfilled natural law and, thus, needed punished correction. Humans derived the knowledge about proper order from the created order, which itself was divine revelation witnessed in these antinomies. Even though God on the cross saved humanity from their worst nature, the law illustrated how God wanted Christians to be good.[60] The goodness developed here was a goodness that justified their own worst intentions and interpretations, which cultivated a place of privilege among certain people and justified maltreatment of those outside the privileged positions (i.e., the criminals).

Criminality informs the public perception of trafficking and impacts social capital in addition to prostitution, namely drug use. Drug use builds upon domestic violence because many individuals who face social insecurity also suffer from substance addiction. According to the Polaris Project, between 2015 and 2017, approximately "2,238 potential victims of human trafficking . . . had drug use induced or exploited as a means of control in their trafficking situation."[61] In Allison's case, trafficking involved drug addiction that led to her exploitation at the hands of James, which only increased domestic violence. The feeding of drug addiction, like the withholding of physical violence, appeared as a kind of love. Since the War on Drugs serves as an essential feature of US domestic politics, those associated with drugs and drug users find themselves bound to one of the most detestable forms of criminality and, thus, perpetuate their social exclusion. The image of the "user" pervades the social imagination as a threat. Competing fears of drug exposure and enabling create a system of vulnerability that perpetuates certain moral assumptions about the nature of the addicted person.

Drug use must be placed within the context of addiction, especially when considering trafficking. As the State Department recently urged, the public must recognize that addiction is a brain chemistry issue. As the Office to Monitor and Combat Trafficking in Persons 2017–2021 report clarifies,

> substance use disorder and addiction are terms used here to describe the stage of the condition where a person's brain and body are chemically dependent on a substance. While the term "substance use disorder" may carry less stigma, the term "addiction"

---

59. Bowler, "Legal Mind of American Christianity," 129.
60. Bowler, "Legal Mind of American Christianity," 128.
61. Polaris Project, "Human Trafficking and the Opioid Crisis."

is used, not pejoratively, in legal and criminal justice cases and by medical experts to describe this complex condition.[62]

The presence of "stigma" illustrates that drug use is a barrier to durable networks for many. However, like domestic violence and substance use disorder, individuals face a real vulnerability to exploitation.[63] Drug use complicates trafficking further in the lack of social networks for those who are addicted and who suffer the stigmas associated with their disorder. Often, these vulnerable people turn to traffickers and abusive relationships to help maintain their addiction.

The Fallen Woman and Purity

The second two images arise from certain theological work arising from constructive terms such as evil, purity, and defilement. These terms shape Christian and non-Christian responses to victims caught in trafficking and often inhibit trafficking relief efforts. Utilizing specifically the language of purity, in this American account and the narrative of the fallen woman, the person caught in the web of trafficking finds themselves caught in a theological torrent. Though the fallen woman in trafficking is a victim, according to its existence inside a matrix of sin, she nonetheless bears the weight of the system of evil in which she unwillingly participates. The issue, then, lies less in the images that tease our imagination. As such, theology lies at the heart of the economic logic of trafficking that seeks to promote and tease out images essential in trafficking.

Amey Victoria Adkins, in her doctoral dissertation *Virgin Territory*, argues that the language of purity is not an innocent and amoral term.[64] Instead, it contains histories of religious meanings which exist today at the heart of sex trafficking. Drawing on the work of anthropologist Mary Douglas, Adkins argues that "purity is not a form . . . purity is a relation."[65] Coupled with the orthodox rationalism of the Second Great Awakening, purity relations hover at the level of truism. Purity presupposes certain norms, social roles, expectations, and qualities from people. It provides a sense of order and calculation to creation and clear boundaries for the social

---

62. U.S. State Department, "Intersection of Human Trafficking and Addiction 2017–2021."

63. U.S. State Department, "Intersection of Human Trafficking and Addiction 2017–2021."

64. Adkins, "Virgin Territory."

65. Adkins, "Virgin Territory," 198.

order.⁶⁶ Purity codes enable humanity to recognize and measure themselves in a social whole to mediate conflict and assuage concerns. Specifically, as Michel Foucault argues, purity organizes bodies so that some "may be subjected, used, transformed and improved."⁶⁷ This *ordo salutis* of bodies encourages bodily discipline so that a central embodied, privileged image might emerge as a measuring stick against which the individual finds their social value. Furthermore, the image of purity serves as the border around which socially acceptable and valuable bodies organize.

A theological locus for purity arises from the traditional fall narrative found in the book Genesis. Utilizing the person of Eve, Adkins argues that Eve's body serves as a prototype for impure, defiled bodies bound to sin and in need of redemption. In short, she is the first fallen woman. Adkins highlights that the true core and beginning of this story with Eve is her boundness to God and Adam in her creation. One cannot read the Genesis account and miss that the "two people together were: One flesh. Naked and unashamed."⁶⁸ The issue arises not through sexual contamination, largely absent from the Eden account, but fruit prohibition. As the narrative goes, Eve eats from the forbidden tree, followed by Adam. When God confronts the pair, Adam shifts the blame to Eve alone, and as such, "the relation of being one flesh collapses beneath the weight of their exposure."⁶⁹ The rupture from the garden is not merely a shift in their life but their relationship. Formerly, Eve was partner, companion, and equal⁷⁰ (Gen 3:12). Eve's former status collapses into a system of exchange, which is the first display of the trafficking impulse. This tendency sees the root of evil inside a gendered hierarchy, wherein the relationship shifts from partner to given and now subordinate.

Adkins notes how Eve's submission to Adam relies heavily on a history of omission in the textual analysis. Translators of this passage take up a theological, patriarchal posture toward the fall by blaming Eve for the transgression. This posture has a long history among theologians since the early church.⁷¹ In short, translators, to support a theological condemnation of Eve, blatantly omit the translation of עמה ("with her") in Genesis 3:6. By omission, it places the total weight of sin on Eve wherein at least Adam was not first to transgress. The sinful subject as a woman projects onto all

---

66. Adkins, "Virgin Territory," 199.
67. Foucault, *Discipline and Punish*, 136.
68. Adkins, "Virgin Territory," 36.
69. Adkins, "Virgin Territory," 40.
70. Adkins, "Virgin Territory," 40.
71. See Adkins, "Virgin Territory," 36–38.

women and creates a "gender hierarchy... codifying the traits and problems already seen as being inherent to the Woman sex."[72] The punishment is that Eve must order her desires toward her husband to whom she is now subject. The sin, transmuted for all humans, is the disordering of desire that must now be rerouted through Adam. The resulting reflection in Christian theology maps onto sex a narrative of impurity.

The emphasis on Eve and impurity finds its counterpart (and correction) in Mary and her purity. Early Christians struggled with Christ's becoming flesh in the wake of the incarnation, and the conversation around Christ's flesh immediately turned to Mary as a source. In many ancient accounts of metaphysics, it would be improper and impure for God to enter the world through a human womb.[73] Nevertheless, Mary would become, in orthodox theology, the source of Christ's pure humanity. Therefore, early theologians made Mary the recapitulation of Eve in the way that Christ was the recapitulation of Adam to address the barrier to the defilement that disturbed metaphysics.[74] In short, Mary's virginity and sole desire for God through her Son is the obedience that undoes the disobedience of Eve.[75]

As Adkins writes, Mary recapitulates the image of Eve to code women's bodies in the sexual purity of Mary.[76] In her purity, Mary exists outside the order of fallenness to remove women from a matrix of impurity. However, one must see how this relates to the male in Christian theology. Mariology is a relation of the female to male as one free from impurity to undo Eve. As Adkins writes, "the coming forth of Christ to redeem the world would not be bound to the sexual rendering of the female body, or the instantiation of fallenness as embodied in Eve's body and actions."[77] There is a "gendered *ordo salutis*" wherein the image of Mary and Eve constantly reproduces one another. Thus, the image of the virgin and the impure map onto all sexuality so as to cultivate a certain sexual capital in profound and meaningful ways.

The language of impurity that guides the distinction between Mary and Eve further complexifies the issues of trafficking. The tropes of pure and impure define an economic space of buying and selling essential to the production of sex trafficking. However, in Christian theology, the perpetual production of Mary and Eve creates a border that draws everyone inside. The survivor or individual caught inside faces the same exclusion

---

72. Adkins, "Virgin Territory," 54.
73. Adkins, "Virgin Territory," 71.
74. Adkins, "Virgin Territory," 76.
75. Adkins, "Virgin Territory," 77.
76. Adkins, "Virgin Territory," 81.
77. Adkins, "Virgin Territory," 88.

because they both break with social conventions perceived as natural order. There remains no gray area. Though we will discuss the agency question concerning sexual ethics at length below, it is essential to note that images capture public imagination more than actions. Thus, the women described in the literature, though dealing with difficult circumstances, are still fallen women according to the rubric of purity. They are classified as threats, sin, and defiled outside the natural moral order. Though the work of evangelical workers attempts to "save" or help, they nonetheless operate from a place of punishment for transgression according to a sexual *ordo salutis*. The result is a system of goodness wherein those inside systems of human trafficking quickly find themselves, victims of labor trafficking, due to well-meaning people.

The Whore of Babylon

Eve is not the only image that presents a treatment of those guilty of sex work. Christian Scripture presents many images that, when paired with a code fetish, take on new life as a justification for mimetic violence. Specific images in Scripture carry authority over others, such as the Whore of Babylon, which sits alongside the fallen woman as an image that codes. This text, while not alone in its power, serves as a guidepost for many sex workers and often women in general, which often justifies forms of mimetic violence.

The Whore of Babylon is an image bathed in apocalyptic language found in Revelation 17. Babylon serves as a biblical image throughout the Scriptures, usually presented as a threat and enemy to the people of God. As biblical scholar Tracy Rowland interprets, Babylon represents the long lineage of "displacement, exile, the threat of idolatry, and the longing for Zion."[78] The Whore of Babylon, on the other hand, is a temptation to follow an idolatrous path and causes John to be amazed (Rev 17:6b-7). However, as the text describes, she is drunk with the blood of the saints and colludes in war. The text images this person as an enemy to the faithful and celebrates her downfall in the following chapters in violent detail. The purpose of the text, as with all apocalyptic texts, is a critique of present realities such as opulence, abuse, and military might as forms of reliance that go against the very ends of God.

Though the text provides a framework for that which is not God, one cannot ignore the image of violence toward this woman. The influence and threat placed at the feet of sex workers and women historically due to this image are numerous. The literalized picture of the Whore of Babylon

78. Rowland, "Revelation," 1060.

presents a difficult challenge. She is the threat to the bride of Christ (Rev 19:8), whom the author describes as the opposite of the Great Whore of Babylon. However, this woman is no ordinary woman, but a sex worker, which is not lost on history. The lust that is the allegory for unfaithfulness finds its embodiment here in the sex worker. As in the text, only violence against her proves one's faithfulness.

The need to find a historical referent for the Whore of Babylon starts in Rome but has always included sex workers and a presumption against them. Since God desired the destruction of Babylon in the most grotesque way (Rev 17:16), there is a referent to the need to destroy the sex worker. As Marion Carson locates, the message from Revelation 17 is that those who embody Babylon on the ground (i.e., sex workers) must be destroyed.[79] Though Revelation encourages that believers patiently endure suffering, individuals have still historically carried out this judgment on the bodies of sex workers.[80]

In sum, images hold us captive both morally and spiritually. The images of criminal, fallen woman, and the Whore of Babylon at once name negative moral codes and how one handles the individuals that at a distance most resemble those images. Due to the images, people struggle to aid those caught in the system of trafficking because they are just prostitutes in their eyes, and prostitution is the epitome of all evil.[81] In the zero-sum game of code ethics, you cannot aid evil but only destroy it. Thus, many women relapse into trafficking because the community lacks the imagination that allow for the reimaging of the survivor's life. Either the fallen woman's narrative or the threat of labor conditions place them back in systems of vulnerability. Many choose sex work precisely because profit drives the system, and one can make more, and the system of goodness does not easily allow for escape.

Minding the Web: A Good Life in a Bad World?

Trafficking, both sociologically and theologically, presents a matrix of issues that create the conditions of exploitation not considered by many who can only see the threat of prostitution. This matrix aims to highlight the inadequacy of present approaches to ethics to account for the moral issues at stake. A sexual ethic of personal responsibility to either partake or abstain from sex does not adequately address the moral system on display

---

79. Carson, "Harlot, the Beast and the Sex Trafficker," 220.
80. Carson, "Harlot, the Beast and the Sex Trafficker," 220.
81. Carson, "Harlot, the Beast and the Sex Trafficker," 220.

in trafficking. Sex for the person caught in the web of trafficking often occurs for material and nonmaterial needs. Language of purity, for example, codes specific aspects of sex into many religious and nonreligious accounts of sexuality that prevent one from seeing the extreme suffering of another in favor of an optic that locates their humanity according to sexual capital. Therefore, the challenge presented to sexual ethics lies in the very structure of the world. If the world presents terrible choices, what can one do? The one, for example, threatened with death or sex work does not receive a good set of choices. In short, specific lives are not allowed according to our systems of goodness.

As philosopher Judith Butler contends, one can discern the life that is not allowed by examining "grievable" life. Butler argues that the vectors of meaning in an imperfect world only support certain life forms. These vectors of meaning give preferential treatment to racial, sexual, and socioeconomic statuses. Recognition of the structures of the bad world requires that the individual pursue a dignified life. As Butler writes,

> When the life that I lead is unlivable, a rather searing paradox follows, for the question, how do I lead a good life?, presumes that *there are lives* to be led; that is, that there are lives recognized as living and that mine is among them ... In other words, this life that is mine reflects back to be a problem of equality and power and, more broadly, the justice or injustice of the allocation of value.[82]

Here one can see whose life matters and if my life numbers among them. Butler suggests an important question: if some pathways close off to particular people who make choices, what does one do if they only receive bad choices? How can they live a good life? Furthermore, a given path to a life that matters emerges, which for some is a living possibility, but for others, is permanently closed off. In short, to fully understand the conditions of trafficking, one must admit that only specific pathways to living are available, and only certain people inhabit the duties and responsibilities necessary to live.

To summarize, the issues perpetuating trafficking arise from material and nonmaterial circumstances in people's lives. Drug addiction does play a role, but domestic violence, sexual abuse, and poverty play an even more significant one. In every circumstance, the aspect of the web indicates a reason for exclusion due to the purity coding of Mary and Eve. As such, the image of the criminal and the addict force those who, according to a cultural aesthetic, fit their description, to become starved from opportunities and

---

82. Butler, "Can One Lead a Good Life in a Bad Life?," 11.

networks necessary to survive. Furthermore, purity cultivates a violence of privilege that manifests in the only relationships available to them, such as domestic violence, where manipulation, coercion, and violence (physical and emotional) often occurs. Human response to "criminality" cultivates the conditions of trafficking rather than discourages it. If the individual commits a crime or becomes addicted, they lose access to job security or even family networks. Attempting to gain security, they turn to any networks available to them, which often involve force, fraud, or coercion, and find themselves caught in the web. In short, social exclusion as a response to "criminality" or "immorality" causes harm in its own way. Considering the trauma and injury one experiences in the web, it is easy to see why one stays in the cycle and struggles to escape. Thus, those who experience trafficking do not find themselves on the web because of a moral deficit but because of trauma (moral injury) or dire circumstances such as poverty (moral luck). The challenge posed by these circumstances makes it difficult to live a good life in an immoral world.

PART III: DISGUST, IMAGES, AND SOCIAL EXCLUSION

Readers might be surprised by how ubiquitous the language of purity and disgust are in the social norms surrounding sexual ethics and trafficking. As moral agents, humans are intrinsically visual in their moral judgments, much to the disappointment of Immanuel Kant. The visual nature of sexual ethics, I argue, inhibits seeing the reality of trafficking. As already noted, evangelical participation in anti-trafficking work arises from a certain moral disgust for evil that breaks a perceived natural order for sex grounded in purity. The language of evil sex, illustrated in Bush's speech, cultivates an attitude toward the survivor so that a moral condescension emerges as a natural result. In short, the "dirty" nature of the fallen woman is all-encompassing. However, evangelicals are not alone in their deployment of purity and disgust. In *The End of Policing*, Alex Vitale argues that the issues perpetuating a zero-sum approach to policing sex work lie in the perceived stain on society's moral order and economic stability.[83] The moral rejection of prostitution does include a strong consideration of the façade of prostitution to hide trafficking by assuming that all sex work is coercive.[84] Nevertheless, even still, the highly moralistic character of policing sex work, according to Vitale,

83. Vitale, *End of Policing*, 108–9.
84. Vitale, *End of Policing*, 108–9.

cannot get past the "behaviors police find personally offensive."[85] Even if the purpose is to rescue an individual from trafficking, they nonetheless justify the brutal treatment of sex workers due to their moral contamination.[86] In short, the purity coding inherent in sexuality begets a treatment from code-abiding citizens. It is not enough to desire the code logic, but one must structure their life so entirely against the disturbance of codes that a natural reflex of disgust emerges in response to concrete humanity. Vitale helpfully identifies the proper place of disgust for many trafficking activists, namely the sexual sins that problematize humanity. The anger at the institution of trafficking, then, manifests often unhelpfully in a collective desire to punish sexual sins even though activists think greater policing will decrease prostitution.[87] Coupled with the language of moral order deployed by President Bush, the individuals who resemble the imbalance to the natural order suffer dire consequences. Thus, purity language, even when attempting to reduce sexual violence, often still increases it.

The role that purity and dirt plays in the social imagination of Christians and non-Christians alike is an important object for consideration. Why does the sexual past disable compassion in many cases or render invisible the suffering experienced by so many? Anthropologist Mary Douglas illustrates how this basic purity impulse remains in contemporary culture through the ever-present human desire to resist defilement. The contemporary manifestation of contagion is, according to Douglas, dirt. Cleanliness is still the operative concern, but the shift in the contemporary world is hygienic. Douglas writes that dirt "is the by-product of a systematic ordering and classification of matter, in so far as ordering involves rejecting inappropriate elements. This idea of dirt takes us straight into the field of symbolism and promises a link up with more symbolic systems of purity."[88] According to Douglas, "dirty" merely denotes that which is out of place and not cherished.[89] Dirt names that which is out of place in a closed system. As Douglas stipulates, this connects moderns and ancients because the idea of a pattern and its disruption is consistent.

The language of dirt and purity emerge from the deeper psychological language of disgust that govern moral activity. Such a claim requires agents to recognize that moral judgments occur not only through rational argument but visual imaging. Following Douglas, humans often rely on images

85. Vitale, *End of Policing*, 109.
86. Vitale, *End of Policing*, 110.
87. Vitale, *End of Policing*, 109.
88. Douglas, *Purity and Danger*, 44.
89. Douglas, *Purity and Danger*, 45.

for their moral judgments that override or short circuit the moral imagination's ability to nuanced perception of another. To be clear, one cannot avoid this in favor of purely rational claims.

Purity and contamination are not inherently immoral words. Purity signals a type of integrity maintained consistently while contamination usually names a transgression of that integrity. However, these terms operate in very innocuous ways when understood, for example, to refer to the consumption of food. When considering possible pollutants, a person with gluten intolerance should very carefully consider the possibility of cross-contamination of food. The food's integrity matters. It is not immoral for those with food allergies to desire clean, pure foods that lack contamination. However, as Richard Beck argues, when purity and contamination become social images and metaphors, problems occur.[90] Purity, as Beck continues, is a metaphor that aids in translating abstract concepts into embodied practices. For example, the purity codes that govern sexuality in Leviticus 18 attempt, at least in part, to participate in a ritual practice to prepare for God's presence.[91] There is a logic in the metaphor that, as Beck continues, "grants us cognitive traction, a means to reason through complex problems or abstractions."[92] In short, it serves as a code to enable decision-making through problematic situations by appealing to experiences such as food, hygiene, and water. One notices this language of purity in many evangelical teachings on sexuality. For example, many supporters of purity codes will claim that sex in marriage with someone who already engaged in sexual activity is metaphorically synonymous with asking someone to chew your already chewed bubble gum. This purity metaphor cultivates a response of revulsion and disgust to resist premarital sex. It is a simple metaphor that translates a purity of food contamination into a purity of sexuality. This language of purity also enables humans to order sexual appetites to avoid sin. A Christian's desire to receive grace and avoid sin and impurity enables a clear metaphor. In the Hebrew imagination, cultivating a language of healthy disgust clearly envisions the path away from sin and toward grace. However, when the disgust impulse becomes fetishized, one missteps into code idolatry. Purity, in this latter sense, encourages structured moral integrity when mobilized into a social reality.

When considering purity and contamination as guiding metaphors, Beck recognizes that a notion of permanence operates within it. In sexual ethics, purity is something that can be lost and not recovered. Beck, drawing

---

90. Beck, *Unclean*, 8–9.

91. Brueggemann, *Theology of the Old Testament*, 192.

92. Beck, *Unclean*, 35.

from the adjacent language of food purity, illustrates that the metaphors for purity operate across experiences with similar rationality. Beck describes a study wherein a clean glass of lemonade is given to a research participant but just before giving it to the participant, the researcher dips an insect into the lemonade. Even though the insect is no longer in the lemonade, the drink is now polluted in the eyes of the consumer. Furthermore, Beck indicates that the study shows that even if the lemonade ran through a water filter, was boiled, and filtered again many people would still not drink the water. Thus, contamination possesses profound weight in the mind of the agent. Once a food item is contaminated, its condition is permanent. Similarly in purity code sexual ethics, once purity is lost, the sexual agent is permanently contaminated with, as Beck argues, "no obvious route to repentance."[93]

Disgust and the "notions of non-rehabilitation" (i.e., permanence) in purity profoundly regulates the behavior of the individual. However, it also regulates the behavior of the community. Purity, as Beck shows, also contains an expulsive tendency toward that which is impure. Purity brackets something holy from the impure. As Douglas writes, "sacred things and places are to be protected from defilement. Holiness and impurity are at opposite poles."[94] Thus, a spatial metaphor exists at the heart of purity preservation in that the holy cannot exist in the same place as the impure. When the impure visually crosses into the holy or pure it requires a sanction or punishment in order to rectify the contamination of the holy. The reflex when confronting the impure is to spit out and push away. In short, purity requires exclusion and rejection by the pure. This exclusion must take the form of social exclusion in the case of impure people.

Though purity and contamination exist at a fundamental level in the human experience, according to Beck, they do emerge from a theological rationale. One source of purity comes to the contemporary world through the Levitical holiness codes of the Hebrew Scriptures. Biblical scholar Jacob Milgrom differentiates between two accounts of holiness, one inclusive of a plurality of people and places and one exclusive to only specific places and people.[95] Holiness in both senses denotes a separation to differentiate between the divine and the human. The holiness tradition never expressed these two in isolation. Even as one sought purity for specific places and people, the tradition required immersing oneself faithfully in the life of others. The original intention challenges more popular accounts of purity and holiness by locating, even in its more restrictive account, as not a possession

---

93. Beck, *Unclean*, 49.
94. Douglas, *Purity and Danger*, 9.
95. Milgrom, *Leviticus 17-22*, 1397.

intrinsic to an agent to the permanent exclusion of others but only as it pertains to a communal reflection of God's holiness to the world.[96] The ancient Hebrew holiness codes do not merely prescribe against taboos but encourage positive ethical commitments of seeking justice, holiness, and righteousness in an unjust and impure world, a seeking that drove Israel's existence.[97]

As such, God called Israel to advance the holy into the impure realm and reduce impurity in its midst.[98] It is not in the absence of others that Israel found its distinction, but the ways in which God called them to pursue justice in their release of those in bondage, as is evident in Leviticus 25. Purity was for the sake of removing the community from the influence of other people wherein this kind of injustice was more common. Life and death were cosmic forces that the Israelites must resist with every aspect of their life.[99] The cosmic forces of life and death emerge as a struggle to refrain (ritual) and engage (moral) for the enjoyment of blessing. To advance holiness and limit impurity thus emerged against the backdrop of this cosmic struggle through people, places, and creation itself.

The themes found in the Hebrew Scriptures carry on into the Christian New Testament. Though the purity/impurity divide becomes upset through passages like Acts 10, the New Testament possesses a qualitative purity structure even as it augments and shifts Jewish culture.[100] As David DeSilva understands, this shift in the New Testament leans heavily into the ethical rather than the ritualistic. He writes that the "process of being set apart for God (made holy) is now an ethical rather than a ritual one. Here it occurs as a person separates himself or herself from sexual looseness and from domination by sexual drives."[101] Sexuality plays a central role in New Testament prescriptions, specifically in the letters of Paul. But more importantly here, as in the Hebrew Scripture, purity is not for a self-enclosed possession, but for important transgressions of justice as purity.[102]

As indicated, purity and contamination create helpful inclinations to avoid substances like poisons that lead to harm. However, projecting this self-preservation onto social relationships creates levels of social capital that

---

96. Milgrom, *Leviticus 17–22*, 1399.

97. Milgrom, *Leviticus 17–22*, 1714.

98. Milgrom, *Leviticus 17–22*, 1720–21.

99. Milgrom, *Leviticus 17–22*, 1721.

100. For my reflections on this shift, see Spaulding III, *Just and Loving Gaze of God with Us*.

101. DeSilva, *Honor*, 295.

102. DeSilva, *Honor*, 314–15.

privileges social or sexual history, as Pierre Bourdieu argues, and transforms them "into signs of recognition . . . through the mutual recognition and the recognition of group membership which it implies, re-produces the group."[103] Purity maintains group membership while contamination eliminates it. One's sexual life thus threatens or deepens one's connection to a group. Social capital is the parent category for sexual capital in that the latter purchases the former. In theological terms, social capital, through the perseverance of purity, perpetuates a natural theology that visualizes divine attributes in social space. In sum, social capital serves as specific kinds of value one possesses. It can be gained and aggregated in an individual's life while maintaining institutions and codes that regulate and consecrate the means of exchange and production. Sexual ethics, when considered as a code, exists for those who have this in excess. The need to maintain and keep durable networks is an essential piece for those in desperate situations. Thus, survival sex and exploitation are aspects of many people's search for a durable network. No one questions the necessity of social capital, only the way one gets it. Social capital and poverty mark out friend and enemy while granting advantage to those who possess it.

In light of trafficking's reinscription of choice, social capital moves to the center of trafficking discourse. The creation of desperation and vulnerability, along with the opportunity of social capital, perpetuates exploitation. The individuals who often suffer trafficking's violence often have no other choice and lack the social capital necessary to maintain relationships. Those caught in the web of trafficking often come from backgrounds of either abject poverty, addiction, or domestic violence.[104] Such cases already trouble the individual's ability to access the social capital required to convert social graces into durable financial and social security networks. Poverty does not indicate trafficking or a lack of social networks; many who lack financial means can still maintain rich social networks. However, some are forced from their social networks and thus lack social capital, namely the lack of community upon which one could build social wealth. The fact that traffickers use social capital as a threat illustrates that social standing matters for the individual to flourish. Thus, traffickers utilize vulnerability to groom victims because they lack the social capital and are prevented from existing in other networks.

Disgust, purity, and contamination all impact our study of trafficking. The language of good and evil along with a psychological and theological image of purity cause disgust when encountering those who fall outside

---

103. Bourdieu, "Forms of Capital," 250.
104. Mehlman-Orozco, *Hidden in Plain Sight*, 90.

the circle. The problem of purity, in the contemporary disgust narratives, arises from its lack of connection to the theological rationale in which it was originally deployed, namely toward the ends of justice. Tragically, it is only a means to exclude. As with the case of the police officers described in Vitale's study, disgust results in maltreatment. When strengthened by a theological rationale, an entire system of goodness found in purity wherein individuals find themselves excluded from the community for fear of contamination. Furthermore, punishing the impure becomes, in this context, a form of piety.

North American Evangelicalism: The Purity Industrial Complex

If purity, disgust, and contamination form a piety, there exists no more pious people than American evangelicals in the twentieth century.[105] During the latter half of this century, evangelicalism composed a large portion of American Christians.[106] However, this movement does not occur in a vacuum. The word *evangelical* has its root in the Greek *euangelion*, meaning gospel or good news. In the United States, evangelical became a famous description of the type of Christianity arising from the revivalism that swept the nation in its early years. George Whitefield, a popular eighteenth-century Reformed preacher, ignited the colonies at the time with fervent zeal for personal heart conversions and the renunciation of Satan's works.[107]

---

105. Though there are many forms of evangelical communities domestically and internationally, my reference is to the white evangelical US domestic community. As indicated previously, this makes up the largest wing of Christians in the US. This is the community most taken with sexual ethics from a privileged position, most concerned with trafficking through a malformed lens (i.e., the *Taken* franchise), and who directly encounter trafficking in the lives of those surveyed for this study. Therefore, by "evangelical," I intend white evangelicalism. Other evangelical ethicists are also important to my study (Stanley Grenz, David Gushee, Lewis Smedes, and many others). However, within white evangelicalism there exists a fundamentalist strand of ethics that deeply penetrates all others. As the most boisterous sexual ethics, fundamentalism should be treated on its own terms.

106. In a recent comprehensive study of religious life in the United States, Pew Research found that in a pool of 35,000 Americans, white Evangelicals make up 25.4 percent of Christians. White Evangelicals are by far the largest number of Christians in the US, with its closest counterpart being Catholic Christians at 20.8 percent and its closest Protestant competitor being mainline Protestants at 14.7 percent. Therefore, the theological and ethical language operative in the United States amongst those who profess the Christian faith is demographically majority white Evangelical. It is essential to consider this language as a primary voice in forming, for better or worse, the American Christian context. See Pew Research Center, "Religious Landscape Study."

107. See Noll, *Rise of Evangelicalism*, 15.

The conversion of the heart led to new affections and zeal for God through the regeneration of the appetites. This emphasis on heart conversion accompanied a larger emphasis on spiritual warfare that characterized much of the evangelical movement. The move to affections and spiritual warfare attempted to correct the rationalist deism of other prominent American Christians like Thomas Jefferson.

The centrality of "spiritual" warfare to the emerging evangelicalism would have a drastic impact not just as an impetus for personal conversion but also on their social circles. To be clear, the "personal" experience of conversion would be the defining feature of evangelicalism. Personal conversion took shape as a decision by the individual for Christ and against Satan and all of his works. An example of such a conversion that illustrates spiritual fervor and fear of contamination lies in the story evangelical preacher William Glendinning. According to historian Christine Heyrman, Glendinning was a "scrawny Scot" Methodist preacher active in the spreading of the evangelical movement in 1784.[108] He, according to Heyrman, felt the need to engage in deep theological education through a desire to grow in "wisdom and truth."[109] However, this new deep wisdom on Christ's divinity, the nature of Scripture, and the reality of original sin led him to doubt what he once believed. Though he overcame these doubts, he began to fear education's impact on his eternal salvation. Entertaining doubt could only be a rejection of God and a surrender to the devil's works. Such thoughts filled Glendinning with a deep dread that drove him away from the church, his family, and even himself, attempting suicide. Though his suicide was unsuccessful, Glendinning illustrates the seriousness by which the evangelical movement takes their decision in faith and the purity of their convictions. One must maintain their faith without entertaining doubts because in so doing one entertains the devil. In short, doubts *contaminate* one's faith and threaten to contaminate the faith of those around you. The Christian life, on this account, survives through the ability to make a decision regardless of circumstances. Nothing, in the evangelical mind, is more important than that decision, because it encapsulates one's place either with Christ or with the devil. Glendinning's subsequent loss of community, family, and mental health through his doubts results from the fear all evangelicals felt. One must distance oneself from the one experiencing such obsession to avoid contamination in their own life through the influence on their decision. Furthermore, it "was expected," as Heyrman argues, "that all who committed themselves to evangelical faiths would . . . explore, regularly and

---

108. Heyrman, *Southern Cross*, 28.
109. Heyrman, *Southern Cross*, 29.

relentlessly, the darkest recesses of their hearts, experience overwhelming guilt and remorse, and search their souls for signs of repentance."[110] Believers must remain alert for such footholds for Satan in their lives through constant inward, spiritual examination.

The emotional distress associated with such rapt attention was too much for many to bear, and not even the choice of the conversion provided relief.[111] Heyrman continues, "to seek evangelical rebirth was to court daunting emotional risks, as even their clergy acknowledged."[112] Furthermore, such a risk then projects itself on every relationship potentially undertaken by the convert. As one explores their inner life, they must explore their outer life so as not to allow a foothold for Satan through other people's impurity and contaminating presence. The Christian life exists through sheer force of will and choice for God and against Satan. Not only are the individual believer's doubts dangerous but their friend, family, and neighbor's doubts and impurity are as well.

The language of impurity and contamination evolves with evangelicalism through the rise of the prosperity gospel. Like evangelical conversion in its fundamentalist instantiation, the prosperity gospel was a sheer force of will. As the historian and theologian Kate Bowler summarizes this evolving movement, "adherents, acting in accordance with divine principles, relied on their minds [and wills] to transform thought and speech into heaven-sent blessings."[113] The inwardness of evangelicalism willed thought and emotion into the outward manifestation of success by correctly choosing God and rejecting Satan. Correct decisions would lead to blessings and wrong ones to curses, which recalls Kant's moral project. In this way, blessing was not merely spiritual term but also material. Prosperity gospel preachers proclaim that heaven-sent blessings are the reward for lack of doubt and the negotiation of relationships that cultivate purity. One's physical and emotional health, economic life, and social status all arose from this sheer force of will "because," as Bowler continues, "all physical [and emotional] imbalances could be traced to demonic influences, [and] for prosperity teachers deliverance—the binding and loosing of spiritual forces—was the most useful interpretive framework."[114]

Since one's interior life is the site of the constant negotiating of spiritual forces that establish one's relationship with God, self, and the world, the risk of contamination through people or media presented a real concern. One

---

110. Heyrman, *Southern Cross*, 33.
111. Heyrman, *Southern Cross*, 39.
112. Heyrman, *Southern Cross*, 39.
113. Bowler, *Blessed*, 11.
114. Bowler, *Blessed*, 169.

must *choose* very carefully what media to consume and what relationships to maintain. What one takes in, naturally, must reflect the correct message about doubt, spiritual warfare, and the path to blessing. As a result, a media empire that catered to this concern boomed in the twentieth century. As Kristin Kobes Du Mez argues, this brand of evangelicalism possessed a wide array of media from books to music and apparel to bumper stickers. One can follow the brand in every way and determine their orthodoxy down to the bracelet on their wrist. As Du Mez writes, many "evangelicals who would be hard-pressed to articulate even the most basic tenets of evangelical theology have nonetheless been immersed in this evangelical popular culture."[115] Evangelicalism, in its prosperity culture, sought a market space in order to perpetuate right messaging and the sure practices that would lead to health, wealth, and success.

One must recognize this shift to prosperity and media as the context for the rise in purity culture as a unique form of sexual ethics. The purity movement emerged from the late twentieth-century rise of teen pregnancy inside and outside the church. In response, prosperity-minded evangelicals drew on a strict history of purity teaching to teach women the modesty necessary to lower pregnancy rates.[116] Though many in the United States first associate purity cultures with the late twentieth century, it is merely a reinterpretation of an early purity culture that occurred through strict policing of racial purity during the first half of the twentieth century.[117] However, as the century progressed, the purity teaching focused on women's purity almost exclusively. With the publications of famed evangelical centerpieces, *I Kissed Dating Goodbye* (1997) by Joshua Harris and *Why Wait? What You Need to Know about the Teen Sexuality Crisis* (1987) by Josh McDowell, a purity revolution began among evangelical families all over the United States.[118] These books quickly became bestselling works that formed evangelical culture around sexuality. Specifically, it formed a market-driven orthodoxy that promised the key to healthy marriages. Fathers and men would protect young women's purity, and young women would, in turn, dress modestly to preserve men from lustful temptation. The goal was for women to maintain their purity (i.e., a virginal state without contamination and a lack of sexual desire) to *give* it to their husband on their wedding night.

Framing sexuality through purity and contamination suggests that sexuality is a spiritual risk that can lead to curses. As such, sexual temptation

---

115. Du Mez, *Jesus and John Wayne*, 7.
116. Du Mez, *Jesus and John Wayne*, 170.
117. See Cone, *Cross and the Lynching Tree*, 7–8, 31, 99.
118. Du Mez, *Jesus and John Wayne*, 171.

is a spiritual battle that possesses the ability to take someone away from their commitment to God, as with Glendinning's temptation with academic study. Through will and agency, the goal of sexual ethics is to strip down one's life, pushing out that which is not pure. The purity culture revolution buried all other sexual ethics in the division between pure and impure with life-or-death consequences. In fact, many young evangelicals grew not according to a healthy diet of doctrine or church teachings, but rather the moral activities essential to find value in the sight of God. As Du Mez rightly understands, many Christians "learned about purity before they learned about sex, and they still have the silver ring to prove it."[119] However, purity culture did not merely sell rings and books, it provided a logic to buy and sell the bodies of young people and groom a self-deprecating image of women and their bodies while also giving the permission for men to accept their own uncontrollable lust. Purity culture urged a theological commitment to value a woman's body as pure specifically and to promote the evil impurity of sexuality. Thus, sex should not be practiced, thought about, or even discussed.

The purity movement was disastrous for young people. As Linda Klein shows, purity culture destroys the view of sexuality by placing it in the zero-sum, commodified matrix. Purity culture's theology of sex did more than condemn the act of sex, it made one receive the entire topic of sex as disgusting. Klein writes, "one does not need to have *sex* to feel this way. The purity movement teaches that *every* sexual activity—from masturbation to kissing if it elicits that special feeling—can make one less pure."[120] In this context, ethics arises from the believer's interior life, as emphasized by the early evangelical and prosperity movement, and illustrates that any sort of sexual feeling can lead to contamination and condemnation. The consequence of such interiorizing toward sexuality creates a fear of bodies (one's own and others) and sexual desires. The only good is the absence of desire.

An example of the ideal, sexually vacuous subject lies in one woman that Klein interviewed for her study. She explained that if, while watching a movie or some form of media, she felt a twinge of sexual desire, she would slap her genital region to make her sexual feelings go numb.[121] Sexual ethics of this kind trains the body against sex itself, which extends beyond sexual desires to the proposed relationships for sexuality in marriage as well. As Klein describes, such rejection of one's sexuality can lead to psychosomatic disorders such as "vaginismus," namely, "an involuntary physical tightening

---

119. Du Mez, *Jesus and John Wayne*, 7.
120. Klein, *Pure*, 12.
121. Klein, *Pure*, 140.

of the vagina that makes sex painful and sometimes even impossible."[122] This disorder can, as Klein argues, "last days, or decades" and is common among women who experience religious pressure to ignore or discourage their sexual desire.[123] This ethic of renunciation led to dissatisfactory sex rather than what it promised.

In addition to sexual dysfunction, many women also experience a new kind of violence inside the confines of marriage. As Klein argues, purity culture teaches women that the development of the vacuum of sexual desire must turn to uncontrollable sexual passion in marriage. Jo, one of Klein's research subjects, refers to this passion as the "tigress" switch. She tells Klein, one needs to move from the absence of sexual urges and temptations to a woman capable of sex anytime or else your husband would have an affair.[124] The story of purity sexual ethics for women illustrates that allowing no room for any sexual desire meant that many Christian women did not "develop sexual desires [toward their husbands] in a normal way."[125] Purity code realism does not bear fruit and only damages healthy sexual desires.

Though the specific purity structure in heterosexual sex primarily impacts women, men also fail to develop healthy sexual desires. According to famous tenets of purity culture, women must possess no sexual desire then become, as evangelical pastor Mark Driscoll urges, porn stars to their husbands.[126] Such objectification of their wives leads to malformation among heterosexual men even in marriage. As Driscoll argues, the "world assaults men with images of beautiful women . . . Male brains house an ever-growing repository of lustful snapshots always on random shuffle."[127] Driscoll echoes the even darker side of classic tenets of purity through arguing that only "free and frequent" sex between husband and wife could keep a husband faithful and the marriage successful.[128] The implication is, in fact, the wife is responsible for her husband's potential infidelity, and the husband is not responsible for his lustful objectification of other women or infidelity. Evangelical purity forms general permission for male predatory behavior, which supports the conditions for patriarchy and sexual abuse. In this system, certain bodies matter and others do not, often disposing of unimportant bodies as a sign of fidelity to the market principle of purity. Such deep-rooted language of sexual disgust clearly benefits some while also harming others,

---

122. Klein, *Pure*, 141.
123. Klein, *Pure*, 141.
124. Klein, *Pure*, 139.
125. Klein, *Pure*, 140.
126. Jessica Johnson unpacks this theme in Driscoll in her work *Biblical Porn*.
127. Mark Driscoll, "Dance of Manaheim," quoted in Johnson, *Biblical Porn*, 7.
128. Mark Driscoll, *Porn Again Christians*, quoted in Johnson, *Biblical Porn*, 7.

which leads to structural violence of violence and exclusion. To summarize, one must choose purity to be pure and blessed (prosperity gospel) and this purity finds its source in God's revelation in creation (Finney). The Christian's only defense against impurity is disgust at everything that is impure.

In purity culture, the desire to remain distinct possesses a grammar that permits immorality in light of the seemingly greater need to fulfill a code. The images that code create a culture of scarcity wherein one must compete and embody one's moral posture by any means necessary, which often leads to tragedy. For example, in March 2021 in a suburb in Georgia, eight people, including six women of Asian descent, were murdered in a massage parlor by a Christian man, Robert Long, who frequented that parlor to prove his own sexual purity.[129] The man admitted to killing the women to avoid sexual temptation and conquer his sexual addiction. Police apprehended the man while on his way to commit a similar crime against women in the porn industry. The man enacts violence against those who tempt him to demonstrate his purity. As with Glendinning, he must will to resist temptation and cut out all temptation by any means necessary. Errant thoughts and peoples' lives go hand in hand in such a calculus. The women in question were not humans in his eyes but fallen women and vessels of temptation in need of eradication. Goodness for him takes the shape of exclusion to the point of murder. Long's case is an extreme one in that not every adherent to purity culture commits murder, but the postures, moral presuppositions, and patterns of exclusion remain indicative of this approach to ethics. Code ethics cultivate a need to be good and fit the most appropriate images, and the more dramatic one's embodiment the better, no matter what violence one must commit. In other words, the only way to be good lies in the fundamental rejection of those who are "contaminations."

Code Ethics

Purity culture best describes the ethics of sexuality centered on disgust. Bodies trained in a disgust model of sexuality cultivate an optic for sex wherein sexuality at all is evil especially as it is present in female bodies. Recalling, for example, the Whore of Babylon, certain images theologically permit certain kinds of violence. One must, then, resemble a specific image (i.e., Mary) and perform a certain code metric to fulfill the standards of an image. The language of coding, as Adkins points out, makes certain images the internal logic that dominates the kind of sexual activity permitted in social circles. Purity proposes that women must be sexually devoid of desire

129. See Fausset, Bogel-Burroughs, and Fazio, "8 Dead in Atlanta Shootings."

and available to men. Thus, purity is a sexual ethic of code, which "codes" certain privileges and condemnations into sexual ethics and women's bodies as a premoral reflex.

Code ethics thus limits the moral imagination and drives humanity to a malformed moral reasoning. Codes are the single source principles that mark acceptable moral behavior by a group and, by extension, unacceptable behaviors in order to present techniques and rules as the exclusive fullness of the moral life. In short, they mark out a visual component in ethics wherein Eve and Mary exist on opposite ends of an optic of sexuality. Charles Taylor terms the mind's occupation with the construction and recognition of codes as "code fetishism." As Taylor writes, a code fetish collapses "the entire spiritual dimension of human life . . . in a moral code."[130] Thus, the depth of human meaning, according to codes, rests in a mere appearance of conduct universally valid for all contexts.

Contrasting code fetishism with an ancient view of ethics, Taylor argues that codes disrupt the original intention for a moral life. The ancients recognized that "situations and events are unforeseeably various . . . This is why the good person with phronesis [practical reason] . . . operates on a deep sense of the goods concerned, plus a flexible ability to discern what the new situation requires."[131] The ancient vision of life and ethics arose from a complex attunement of one's loves and affections toward the good beyond being in order to form moral reasoning in such a way as to commit moral activity amongst competing claims.[132] Such attunement allows for the moral being to negotiate a world with a "plurality of goods" that often "conflict in certain circumstances" (e.g., liberty and equality; justice and mercy; communicative justice and community).[133] The disappearance of this kind of practical reason in modernity funds a search for a "single-source principle" (i.e., a code) that does not recognize the conflicting goods in varying situations.[134] The competing goods, for example, are the impossible choices that many women have to make in their search for subsistence that often leads them into trafficking relationships. For example, Immanuel Kant rejected that any external contingencies should impact one's various duties. Moral luck, the term for such contingencies, should not impact the moral choices one makes. As a result, modern attempts at practical reason, for the most part, fall short of nuanced wisdom because moral thinking must take a

---

130. Taylor, "Perils of Moralism," 353.
131. Taylor, "Perils of Moralism," 348.
132. See Plato, *Republic*, 205.
133. Taylor, "Perils of Moralism," 348.
134. Taylor, "Perils of Moralism," 348.

specific shape without negotiating contingencies. The fetishization of the code simplifies the moral life and guides moral agents in the perfection of their natural capacity through the constant rehearsal of a code.

A helpful description of code ethics arises from the work of Paul Ramsey. Utilizing the example of legalism present in some strains of first-century Judaism, code morality, according to Ramsey, places "fences around the law [that] serve to guarantee righteousness."[135] Thus, code morality is not merely a rule or moral prescription. Code morality, instead, arises from a single-source principle in a rule or law that includes a fundamental set of complementary rules that "hedge" specific interpretations of the principle to maintain a narrow meaning of it to adjudicate an "order of preference . . . in case of conflict" with other competing goods.[136] Such an order of preference does not entail a true practical reason but merely a set of techniques to memorize. Ramsey exemplifies this ethic through accompanying descriptions surrounding the law prohibiting work on the Sabbath. The existence of the rule to rest alone does not satisfy all the conflicts that arise from it, but rather the accumulation of exact code prescriptions that replace practical reason to aid the agent in the exact execution of the law. The purpose of order of preference for the rabbis of the day consisted in aiding the common person's understanding of the Sabbath through the adherence to the specific rules required to inhabit it. The extreme manifestation of this custom in legalism flipped the order of meaning in the covenant and turned righteousness into a technique.

The language of technique is an important aspect of code ethics in general. Jacques Ellul, a French theologian, provides a description of technical ethics, which argues that code morality no longer concerns the development of a practical reason and character but rather the perfection of a specific technique. The agent's "behavior," as Ellul writes, "must be exact, precise; his acts must be coordinated with the play of the various kinds of techniques that proliferate in our society. And this behavior must be decided not in virtue of moral principles, but as a function of precise . . . rules."[137] Thus, sexual ethics is no longer concerned with discerning the meaning of sexuality and its contribution to the good life, but rather a technique that one can practice, such as avoiding all sexuality in thought, word, and deed before matrimony. Ellul describes the technique as the commodified version of ethics collapsed into specific decisions and actions capable of gaining a habitus for the agent. The motivations of the agent causes satisfaction in the

---

135. Ramsey, *Basic Christian Ethics*, 46.
136. Ramsey, *Basic Christian Ethics*, 47.
137. Ellul, *To Will & To Do: Volume I*, 174.

very use of the technique itself. The agent "must adhere to [the technique, the code] for moral reasons."[138]

The result of the technique is the elimination of the moral in favor of the normal, which codes actions as particular behavior rather than the good.[139] The normal becomes a means that the agent can maintain social capital and durable networks through visualizing the code in their body. The perpetuation and desire to be normal serve as labor that confers meaning on social capital as the cost to maintain group membership. The pure are granted access while the impure are not. One should recognize by now why the mistreatment of those caught in the web becomes such an easy temptation. The one without social capital, namely the one who exists outside the durable network, "is not considered to be a [person] who has done wrong, but a sick or abnormal person who must be cured, to bring them back to average behavior."[140] Normalcy, as such, cultivates a society capable of adaptation wherein conformity is the only true virtue.

Normal behavior must possess a precise mechanism to measure normal versus abnormal, pure versus impure actions. The importance of the technical society is precisely the behavior proscribed for measurement, and Ellul argues that this is material and measured according to two values: success and failure.[141] In the technical society, the virtuous individual is the most successful person, and the immoral is the one who is not.[142] As Ellul states, "every success of technique participates in the ultimate Good; and to oppose this development is truly to do Evil, and to be demonic."[143] The result of this technological society is the construction of ethics wherein goodness and evil are zero-sum games. Failure to adhere to the codes to embody "normal" behavior results in a strict division and hierarchy in society.

Thus, as Ellul describes a central feature of the technological society, one must able be to identify those who do not fit the code, not only to cast them out but also to measure ourselves. Furthermore, it is not enough to merely succeed where others fail but also to punish those who fail. This aspect beyond the mere desire to succeed mirrors what James Alison calls a "system of goodness."[144] In such a system, "I rely, for my goodness, on holding onto, and obeying, everything in the system, then that means my

138. Ellul, *To Will & To Do: Volume I*, 175.
139. Ellul, *To Will & To Do: Volume I*, 177.
140. Ellul, *To Will & To Do: Volume I*, 177.
141. Ellul, *To Will & To Do: Volume I*, 178.
142. Ellul, *To Will & To Do: Volume I*, 178–79.
143. Ellul, *To Will & To Do: Volume I*, 179.
144. See Alison, "Place of Shame and the Giving of the Spirit."

goodness is 'over against' someone else's badness, and thus, being dependent on it, is part of it."[145] What the code secures for one must mean punishment for others. The only way to maintain the pure/impure distinction is through the prosperity posture of success and reward. It is not enough to merely succeed, but if the code measures success, it must mean damnation for the contaminated other.

Social Exclusion: Toxic Goodness

As should be clear, the punishment/reward system creates a toxic goodness at the center of ethics. Rowan Williams notes that toxic goodness is "that humans do things in order to be good—or perhaps to *seem* to be good."[146] The people who practice toxic goodness "are those who don't always see what they're *implicated* in."[147] This remarkable statement by Williams shows the true banality of what many term goodness today. Humans delight in their embodiment of goodness in order to claim that their actions arise from good motivations. "But," as Williams continues, "this can blind us to the ways in which we are shaped by what we don't know. As a self, I am already implicated in what I don't know and what I don't see, and simply to focus on goodness in a narrow and self-defining way can be a problem rather than a blessing."[148] Since humanity desires the appearance of goodness, or normality, they define the terms of goodness to match their actions and judgments.

As such, the issue of Christian sexual ethics lies in our code construction of the moral life in which goodness becomes something one can *seem* to be as markedly different from one's abnormal neighbor. Critics might balk at such a claim, citing the church's call to be "set apart" in holiness. However, upon further examination, the call to holiness of Christ's church always closely connects to the being of God, which is "made known" in the person of Jesus Christ (John 1:18, NRSV). Christ makes known the being of God through a myriad of seemingly immoral tasks among God's people in direct opposition to their systems of toxic goodness. As theologian Sarah Bachelard acknowledges,

> Instead of working to stay on the right side of the religious authorities, the enforcers of the system, Jesus goes to the space of

---

145. Alison, "Place of Shame and the Giving of the Spirit," 201.
146. Williams, "Beyond Goodness," 157.
147. Williams, "Beyond Goodness," 158.
148. Williams, "Beyond Goodness," 158.

being cursed by them. In doing so, he unmasks the mechanism through which the identity and goodness of the group is secured over against its designated "other." This revelation pertains not simply to the actions of this particular system of goodness in this particular case, but to all systems of goodness that maintain themselves by creating victims.[149]

Bachelard articulates a theological critique of toxic goodness embedded within the very life of God. Christ's solidarity with the criminal and the immoral leads to a radically provocative claim that God shares in the "implicatedness" of a system that God sees, but humanity does not. In other words, God allows Godself to be implicated in a system of toxic goodness that God did not create in a world imbued with sin. Rather than uphold these systems, Jesus brings them to an apocalyptic rupture by rejecting such means to achieve goodness altogether. Instead, those who follow Christ must do so through participation in Christ's life at the site of the rejected. Purity and disgust create the places of Christ's rejection. Even among those tasked with helping people caught in the web of trafficking there remains a disgust of those they help. Disgust posture is premoral, a reflex embedded within the human community based on coordinated social norms. Many use this reflex to reject certain forms of life outright, namely the rejection of people who lack the codes to exist within the circle of durable networks. As such, codes render invisible the myriad of issues that cultivate trafficking and can only focus on the sexual impurity.

CONCLUSION: IMAGES

As stated in the introduction to this chapter, ethics suffers from an image problem. The images that drive Christian sexual ethics haunt those caught in the web yet render invisible the suffering of those caught in the web. Images, in short, code experience to privileged bodies and exclude those who bear the wrong image. Mary, Eve, the Whore of Babylon, and the fallen woman all swirl around the lives of those caught in the web and justify exclusion. Furthermore, it creates an economy of images with strict borders and an aesthetics of sexuality. When coupled with purity, it utilizes a compulsion of disgust in order to police sexual behavior and drive out those who do not fit. This ethics of purity, popular among evangelicals, must experience defamation.

---

149. Bachelard, *Resurrection and Moral Imagination*, 75.

2

Hearing from Survivors

Trafficking and Purity Codes

INTRODUCTION: PHENOMENOLOGICAL RESEARCH

IN CHAPTER 1, I established the history and terminology around sexuality and trafficking while highlighting central pre-moral impulses, namely purity and disgust. Ethics in the Christian and non-Christian world possess a code approach that depends less on the cultivation of virtue than on the learning of a technique. In this chapter, I will tease out the implications of these terms through a series of qualitative interviews. The qualitative method deployed in this chapter is phenomenological; namely, it seeks to establish a phenomenon's essence and terms related to it to suspend a researcher's bias. In terms of phenomenology, I draw from the research method of the twentieth-century philosopher Martin Heidegger, wherein "something shows itself."[1] Specifically, Heidegger envisions research that not only considers terms but "establish[es] the sense in which that fact of the matter is meant by the word."[2] In short, phenomenological research considers the perspective of individuals as a means to establish our understanding of terms. Though many of the sources and resources utilized in chapter 1 use primary research data, I wish to explore whether the one who experiences trafficking shares any experience of sex or sexuality with those who grew up under strict purity culture. I establish terms such as *purity, trafficking, code ethics,* and *disgust* in response to the lives of research participants.

---

1. Heidegger, *Introduction to Phenomenological Research*, 4.
2. Heidegger, *Introduction to Phenomenological Research*, 4.

Thus, I ask a singular question: is there a shared experience around "code ethics" between these two groups?

The answer to this question is yes. Participants admit to similar patterns of social exclusion based on their ability to fulfill or fail certain codes centered around sex and sexuality.

This chapter will present a study of eight women, with half composed of survivors of trafficking and the other half composed of women who grew up in a traditional purity culture context. As the proceeding analysis will indicate, each participant will self-narrate their life and identify the expectations imposed on them and the consequences or benefits of failing to or successfully meeting them. In each case, sex is an avenue to community so long as one performs according to expectations. Furthermore, women on both sides experience a tremendous amount of pressure and policing around sexuality, as well as significant impact to their moral consciousness.

PART I: TESTIMONIES

The following study unpacks the phenomenon of sexuality through the lens of survivors of trafficking. The testimonies offered here contain many difficult stories but nonetheless offer a clearer perspective on certain issues covered in chapter 1. The structuring of ethics according to code and disgust impacts people's material lives. These testimonies show the cost and simultaneously offer a chance at reorientation. Thus, to summarize, there are certain social factors (social capital), material factors (moral luck), and psychological factors (moral injury) that shape a world where maltreatment finds the vulnerable. As we proceed with our study, many who experience trafficking do so, as Howard Thurman describes, with their backs against the wall.[3] Theology must speak from this posture and, as with Paul and Silas, hear these voices.

To be clear, what follows is testimony. Not all women interviewed are Christians, but all witness to a new way. What cannot be lost in a study such as this is the agency that these women exhibit. They resist definition, call systems into question, and do not collapse into other ill-fitting accounts of their humanity. Theology done well speaks from these testimonies to better articulate the prevenient work of God in the world. Thus, theology is far richer when considering these testimonies. Only by bringing these testimonies deep inside our communities can social exclusion be challenged.

---

3. Thurman, *Jesus and the Disinherited*, xix, 1–3.

THE STUDY

Before exploring the findings, I wish to outline the study. An invitation went out to organizations that worked with survivors of trafficking and purity culture. Only graduates no longer dependent on the resources from the organizations were solicited to participate in the study. In the end, eight women participated in the study. Half of the women were survivors of trafficking and the other half grew up under purity culture teaching, but all participants were given pseudonyms. The participants were selected from a pool of applicants who graduated programs for reintegration and now volunteer through mentoring women coming out of trafficking or who can openly speak about purity culture. In addition, each participant took the Adverse Childhood Experiences (ACEs) test in order to indicate the level of trauma from during their childhood years. High numbers, greater than 4, indicate a high level of abuse and lingering mental and emotional strain later in life. All participants selected took a trauma response test before and after the survey to gauge the strain on their mental health. All participants were then asked to narrate their lives from childhood through their adulthood, allowing the participants to name and describe each major milestone of their lives. Along the way, participants were asked the major influences, expectations, and consequences/rewards for meeting those expectations. Next, the survey asked participants to narrate, as with their milestones, their history with sex and sexuality. Participants began with their first sexual opportunity, which could be a kiss or even speaking about it with parents or family. After describing this first experience, the participants named the influential voices and expectations as well as the consequences and rewards for meeting expectations. As with the milestones of their life, the participants then narrated through the major milestones of their experiences with sexuality. In the final portion of the survey, participants narrated their hopes and dreams as well as reflected on the survey itself. Though much can be said about the results, the finding of this study is that trafficking and purity culture share a similar internal logic. At best, purity culture realism merely reflects trafficking back at itself, and at worst purity culture grooms young women *for* trafficking.

Hearing from the Survivors: Trafficking

The study begins with those who are survivors of trafficking. Beginning with childhood, all participants named a significant amount of trauma emerging from their childhood experiences. The ACEs score for this group ranged from 3 to 8 with an average of 6.25. The high levels of abuse are coupled with a lack of family love and support necessary for a child's development. The majority of the participants (3/4) remembered the negative attributes about themselves. In addition, the hopes and needs expressed during this period are immediate and not long-term. One survivor remembers a specific career that she wanted, but she also wanted the more immediate attention or lack of abuse from a family member.

The expectations of these participants in their youth largely included their silence about their abuse and submission to continued abuse. The expectation was that abuse would occur and that the young girl should behave, be quiet, and accept their fate. The abuse experienced by the women was verbal, physical, and sexual in nature. It was at this stage that they learned two important things. First, the women learned that sex was a means of receiving things of value. To be clear, the exchange was not consensual but coerced and constantly under threat. In two cases, participants recounted that silence and not resisting abuse met positive reinforcement through material gifts. As one participant indicated, this instilled a feeling that she was never good enough, that her body meant nothing, and that she must continue to perform. In other cases, material items of value were not received in exchange for sex but rather nonmaterial such as the cessation of abuse. If a participant went along with the abuse, no more harm would come to them. If she refused, she would be beaten or more violently sexually assaulted.

Second, the participants, through their abuse, lost trust or formed untrusting images of men and authority. In all cases, the abuse came from an older male member of the family. In one case, female members of the family participated in the abuse. The messaging received during this time was that the young women could not talk about their sexual encounters or bad things would happen to them or their loved ones. In one case, for example, a participant's stepfather threatened to kill the young woman and her mother if she told anyone about her abuse. This same participant, once she did testify against her stepfather, was then abused by her uncle and aunt for a period. In short, the women articulated that sharing about one's sexual experiences only led to worse punishments.

As the survivors moved into their adolescent and teen years, a wound developed in their psyches. A deep yearning for connection and belonging emerged as a significant theme in all of the participants. During this period, the women found belonging outside of their family structures. The people that all of the women met gave them a sense of belonging that they did not possess in their traditional family structure. They transitioned from articulating a sense of meaninglessness and loneliness as children, but during this period, among new social circles, they received attention. The relationships encouraged delinquency, such as skipping school, misbehaving, and low-level criminal activity. Furthermore, through these relationships, early drug activity began.

Every survivor indicated that their trafficking relationships began during this time. In most cases (3/4), the trafficking relationship was a romantic one wherein sex was an avenue to fuel addiction. The wound that formed during their childhood was numbed through substance use and toxic relationships that granted attention. Drug addiction, thus, was a response to this moral wound, namely a way to cope with the deep trauma they experienced as children and continued to experience as young adults. Traditional structures of therapeutic care were absent during this period.

The expectations of this time mirrored their life as children. Women must do as they are told in order to gain access to things such as housing, drugs, food, and water. There was another element significant during this time, namely the women beginning to have children of their own. Most of the women (3/4) articulated that they wanted kids so as to not repeat the mistakes of their parents. However, due to life circumstances and external manipulation these women all lost their children. The cycles of trauma and addiction inhibited their ability to be fully present and their lack of social support led to estrangement from their children.

Due to these new traumas, the women went further into the realm of delinquency and crime to support their addictions. Some women turned to the streets during this period and overall, the women expressed a severe lack of hope, only searching to meet immediate needs. The women mostly adopted negative expectations and found worse and worse social circles, with some notable exceptions along the way. This shift, however, is not surprising. One of the main opportunities for trafficking arises from a lack of other adequate social supports. Survivors of trafficking note a lack of social networks in traditional settings due to abuse or delinquency from direct family members. This leads the survivors to find new social networks for a sense of belonging and stability, but the assumption among survivors is that these networks will fail too. However, they nevertheless seek to entrench themselves in networks that provide durable access to material and emotional needs.

With the emotional and material needs met, the most fascinating aspect of the survey involved the perceptions and changing perceptions around sexuality throughout their lives as they sought communities of support. As already indicated, the first sexual experiences for survivors were sexual abuses early in their life. This experience shaped them significantly. Submitting to abuse led to rewards such as material gifts and nonmaterial gifts such as safety. Sex, as a kid, was a code to gain something even if they did not want to use their bodies this way. Such an expectation continued into their later lives, where sex served to gain attention and maintain subsistence in durable social networks. Even in their stages of healing, half of the survivors felt that at some point, their current romantic partners required sex in exchange for some other good. Their body, as such, was a means to get what one needed both materially and nonmaterially. The trauma experienced in trafficking led to a negative self-perception, further drug addiction, and increased dependence on trafficking to continue addiction to numb their pain.

In each case, survivors only found a way out after jail, rehab, and the discovery of new social circles. To be clear, this last factor is the most significant. Each individual went through cycles of incarceration, rehab, and sobriety, but only a period of sobriety coupled with new, positive social networks would lead to lasting change. The elements that characterized these salutary communities were their willingness to embrace the women as they were and only desire their healing. Here the women found the ability to share their stories empoweringly. Each found places where they could express their feelings and find more healthy means for dealing with them. In many of these cases, the organizations were religious. But, as we will see with purity culture, religious organizations do not have a monopoly on the kind of goodness required to contribute to healing even though, as I argue, they are ideally placed to do this work. The important central theme identified by the participants is that these organizations did not require that the survivors use their bodies or assets to gain access to the community and that their bodies were not meaningless.

In conclusion, the survey lined up largely with the themes found in our literature review (chapter 1). The overarching theme is a process of formation from childhood into adulthood of expecting to use one's body to secure goods and durable networks. This expectation and the experience of these expectations led to addiction and trafficking for these women. Though choice does exist in these scenarios, a choice must be considered under the structures of power that shape and form. Specifically, that love looks like giving sex for material and nonmaterial blessing and the perception that one cannot opt out of the system as it is. This leaves a wound through trauma that influences how one lives their life and the choices that they make. The path to healing requires acceptance, love, and patience, where the communities do not base *correction* on bad behavior.

Hearing from Survivors II: Purity Culture

The participants recruited from the purity culture group answered the same questions as their trafficking counterparts. The ACEs scores for this group were much lower than the trafficking group with a range of 0 to 3 with an average of 0.75. One participant identified significant abuse, both verbal and physical, as a child, but this was not prevalent in all participants. Also, unlike the survivors of trafficking, purity culture participants indicated more future-oriented aspirations rather than immediate needs. They all expressed career aspirations and the majority (3/4) expressed a desire for Christian mission work from an early age. The people of influence in the lives of these participants were primarily family and church. Grandparents played a large role in two of the women surveyed, often modeling more healthy forms of love and care than more immediate caregivers.

The expectations of these primary influences were largely religious, but all centered on achievements. The expectation was that the participants would act a certain way to gain spiritual blessing. As one participant put it, they must achieve certain spiritual platitudes to "be church worthy" (Terry). The grandparent's influence in two cases offered more narratives of acceptance. Caregivers expected certain types of behavior and dress. The rewards for adherence to expectations were spiritual and material blessings. If one behaved, then toys and even heaven were promised rewards.

The majority of expressed expectations concerned sexuality. Purity, even from a young age, was a significant expectation. All of the participants identified certain expectations to dress modestly, to abstain from all sexual thoughts and activity, and to not talk about sex at all. In addition, expectations around romance caused a great deal of anxiety for the participants as children. The families and churches of the participants expressed dire consequences for a failure to meet codes. If one failed to meet purity code requirements, one would either "get pregnant and die" (Phoebe) or they would go to "hell" (Terry). The stakes were high and since many purity culture teachers claimed that even having sexual thoughts or urges would transgress the purity code, one could not afford a mistake. Though some might balk at the fear of pregnancy and death, the participants expressed that their childhood selves were not allowed to know about how sex or their bodies worked so as to not invite intrusive thoughts about sex. This inability to talk about sex coupled with the fear of punishment for sexuality, created an atmosphere where abuse can easily occur. Emily Joy Allison, author of *#ChurchToo: How Purity Culture Upholds Abuse and How to Find Healing*, recalls a conversation with therapist and author Dr. Tina Schermer Sellers, who presents the connection between this purity paradigm and sexual abuse. Dr. Sellers argues that the purity response in Christian and non-Christian contexts attempts to discourage sexual feelings so that bad consequences (i.e., impurity) do not follow. She continues,

> And you've given them no knowledge . . . no resources, nothing to equip them to protect themselves . . . And you are now no longer a resource, because you've made it clear that if they come to you, you'll only punish them. So now they're out in this world where there is exploitation at every turn. And they can't recognize the exploitation because you've given them no tools to recognize the exploitation.[4]

Phoebe, a participant in the study, confirms this perspective. Sex was such an evil activity that it felt like a crime to have sex. She ended up in an abusive relationship and felt isolated because her support system only expressed condemnation of her if she ever did transgress. Furthermore, when she did escape the relationship, that support system responded exactly as she expected—with disgust and anger at *her* choices, even asking Phoebe to get tested for AIDS and take a pregnancy test although the relationship ended over a year prior. Without resources, abuse is a distinct possibility.

The largest impact of purity culture messaging was the meaning it placed on the female body. For most (3/4), there was a deep-seeded anxiety and for the remainder there was confusion. Their body, as articulated by the participants, is dangerous because of the capability to transgress the codes. Furthermore, as they were told by their superiors, their body is a gift for their husband. The code givers (e.g., family, church) coded the body into a possession for their future husband, which led to a disempowering posture toward their body. The only one who has a right to know it and explore it is the husband. This is a right that not even the participant has. One's purity thus is how one secures a husband. The code of exchange, purity for matrimony, finds expression through now classic illustrations such as asking if someone wants to drink water from a cup with another's spit in it to explain how one's future husband would feel when having sex with anyone other than a virgin (Phoebe).

In addition to romantic achievements through purity, it was also a means toward great esteem and praise inside the participant's social circles, such as the church. One participant highlighted how her modest dress allowed her to gain leadership positions at her church. The church leadership even asked her to provide peers with more modest clothing since she was the example of modesty. However, the moment that she wore tight leggings she gained a bad reputation and lost all positions of authority. The optic of purity culture visualizes the perfect female body. It is chaste, modest, and submissive in that it can follow the rules. The rules are absolute and thus offer no room for nuance.

4. Allison, *#ChurchToo*, 61.

Much like survivors of trafficking, the participants found a way out of purity culture through new social networks. For at least half, this led them away from the church. For the majority (3/4), it at least led to romantic partners who did not hold the participants to the standard of purity culture. Furthermore, the husbands and partners of these participants did not treat their bodies or sex as a right or possession. To be clear, the participant's understanding of sex is still deeply complicated. The journey of learning to know their bodies and explore sexuality with their partners remains a tricky affair. Even though this is the one prescribed relationship wherein one can have sex, they cannot shake the stigmas cultivated by the mindset that sex is evil.

One element that appears also throughout the milestones of each participant is the discovery of new social networks other than romantic ones. One of the pressures present in all participants is the implicit fear that their sexual experience might lead to a loss of primary support. This makes the person's status in their social networks insecure. As with the survivors of trafficking, after separating from primary support, the participants sought new social circles that might be secure. As children, even though they did not score high on ACEs across the board, the purity culture adherents expressed a lower sense of self-worth. The strong emphasis on achievement without an equally strong sense of worth complicated the participants' desires once they found new social structures. A failure to meet expectations threatened expulsion from the primary family. However, the difference between the purity culture participants and the trafficking survivors lies in the different social groups that they found. In the case of survivors of trafficking, these circles were ultimately the same as their childhood with steep expectations to give of oneself at the cost of one's well-being. They were conditional, harmful, and malformed. The purity culture adherents also found some of these circles but ultimately found places of safety and belonging with people who only desired their health and wellness. The themes of these groups were not to create strict conditions for group membership but rather the embrace of differences and partnering to flourish.

The overarching theme of purity culture is twofold. First, it is the fear of sexuality that drives it into silence and stigma. This resulted in a lack of resources and tools to understand and articulate healthy sexuality. Second, purity culture participants learned a negative sexuality in which exchange operates to earn access to social networks, spiritual blessing, and material gifts through their bodies. It is negative in that they do not engage in sexual activity, but rather use their lack of sexuality to gain access to reward. Furthermore, one cannot opt out of this system. It is total. One must adhere to secure a place or be cast out from the community.

Conclusions: Connecting Stories

In conclusion, the finding of the survey led to many unique findings. However, for the purpose of this study, I limit my engagement to the understanding of sex, codes, the body, and social influence. As such, even in this area one finds immense overlap between the two groups. Both express a feeling as if they are not enough as children from primary support systems. This is more universal in the trafficking group than purity culture, but it exists there as well. As children, the clear code for each of them was to meet an expectation from at least one primary caregiver. The distinction between future aspirations and immediate need rings as the biggest difference between the groups, even though both groups expressed a childhood unease with themselves. The participants state that their childhood selves, even if outgoing socially, feel an inner insecurity when it came to the articulation of self-images.

The consequences of not meeting expectations also proves to be an important area of exploration. In many cases, isolation and direct harm emerged as a result from a failure to adhere to given codes. To be clear, belonging is a basic human desire. However, the communal expectations surrounding one's place, as illustrated in this study, is the problem. The universal feeling across all eight participants was that they at one point or another must purchase their place in a community through a type of code adherence (silence, sex or lack of sex, or even consent to abuse). To be clear, there are expectations in the healthy communities described, but the difference is an open acceptance and a partnering with each in a way that honors dignity and agency. Unhealthy means create a deeper desire for belonging in a way that those with ill intent can exploit. Consequences shape a self-image, resulting from the communities that set expectations, benefits, and consequences.

Another overlap is the trauma expressed by both groups though the difference between the types of trauma remains notable. In each case, the trauma largely revolves around sexuality. For survivors of trafficking, the trauma emerges first through childhood sexual abuse and the way this shapes their picture of sex in general and men particularly. If one learns that "no" is not an option, then one's body is available to another. This mirrors the theme expressed by purity culture participants in that their body was a possession of their future husband. Purity culture and trafficking both favor men in that both systems, for the most part, privilege the male experience. The trauma thus appears through the expectation of abuse or misuse of sex in their lives. As different participants from both groups indicate, not only is sexual abuse possible from a man, but it is expected. This kind of trauma influences decisions and cultivates habits about sexuality in the world.

The biggest finding already alluded to in the emphasis on consequences lies in the way that sex is the same for trafficking and purity culture. This shocking claim emerges from the basic impulse to use sexuality to get something. Thus, purity and trafficking exist at different points on a similar trajectory. If purity code transgression can equal loss of community and trafficking arises from a desire to belong in the absence of primary social networks, then Christians should ask whether purity culture ideologically grooms women for trafficking relationships. Whether one uses sexual favors to earn material and nonmaterial gifts or uses the absence of sexuality to do the same, one must recognize that both logics exist as opposite sides of the same coin. One's worth emerges from the ability to secure certain things and causes a loss of intrinsic self-worth.

It would be a mistake to assume that the formations experienced by both groups remain isolated to their own individual experiences. As already illustrated, the expectations of both groups carry on into other aspects. For both groups, sex with a spouse must reckon with the trauma of past sexual experiences. In both groups, sex served in their past life as a means to secure a relationship. Furthermore, the larger community experiences this formation as well. It takes a system of people to sustain the expectations experienced by both parties. Churches, traffickers, parents, friends, and partners all expect specific activity from these women, albeit in different ways. Thus, only an entire rewrite of the moral imagination that funds such a code fetish can finally overcome the issues presented here. The inordinate pressure placed on sex to secure one's place in a relationship or even a larger community causes great harm. In short, sex cannot bear this weight.

PART II: UNPACKING THEMES IN THE RESEARCH

The research bears many themes for consideration, but I choose to focus on three as they directly confront the issues of code ethics, purity, and disgust. The phenomenon of trafficking and purity culture bear on specific terms found already in the research from chapter 1. In each theme, code ethics finds an important dialogue partner. Individual accountability craves a code ethics approach, but these themes highlight that exterior factors influence situations that do not lend themselves to black-and-white interpretations of ethics. Rather, as these themes suggest, choice and autonomy exist in a matrix of external social pressures and circumstances that lead to transgressing of codes and, thus, disgust at another's humanity. Such a socially unjust ordering of social space must be addressed not to perform code ethics more efficiently but rather to open up new pathways to freedom that do not include social exclusion.

Social Capital and Belonging

The first theme to emerge from our study is social capital and belonging. As stated in the Introduction, social capital is the parent category for sexual capital, which is the main source of meaning traded between participants. Each participant, in different yet complementary ways, stated sex and other aspects of their humanity served a purpose to accrue, maintain, or lose access to social networks. Sex, for example, served as a means to secure housing, food, or even drugs for trafficking survivors. In addition, those who grew up under strict purity codes confessed that a lack of sexuality maintained their status in church leadership, at home, and even before God.

The women surveyed in this study communicate their own experience of social capital in different ways, but all do so through a language of belonging and worth. When asked how she responded to expectations placed on her, one participant, Bobo, stated that she only performed actions to feel worthy of love and community. She was not *intrinsically* "enough" to those around her and thus had to perform certain actions to ensure that her place with her family or network could continue. Stacy, another participant, describes that sex felt like an obligation to those who provided for her: "I felt like I had to [let someone touch me sexually] if [they] bought me something . . . I felt obligated to have sex with them. It was never free will." Stacy represents all survivors in this study by naming the process whereby their trafficker maintained control over them. The deep-seeded anxiety surrounding the need to earn her worthiness impacted Bobo for her entire life. She explains, "[It has] carried over into my life. Like I have to remind myself today like I am enough, like nothing I do or say will make me more enough. I already am enough." Thus, social capital psychologically forms the individual to a self-deprecating picture of themselves that can only resolve through earning what Bobo terms "enoughness."

Social capital and belonging also emerge in purity culture participants. For the trafficking survivors, they exchanged sexual acts for durable networks. This pattern appears also in the purity culture participants but the order of expectation around sex inverts. Instead of sexual activity exchanging for durable networks, the absence of sexual activity or sexuality served as the sexual capital that purity culture participants traded in their durable networks. One such participant, Regina, notes just how valuable it was to present an absence of sexuality. Speaking of her experience with modesty, Regina recognized that when she dressed modestly, she earned leadership positions and esteem from her parents and church. Yet when she dressed in a way that no longer fit that description in the eyes of her community, she lost those privileged positions. As with all social capital, the social group (e.g., church, traffickers) must internally police their metrics to consecrate and reconsecrate the exchange as valuable, thus granting the possessor the rights and privileges guaranteed therein. In short, sex or its absence serves as a metric that secures one's place into durable network.

In sum, social capital serves as specific kinds of value one possesses. It can be gained and aggregated in an individual's life while maintaining the social institutions that regulate and consecrate the means of exchange and production. Sexual ethics, when considered in this code, exists for those who have this in excess. The need to maintain and keep durable networks is an essential piece for those in desperate situations. Thus, survival sex is a part of many people's search for a durable network. No one questions the necessity of social capital, only the way one gets it. Social capital thus marks out friend and enemy while granting advantage to those who possess it.

Moral Injury

In distinction from social capital, moral injury is a theme less about what one possesses and more about the negative self-picture one possesses of oneself and the trauma arising from certain experiences as a contributing factor to trafficking. Moral injury does not suggest that trauma survivors are incapable of moral activity, but that trauma experienced can harm the internal picture of oneself. Moral injury, to recall, is a central topic of study in the ethics of war indicating a bruise on the soul as a result of acts committed or experienced in a given militarized conflict. However, the bruise on the soul indicated moral injury also appears in trafficking survivors. Many of the survivors of trafficking surveyed in the preceding analysis identify domestic violence as a central part of their journey. The moral injury that emerges within the context of domestic violence and the actions they committed as a result of this relationship harms the humanity within the victim. As Margret Farley writes, the crimes associated with domestic violence are "not just against one's political or ideological enemies, but crimes against what makes humans, 'human.'"[5] The physical and psychological scars resulting from it and its power dynamics lead to a hurt in the individual's humanity. For purity culture the bruise was their fear of sex resulting from the

---

5. Farley, "Forgiveness in Service of Justice and Love," 326.

acceptance and perpetuation that it was evil, for survivors of trafficking it was addiction and trauma from abuse and the acts they participated in during their trafficking. While this hurt does not eliminate agency and the ability to make moral decisions, it does leave its mark. In short, it aims to destroy that sacredness at the heart of the human.[6]

An example of moral injury from our interviews lies in the story of Tracy. She experienced domestic abuse in her childhood. Tracy and her siblings were bound, beaten with belts and boards, tied up and locked in rooms unable to move for hours and sometimes an entire evening. Tracy mentions that in these moments she lost a chance to be a child in a way that would aid in her development as an adult. Specifically, she mentions the experience of being locked away impacting her positive self-worth and even her conduct throughout the course of her life. She recalls,

> I'm locked in this room. [And I feel like] I'm no good . . . So . . . I'm not of any value to be around the rest of the family and [they're] locking me away [and] into my adult life when I did something that I felt wasn't right . . . I continued doing it anyways [and] I feel like I kept doing things to get myself locked away.

Tracy notes the internal feeling created in her childhood lasted into her adulthood. An internal wound lasts a lifetime.

Moral injury is not just a feature of the survivors of trafficking but also among the women surveyed from a purity culture context. Twyla, who grew up under strict purity codes, also experienced significant abuse and trauma. Twyla's mother physically, emotionally, and verbally abused her from age six into her teen years. The abuse took its toll. As Twyla states, "[My mother] like really drilled into my head that you are worthless. You deserve bad things you know, like you [are] ruining my life and it's like I didn't freakin' choose to [live]." This began a negative feedback loop that would mirror her direct experience of purity culture. When Twyla attended church and heard messages about sex, she already believed that she only deserved bad things. As Twyla began to experience sexual feelings, she met the messaging around purity codes. These feelings, as she was told, were impure and thus threatened her standing before God. Thus, Twyla had to actively participate in this code ethic to maintain her standing. The consequences of her feelings or failing to wait until marriage for sex led to her "impurity," which meant she would be, as she states, "dirty for the rest of my life." Thus, when Twyla experienced sexual sensations, the environment of purity culture messaging cultivated a low self-worth.

6. Farley, "Forgiveness in Service of Justice and Love," 327.

In sum, moral injury arises from negative images cultivated by negative experiences, abuse, and trauma. When verbal and physical abuse becomes internalized, the one abused assents to the trauma as a form of self-hatred. As Tracy and Twyla equally state, their abuse leads them to believe that they are no good and worthless. However, when the wider culture, especially Christian culture, only sees the Whore of Babylon in the face of every person who trades sex for goods, then the shame is more deeply entrenched in their humanity. Moral injury creates a negative feedback loop wherein the victim of abuse assents to further abuse or only believes the worst about themselves.

Moral Luck

A third theme that emerged in the interviews was moral luck, which accounts for how circumstances outside of the individuals control impacts their pursuit of virtue.[7] Poverty, for example, deeply impacts the way humans develop virtue and how one chooses between competing goods. To be clear, moral luck, and for that matter moral injury as well, does not claim that those who experience great calamity are incapable of virtue, which would merely be victim blaming. Rather, moral luck, as Kate Ward clarifies, "offers a tool to assess whether communities are truly offering all their members the opportunity to flourish as full human beings with moral agency, or whether some members of the community are expected to pull themselves up by their own bootstraps morally speaking."[8] Moral luck, then, is as much a way to think through the unjust punishing of individuals for failing a moral code when in fact they could not fulfill it due to various obstacles.

To explain a situation of moral luck, I return to the story of Tracy. After her abuse, Tracy began acting out, leading to incarceration and expulsion from her home. During this period, Tracy ended up living with her first trafficker, who coerced her to turn tricks to get drugs for the pair. Tracy gave birth to her first child at age seventeen. To support her child, Tracy worked a demanding food service job that required a lot of her time. While at work Tracy left her child with a family member of the child's father. One day while at work, this family member took advantage of Tracy's age and tricked her into giving custody of her child away. This was a devastating blow and due to her lack of money and social capital, she lacked the resources to regain her child. Shortly after this episode, Tracy bore her second child and became

---

7. See Ward, *Wealth, Virtue, and Moral Luck*, 5.
8. Ward, *Wealth, Virtue, and Moral Luck*, 87.

immediately afraid she would lose them. Desperate for a well-paying job, yet lacking the education required as well as possessing a criminal record, Tracy saw an ad for nude dancing that guaranteed one hundred dollars a night. Tracy took this job to maintain custody of her new child. Onlookers can scoff at this choice. However, for a seventeen-year-old girl with no social network who did not understand the complexity of the child welfare system and no one to recommend different options, one can understand the impossible situation that stood behind her choice. This is moral luck; her life circumstances drove her to a choice. She needed money to support and keep her child. She states quite clearly and powerfully the dynamic of moral luck:

> I've always wanted . . . to get my kids and be a good mom and . . . that was always my heart's desire, and I just never . . . liked being out there. It's . . . a big hole. And when you have nothing . . . I don't even know where to begin, or how to get there if I didn't know where to begin . . . So like I had these deep-rooted desires and wants . . . and didn't have a social support system that . . . helped me find my way out of the deep hole that I had gotten myself in.

She was in a hole and could not see a way out, so she made the only choices available to her in her mind. Recalling Judith Butler's description of biopolitics, how can one live a good life when they are only given bad choices?

Neutral observers without this information would look on Tracy with apathy as merely a criminal, sex worker, stripper who deserves her low status. This apathy arises from what Ward calls hyperagency, namely the "abundance of power, freedom, and choice beyond that enjoyed by other members of society."[9] One should recognize the similarity between the hyper agent and Kant's ideal agent. The problem in hyperagency is not that one possesses freedom, but rather than one's exclusive ability to determine structures and that those structures should adapt to the hyper agent's needs and concerns.[10] In short, the hyper agent has tools to not fall on hard times and the system of recognition whereby one gains or loses social capital favors them. The assumption that the structure of the world should adhere to the hyper agent's specific experience and wealth moves one's moral formation from a place of virtue acquisition to a place of preservation of assets. The judgment on Tracy's life arises from a place where an individual who never knows the kind of desperation experienced by Tracy nevertheless judges her life decisions as worthy of condemnation.[11]

9. Ward, *Wealth, Virtue, and Moral Luck*, 133.
10. Ward, *Wealth, Virtue, and Moral Luck*, 134.
11. Ward, *Wealth, Virtue, and Moral Luck*, 136.

Hyperagency and moral luck appear in the lives of survivors of trafficking and those who grew up in traditional purity culture contexts. One interview participant, Terry, noted a particularly troubling lesson from a youth pastor on purity codes. She recalls the lesson stated, "If you've experienced any sexual intimacy before marriage, even if you were, you know, raped or something like that, [the] . . . youth leader just like grabbed a piece of paper and crumpled it up and was like, yes, you can open that piece of paper up, but it's always going to have those wrinkles and imperfections, and they'll always be broken and ripped." Terry then recounts that a friend in attendance, who was a victim of sexual assault, was disturbed by this teaching. She stated, "I can't believe they're telling me I'll always be broken and ripped." The internalization of this moral injury finds a negative feedback loop in this teaching. The pain experienced in sexual assault doubles down in the failure to meet a purity code. This form of moral luck, a negative experience, shapes an equally negative self-perception and affects how others perceive the failure to meet a purity code. Terry admits that the purity code bound up in her perception at the time led her to defend the code in the face of her friend's pain. In this sense, a tragedy such as sexual assault is the victim's fault because the code cannot accommodate exceptions. Any sexual activity, even when forced or coerced, leads to impurity. The moral luck experienced by Terry's friend impacts how others perceive her. Those who perfectly fit the codes are hyper agents and cannot imagine life outside of it. There is the broken and whole, the impure and pure, and the immoral and hyper agent.

Moral luck offers a true barrier that must be considered. When the moral agent appears in the most ideal state abstracted from context, ethics takes shape as a practice of the hyper agents. Against this structure, the contexts and circumstances of the agent's life must be considered. Poverty can be a problem that shapes the evaluation of various goods. However, the circumstances of those who gaze upon the choices of others must also be considered. The same circumstances do not always shape all people. Furthermore, the hyper agent controls the formation of the moral landscape because from their perspective, the articulation of ethics emerges. This way of moral formation lacks the ability to articulate the goods necessary to human flourishing. Rather, it only creates certain pictures of privilege cast over the moral landscape and competing goods.

THE PATHWAY OF ESCAPE

Before concluding this chapter, it is important to name two important shifts that must occur that address the moral ills of trafficking and purity culture.

I highlight these here in order to set the stage for the following exploration of sexual ethics. Much of the preceding analysis of purity culture and trafficking illustrate two points of observation. First, sexuality, both in the experience of trafficking and purity culture, flows down from a male-dominated hierarchy. A shift to a feminist perspective will work to undo many problems, including the Kantian agency at the heart of the misunderstandings around both purity culture and trafficking. Second, the rescue mindset observably does not work. Rescue only secures the patriarchal approach critiqued in the first observation. Only a shift from rescue to solidarity, as illustrated in all participants, will aid those caught in the web of trafficking and in purity culture.

Feminism and Agency

To begin, I propose that Christian ethics make a shift to the feminist perspective.[12] Karen Peterson-Iyer articulates that a feminist sexual ethic not only promotes "sexual freedom and agency," but also "broader dimensions of well-being, including physical health, emotional integrity, relational intimacy, and mutuality and equal regard as they intersect with and bolster agency."[13] In short, this shift promotes a wholeness for sexuality that integrates spirituality, ethics, and well-being into a single approach to ethics. Rather than merely remaining captive to a purity/disgust mindset about sexuality, a feminist approach considers the person and their needs as well as a vision for justice and love that transcends the immanent picture created by purity. By listening to the voices of these women and considering their needs, a new pathway for sexual ethics will emerge. All ethics should mirror strategies that listen to those who find ethical teachings a matter of life and death.

Though I will unpack the feminist approach in conversation with feminist scholars in the proceeding analysis, I highlight one specific theme that is particularly illuminating for this study, namely agency. In Western accounts of moral philosophy, agency and the ability to follow rules or principles serves as the highest expression of agency. However, feminist scholars point to a different voice in the tradition. Feminist scholar Carol Gilligan argues, for example, that a shift to feminist voice changes the dominance of

---

12. I am not alone in this recommendation and follow the lead of many brilliant feminist scholars. I especially draw from the work of Margret Farley, Karen Peterson-Iyer, and Lisa Sowell Cahill, but they have many companions as well. I merely join their voices.

13. Peterson-Iyer, *Reenvisioning Sexual Ethics*, 21.

this account of agency.[14] Gilligan found that a feminist approach reveals less adherence or lack of adherence as the metric of the moral life, but rather *"responsibility."*[15] This recognition is significant in Gilligan's approach because it offers a new way to ethical thinking, one based on negotiating relationships rather than rules exclusively.[16] Therefore, the decisions were made in the context of the community and agent's relationships rather than rules. "There was," Gilligan continues, "no way to separate self and other into a distinct opposition."[17] Any rules or norms are negotiated not in isolation from one's support community but only within them.

Thus, agency is not understood in relationship to autonomy alone, but uncovers a central virtue: dependence. Dependence carries significant baggage because autonomy is often viewed as the highest virtue, and dependence is the greatest weakness.[18] However, when Gilligan asks a group of young women the meaning of dependence, they reveal "the assumption that dependence is positive, that the human condition *is* a condition of dependence, and that people need to rely on one another for understanding, comfort, and support . . . Dependence, rather, was created by choices to be there for others, to take care of them, to listen, to try to understand, and to help."[19] Dependence, then, expresses care and means that "[s]omeone would be there when you need them."[20] Therefore, dependence is an "active" choice that sustains relationships of moral community and care.[21]

For the study of survivors of trafficking and purity culture participants, agency and autonomy are a significant concern. For example, the agency of a person in the midst of trafficking is complex. However, one must be careful to not completely negate agency and only elevate dependence. Thus, any conversation about the agency of a person in the web of trafficking must proceed with caution. As Karen Peterson-Iyer understands, trafficked persons are not merely "objects of pity" but "bona-fide moral agents caught in systems of oppression."[22] As such, the purpose of ethics is not the maintenance of a patriarchal order where survivors and those still in the web are acted upon, but rather sexual ethics in a feminist expression must promote

---

14. Gilligan, "Different Voice in Moral Decisions," 172.
15. Gilligan, "Different Voice in Moral Decisions," 173. Emphasis original.
16. Gilligan, "Different Voice in Moral Decisions," 173.
17. Gilligan, "Different Voice in Moral Decisions," 173.
18. Gilligan, "Different Voice in Moral Decisions," 175.
19. Gilligan, "Different Voice in Moral Decisions," 175.
20. Gilligan, "Different Voice in Moral Decisions," 175.
21. Gilligan, "Different Voice in Moral Decisions," 176.
22. Peterson-Iyer, *Reenvisioning Sexual Ethics*, 149.

a language of mutuality that empowers agency rather than diminishes it. If not dependence, then interdependence works to aid an understanding of ethical choice. Freedom, in the Augustinian sense, means the freedom to choose the Good. Thus, partnering with agency, in response to Butler, involves a solidarity that cultivates a world where choices for healing and wholeness can occur. The sexual ethics offered below will encourage a language of free response that meets each in response to God's command and a loving solidarity that partners with agency and does not make behavior a barrier to community. Thus, a language of mutuality must move to the center of sexual ethics without negating ethical concerns such as consent and theological concepts like covenant.

Solidarity over Rescue: The Way Out

Feminist approaches to ethics also call for a shift to solidarity rather than rescue. Overall, a pattern of solidarity fits well within the responsibilities of the Christian community. Many evangelicals, as already indicated, think rescue of a "slave" somewhere far away is the only way to end trafficking. However, the situation is far more local and far more personal than this approach allows. As such a model for solidarity emerges from the work of gang activist Greg Boyle, when he writes,

> You actually abolish slavery by accompanying the slave. We don't strategize our way out of slavery, we solidarize, if you will, our way toward its demise. We stand in solidarity with the slave, and by so doing, we diminish slavery's ability to stand. By casting our lot with the gang member, we hasten the demise of demonizing. All Jesus asks is, *"where are you standing?"* After chilling defeat and soul numbing failure, He asks again, "Are you still standing there?"[23]

Iconoclastic ethics asks this exact question, namely where do you stand? Solidarity that leads to empowerment and the end of demonizing through images such as the addict and the criminal do more than rescuing to end the practice of trafficking. What remains is a vision of God's indicative that motives solidarity more powerfully than exclusion.

Solidarity for its own sake is the beginning expression of another important element of sexual ethics, namely mutuality. In solidarity, the community comes alongside to be with the person who experiences trafficking or purity culture. Coming alongside requires relationship and mutual care

---

23. Boyle, *Tattoos on the Heart*, 173.

that empowers agency rather than diminishes it and solidarity is primarily the activity done with another rather than through shared experience or identity. As Peterson-Iyer writes in regard to trafficking, communities of mutuality work "more holistically, at the fulfillment of their ongoing needs so that they may take control over their own recovery."[24] Such efforts realize what our participants expressed as essential, namely communities that base communal acceptance not on behavior where work can be performed together. Healing is thus not a non-survivor performing for another but the shared activity that cultivates an environment of empowerment and discovery. This is expressed well in the way that one organization helped a survivor of trafficking, Darla. She describes the expectations associated with this organization,

> I really don't know . . . what they expected from me. Besides to do better than I did yesterday. And so different, like when you think of . . . all that like it was more what can we do to help you instead of you're doing this, this, this, and this wrong and just throw you in here and lock you up. No, but it was more of how can we help you become better?

Darla continues that the result of this kind of acceptance to her finding herself and even discovering herself in ways made impossible previously. As she describes, "For the longest time I didn't even know my favorite color was . . . [It's] turquoise, [it's] nice finding the things that you'd like to do. Because [before] I was just lost. I didn't know any of [the things I like]." Mutuality and solidarity empower where rescue truncates. The move to solidarity and community with survivors is not condescending but participates in the kind of communities capable of addressing a world of trafficking. Sexual ethics must promote this mutuality in every aspect of its prescriptions.

CONCLUSION

In the end, theology may only escape the lure of social exclusion by refusing to repeat the errors of previous generations. However, theology must seek a moral taste averse to the savage realm of purity. For example, the desire for community is not wrong, but the sinful human propensity to durable networks to the inclusion of some over others often robs humans of basic human dignity. Even the reflections provided in this work require the continued reflection and deliberation of the people impacted by it. The interludes that lead to a place of retreat from the theological foundations of

---

24. Peterson-Iyer, *Reenvisioning Sexual Ethics*, 153.

code fetishism must be explored, which I will take up in the next chapter. Uncoupling the codes from Christian ethics will most likely be an unending task, but it is a task that nonetheless leans into the eschatological imagination essential to all Christian theology. The tradition of social exclusion ever-present in the church's history exists in tension with its inclusive strains. Nevertheless, I challenge Christians not to look away from the negative aspects of the tradition. The goal is not a better code but a different moral world. Sexual ethics cannot include the moral imagination of the old world disguised as something new. Giving a better use of capital, sex, and purity only perpetuates the death of its current structure. As poet Audre Lorde rightly diagnoses, "*the master's tools will never dismantle the master's house.*"[25] This fugitive logic will empower the remainder of the study. Purity and social exclusion cannot fix purity and social exclusion. Instead, as Lorde continues, one must "make common cause with those others identified as outside the structures in order to define and seek a world in which we can all flourish."[26] The interludes to the code fetishes offered throughout history are the cracks at the corner of the long development of code reasoning. All flourishing only occurs when the cracks splinter the door that holds humanity captive. In short, human flourishing can emerge only by breaking the codes and idols that hold us captive.

---

25. Lorde, *Master's Tools*, 19. Emphasis original.
26. Lorde, *Master's Tools*, 19.

3

Iconoclastic Bodies

Karl Barth and the Indicative of Reconciliation

INTRODUCTION

As Margaret Farley notes, ethicists rarely set the moral agenda for their day.[1] The testimonies of survivors and those who experienced purity codes demands the ethicist address their experience as a part of the moral agenda of today. The constructive task of this work, beginning in this chapter, considers the role that iconoclasm must play in breaking the image that undergirds code fetishism. Iconoclasm breaks the cultural and moral images that limit Christian ethics and opens the way to new modes of ethical praxis. This requires a mood shift from the imperative to the indicative in order to relieve the pressure placed on moral action.

I begin this chapter by outlining the indicative mood in contrast to the imperative. I encourage a meaningful mood switch in ethics with a brief reflection on the expressive lens of iconoclasm. The use of heresy here will open humanity to an all-embracing indicative reality for moral formation rather than code-specific forms of life. After providing the role of expressive in moral formation, I draw on the theology of Karl Barth, which as John Webster indicates, articulates a "moral ontology" that does not merely tell humanity what to do, but what is the Good.[2] Barth's teasing out of the indicative of reconciliation will be the central theme of iconoclastic Christian

1. Farley, *Just Love*, xi.
2. See Webster, *Barth's Ethics of Reconciliation*, 1.

sexual ethics in order to motivate a deep desire for belonging and fellowship in the place of exclusion.

PART I: FROM CODE TO INDICATIVE

The code fetish central to purity code sexual ethics collapses the gospel into the imperative mood. For example, consider the purity code realism that faced our participants wherein hell was the punishment for transgression. To be clear, one cannot abandon the imperative mood in ethics. But the imperative mood is not the central mood of the Christian faith. Instead, the Christian faith relies on the indicative mood to guide its way. As Ted Smith argues, "An imperative might be enforced, whether on someone else or on oneself. An indicative, on the other hand, just *is*."[3] When lacking connection to the indicative, the imperative mood becomes a harsh moral code lacking grace or Spirit. Smith offers a succinct and essential indictment of code fetishism and its impact on moral theology. He writes,

> For the church, code fetishism has often turned the Beatitudes, those great indicative declarations of blessedness, into lists of things to do. It has shown the ability to make Psalm 119—a long declaration of love for the law—into the self-satisfied song of a prig. Nomolatry has made sermons feel "relevant" only when they end in exhortations of some kind, whether to give your life to Christ, live your best life now, or get to know the sources of your food.[4]

Locating Christian ethics *exclusively* in the imperative inaugurates ethics tempted by coercion. When the fulfillment of blessedness lies in a code, the means to fulfill the code become self-justifying and self-serving. In short, codes are a zero-sum game and require absolute adherence by any means necessary, including acting in ways inconsistent with the indicative from which they derive. Thus, to break the image of the code, Christian sexual ethics requires a return to the indicative of the gospel to reorient the moral imagination. Such a claim is bold but provokes an exciting dialogue for ethics. I look at two critical indicative examples in Smith's account to explore his claim.

First, the indicative is positive because it contains images that gesture toward a reality not captured in an imperative. The indicative provides the content that resists code fetish as "the wolf lies down with the lamb; the

---

3. Smith, *Weird John Brown*, 117. Emphasis original.
4. Smith, *Weird John Brown*, 110.

law is written on people's hearts; the dwelling place of God is with humans, and God shall wipe every tear from their eyes, and death shall be no more . . . there is something these visions, even if known only in hope . . . they have direction."[5] Smith clearly states the indicative invites a free response and fidelity rather than a mere code to repeat. The posture of fidelity *forms* more than it prescribes, and one's proximity to the indicative creates a new coordinate reality that grows from it. As such, the indicative encourages a moral imagination where a plurality of actions can emerge from a central indicative logic.

Second, the indicative mood presents something positive and negates codes. In this way, the indicative disentangles Christian ethics from the coercion inherent in code-making. The indicative only relates to code by way of negation, namely by relativizing every specific rule and the entire "imperative mood."[6] This shift is crucial because the indicative is not without moral content, to be sure, but it does not merely replace the moral code with a new one. Smith uses the indicative of the cross to illustrate this point. He writes,

> because the sign of the Kingdom is the cross, new obligations do not arise to fill the little gaps left by the old. In the cross, Jesus does not squeeze himself into Caesar's throne. The indicative . . . breaks the absolute hold of every earthly imperative without establishing new ones in their place.[7]

All Christian ethics must absorb the weight of this claim. The indicative relocates moral activity as a reflex and free response that claims no earthly authority and instead gropes for a kingdom not yet fully realized. This lack of possession of codes frees humans from the need to secure one's place metaphorically on Caesar's throne which inevitably must use coercion, violence, and codes to police the boundaries between surplus and lack.

Taking together the positive and negative aspects of the indicative mood, the moral activity that follows from indicative resembles the work of testimony. Locating testimonies of participants within this account will help orient a new moral activity. The reason for this liturgical expression is that the indicative is itself already a fulfillment. It is: justification, reconciliation, redemption, creation, sanctification, and the fulfillment of the law. Moral activity rests in testimony "not only because [it] points toward the

---

5. Smith, *Weird John Brown*, 119.
6. Smith, *Weird John Brown*, 118.
7. Smith, *Weird John Brown*, 118.

fulfillment of the law but also because [it comes] *from* the fulfillment of the law."[8] Because the justified need not fulfill an imperative to *achieve* the indicative, the moral activity subsequent to justification is freedom. The presence of God in such an indicative is never fully identical with the testimony but rather enables the plurality of testimony to arise from the community of the justified. Testimony allows individuals "to imagine the presence of God in a new way. God is present not where the world lives up to some imperatives that God has given but in the fact of free responses" to the indicative of grace and reconciliation.[9] In short, the tendency to measure like for like in code fetishism is absent in the indicative of grace. As such, God is not identical with a particular group based on their social capital, but rather God shows grace even to those not identical in any measurable way according to the logic of code fulfillment. Instead, the freedom and testimony of the indicative resemble less a political order that attempts a one-to-one correspondence between God and the order of power and more the ascension of Jesus proceeding the cross, tomb, and resurrection. Christ is absent from these so that Christ can be present to all. The indicative mood does not encourage and affirm all actions or codes but does not make one's social/sexual capital or proximate fulfillment of the code the mark of God's presence. In the end, only a switch to this moral imagination dislodges bodies from the vice grip of code fetishism.

ICONOCLASM: DISMANTLING THE METAPHYSICS OF CODE

To further put a point on the posture cultivated by the indicative, I turn to iconoclasm. The language of iconoclasm exists in a variety of cultural and religious ideas. The central element of our study is that the indicative not only presents a reality but also robs others of their power. Directing the indicative toward the realities of purity culture and human trafficking requires defaming the images that hold them in place (i.e., the fallen woman, the Whore of Babylon, purity culture). Thus, iconoclasm will provide nuance as to the indicative that invites free response.

Iconoclasm as a set of theological concepts first appeared in the Christian tradition around the sixteenth century to describe a phenomenon in the late ninth century. The word first appears in Latin, but appears in English to describe a French Protestant movement.[10] However, theologians

8. Smith, *Weird John Brown*, 119. Emphasis mine.
9. Smith, *Weird John Brown*, 120.
10. See Carnes, *Image and Presence*, 9.

mostly associated iconoclasm with the Byzantine image controversy of the eighth century, described as such in 1953.[11] By utilizing this term, I do not intentionally align with any of these movements or figures of the Byzantine controversy. Instead, with Natalie Carnes, I use this term "to capture a sense of 'breaking' an image."[12] The dynamic of image breaking is not merely a deposition of an image but, as James Simpson argues, the need to expose the ideologies of an image.[13] This latter sense appears more in the modern sense but resonates with deep scriptural themes. Carnes states, the iconoclast

> as a breaker of cultural images—a blasphemer—is additionally important because it resonates with Scriptural descriptions of Christ as a *skandalon* or stumbling block (1 Corinthians 1:23). These accusations of blasphemy leveled at Jesus by some of his contemporaries figure him as an iconoclast, in the modern sense that . . . breaks cultural expectations and institutional mores. In some cases, iconoclastic breaking injures; in others, it renews.[14]

This last distinction remains crucial for our work because it recognizes that not all iconoclasms are good. Iconoclasms that renew and heal help dissolve the dichotomies essential in code fetishism.[15]

Carnes identifies two main types of iconoclasms that serve as indicatives of healing or injury. Following her lead, I use this distinction to show the difference between the present work and the code fetish approach. First, an iconoclasm of fidelity names the place of images and imaging in breaking specific images and conceiving images in light of the Christ image. As Carnes writes, "in Christ desires, possibilities, and *telos*, humanity expresses not only what it is (humanity) but also what it is not (very God)."[16] In Carnes's assessment, the centrality of Christ, as *homoousios*, is essential. Christ is God and perfectly images the Father (John 14:9) but also fulfills the Father's will (John 5:36–38, 8:19, 28–29; Luke 22:42; Mark 14:36; Matt 26:39, 42), founds the Father's kingdom (Luke 11:2; Matt 6:10), glorifies the Father's name (John 12:28, 17:1) and performs the Father's work (John 5:36, 10:32). Christ performs this work as fully human with humans in order to open the way to the Father. As Carnes continues, humanity "is negated in Christ, ordered beyond itself to reveal very God, the very human is also

---

11. Carnes, *Image and Presence*, 9.
12. Carnes, *Image and Presence*, 9.
13. Simpson, *Under the Hammer*, 11, 14.
14. Carnes, *Image and Presence*, 10.
15. Carnes, *Image and Presence*, 10.
16. Carnes, *Image and Presence*, 13.

revealed."[17] Christ is exclusive in this regard, revealing and negating what only he can reveal and negate. This dialectic of revelation and negation protects humans from attempting to negate their humanity to the point of self-abasement, and it also discourages them from trying to "perform" the image God in their humanity.

Though the Son is of one substance (*homoousios*) *with* the Father, he is not God the Father in his personhood (*hypostasis*). As Carnes helpfully recognizes, "this 'is' and 'is not,' 'likeness' and 'unlikeness,' 'presence' and 'absence' that makes an image *image* is the negation at the heart of imaging."[18] Therefore, an iconoclasm of fidelity negates the visible to gesture beyond it to a transcendent reality. By negating in favor of the transcendent Father, Christ reclaims humanity as the Son by indicating its "not God" status. The negation of Christ's humanity is not an abasement of humanity but rather the reclamation that humanity as humanity, which, according to Chalcedon, Christ shares co-substantially *with* humanity.

An iconoclasm of fidelity breaks the image to gesture to a transcendent reality, which is how it does not merely code new forms of life into ethics. However, the iconoclasm of fidelity returns to the image in order to open its former negation to realize it anew. The transcendent still claims the goodness local to it but claims its status as creaturely. An error occurs when an iconoclasm opens the immanent to the transcendent *at the expense of the immanent*. The negation of an image in this way contrasts with an idol, which is an image fully immanent to itself. Nothing exists beyond it even though it claims transcendence. The only way to fulfill the imperative in the indicative is to "image" the code and idol perfectly. In short, it is a closed system of imaging without grace or forgiveness. Therefore, a further fidelity to Christ and his imaging locates humanity in its creaturely place and allows God to be immanent to all creaturely realities, not to be synonymous with them and, thus, to love them equally.

An iconoclasm of temptation, secondarily, works in the opposite direction of an iconoclasm of fidelity, which "literalizes" the image and its affections and desires. As Carnes clarifies, an iconoclasm of temptation "attempts to be both more and less than an image: seeking to substitute for the prototype (more) and closing itself off from transformation beyond itself (less)."[19] The image, in this case, is Christ in his imaging, but through this imaging closes itself off from grace outside of itself.

---

17. Carnes, *Image and Presence*, 13.
18. Carnes, *Image and Presence*, 14.
19. Carnes, *Image and Presence*, 50.

An iconoclasm of temptation fails to account for the deep resonance of literal and nonliteral desire. Literal desire obsesses with a material good (e.g., sex, food, sensual delight), while nonliteral desire is associated with the desire for divinity.[20] Nestorius, for example, disassociates (i.e., literalizes) literal desire from the nonliteral desire by sanitizing Christ's humanity from his divinity at the point of his conception. Purity works in this way as well by sanitizing through literalizing the absence of sexual desire thereby closing humanity off from God.

An iconoclasm of temptation absolutizes literal desire even as one attempts to sanitize nonliteral desire. Purity code realism is a crucial example of an iconoclasm of temptation. Purity codes literalize desire in that they are for their own sake "gratifying the one who desires it."[21] In other words, purity is only consumptive; namely, it forecloses any meaning not immanent to its material consumption or practices.[22] The codes are closed to nonliteral desires, preventing the body's access to grace. The image of purity operates as sexual capital able to purchase social capital and, thus, durable networks. Though purity can purchase divine favor (according to its defenders), purity is a prize on its own. It is removed from nonliteral desire entirely because the nonliteral must sanitize itself from the literal desire of sex. As such, the body imaging purity is cut off from nonliteral desire insofar as a final determination of the body exists exclusively within this literal desire. However, the iconoclasm of temptation arises from fear. It arises from a human desire to know right from wrong and contributes to code fetishism. The iconoclasm of temptation seeks the preservation of an image that guards and creates permissible forms of life. In short, the iconoclasm of temptation takes over "when fear overrules hope."[23]

The difference between iconoclasms of fidelity and temptation is significant yet nuanced. In fidelity, the negation of the image does exclude its transformation by that which is beyond it. Temptation, on the other hand, negates all meanings exterior to the image. Unlike Christ, who negates the immanent to reveal the transcendent without losing the immanent, temptation negates the transcendent to consume the image entirely. All that matters is the immanent process, and the image loses the chance at transformation with a zero-remainder outcome. In short, nothing remains after the image.

To put the difference between the two in terms already established by purity code realism, sexual ethics toward the ends of purity code

---

20. Carnes, *Image and Presence*, 22–23.
21. Carnes, *Image and Presence*, 23.
22. Carnes, *Image and Presence*, 23.
23. Carnes, *Image and Presence*, 30.

maintenance is an iconoclasm of temptation. One detects this at the site of losing virginity outside of marriage. According to the teaching, the image at this point becomes corrupted and bad, unable to be correctly offered to their future spouse. Furthermore, this does not allow contingency (Kantian agency) for events such as sexual assault because the image of perfect sexuality is entirely immanent to the pure virgin herself. Thus, there is no meaning beyond it other than its immanent process.

The rest of the work will emerge as a distinction between these two forms of iconoclasm. How might the Christ image perform an iconoclasm of fidelity? The only way forward is the iconoclasm of these images and idols that opens up the literal to the nonliteral in a way that restores and does not injure. In this way, iconoclasm harkens back to Christianity's beginnings, reflected in recent literature, that Christians must learn a kind of atheism, namely by refusing to believe in false gods.[24] This new rejection of the gods must emerge as a rejection of the god forged in the fires of code fetishes. The power of code forms the gospel in a way that chokes out life except for the very few. An iconoclasm of code-driven Christianity rends everything to the floor so the gospel may speak again. Only here can a constructive sexual ethic emerge untied from its service to social capital.

PART II: KARL BARTH'S DOCTRINE OF RECONCILIATION

Iconoclasm causes a fundamental rupture in theology that aids the necessary rejection of codes and coding and the social exclusion resulting from it. Though indicatively driven, iconoclasm offers a new place from which to think. However, what is this indicative that performs this reality? Smith hints that a "code commands obedience," but the goal of iconoclasm is the creation of many "faithful, free responses, which become testimonies to God's great indicative of reconciliation."[25] Reconciliation, thus, is the indicative that does the work of iconoclasm. If the social exclusion model is the moral posture of code ethics, then reconciliation must defame the alluring power of purity codes and privilege. In short, an even deeper desire for reconciliation and solidarity must overcome the impulse to reject others based on a code-formed disgust. Reconciliation is a community, togetherness, and the most profound commitment to being with another person. It opens up a desire to be with one another to a transformation beyond itself. Reconciliation aids a theology of sex to constructively address sex trafficking

---

24. This call to atheism is the argument of Larry Hurtado's *Destroyer of the gods*.
25. Smith, *Weird John Brown*, 119.

because sexual and social capital should not be how one arrives at the beloved community. These new pathways will resist places of privilege and, as presented in the iconoclasm of fidelity, think from the place of the crucified, the enslaved person, and the trafficked to work for their liberation.

To this end, I turn to the work of Karl Barth and his account of the doctrine of reconciliation. Barth's theology tears human idols asunder and recenters moral communities around God's reconciling work that opens it to transformation. Thus, Barth presents an indication of reconciliatory intimacy that tears down, binds, and reorients the community toward the end of God's love for and fulfillment of creation. Barth's account of the doctrine of reconciliation provides a thick description of Christ's life, death, and resurrection, again illustrating that central to Barth's ethics is a moral ontology. However, Barth provides many provocative and unique images accompanying his account of the doctrine of reconciliation. These include Christ's acceptance of judgment in solidarity with the oppressed, a resurrection of the body as freedom from oppression, and the freedom not only of Christ's resurrected body but also of other human bodies. Barth's account of reconciliation runs through these images and, thus, serves as the basis of Christian ethics that binds communities of difference into one community of solidarity with the neighbor. Reconciliation thus motivates a sexual ethic.

Before turning to reconciliation, a word of clarity remains for the task of reconciliation. As theologian Willie James Jennings writes, reconciliation is a troubling concept because it is essential to many failed theological projects in the history of racism, sexism, and colonialism.[26] The rescue narratives around sex trafficking arise from a certain understanding of God as outside agent who motivates a colonial capture. I share this concern over reconciliation with Jennings that one cannot recover reconciliation until one "first articulate[s] the profound deformities of Christian intimacy and identity in modernity."[27] Jennings contends that the soil in which Christian theology grows lacks the nutrients necessary for survival.[28] The nutrients currently in the soil suffer from a structural deformation that creates patterns of intimacy bound to death. Drawing on the legacy of Gomes Eanes de Azurara (Zurara), royal chronicler to Prince Henry of Portugal in 1444, Jennings presents an aesthetic of racial becoming that locates the necessity of slave suffering and death inside the story of reconciliation and crucifixion. Such a position crushes those, such as the survivor, caught inside the matrix of suffering and death. Zurara provides an account of the ancient

---

26. Jennings, *Christian Imagination*, 10.
27. Jennings, *Christian Imagination*, 10.
28. Jennings, *Christian Imagination*, 7.

ICONOCLASTIC BODIES   89

slave practices that united white and black bodies through a theological account of the crucifixion. He literalizes the desire for Christ crucified as a simultaneous desire for the European. Utilizing the passion narratives of the Gospels, Zurara narrates Christ's slow walk to Golgotha as the interpretive key for the bodies of enslaved people now joined to the Portuguese people.[29] Zurara recognizes the enslaved person inside the crucifixion of Christ and their shared cries of dereliction.[30] However, Zurara does not allow the suffering of Christ to be joined to the enslaved person as an act of liberation but cruelly uses death as the reconciling bond between them.

Jennings presents how this form of reconciliation also generates an aesthetic of social existence with white on one end and black on another. As the Portuguese joined themselves with other Western nations in conquest and discovery, the aesthetic of skin color emerged as a false science that nonetheless joins itself to Christian ways of knowing. According to the aesthetic as it emerges from the European colonial imagination, the Christian must overcome blackness.[31] The description of African bodies and black skin suffers the gaze of a black-to-white aesthetic wherein the Christian must overcome the former.[32] Christian, thus, codes as white and sinful codes as black. Adkins already established that this coding leads to life and death for others. This form of reconciliation is violent and assimilating, necessitating a social death for those not coded as life. There are those in charge that must be saved by any means necessary. Furthermore, it justifies all kinds of violence toward the bodies coded and bound to death as a mere extension of their humanity. Thus, as Jennings suggested, reconciliation that cannot perform iconoclasms of fidelity to tear down false images of colonial literalized desire must be rejected.

To this end, Barth's theology of reconciliation that rests in the indicative bearing, iconoclastic destructiveness of the incarnation, moves ethics in a new direction. Barth's theology is dialectical in that it assumes a Wholly Other God whose actions are entirely unique and separate from humanity. Barth's account of reconciliation does not encourage our repetition of reconciliation as a divine agent, but rather only commands a participation in a community where each mutually receives from God what only God can give. One can see how the colonial imagination still exists by exploring the images that bind bodies to human trafficking. The Whore of Babylon, for example, cultivates a fear in service of social exclusion for those who

29. Jennings, *Christian Imagination*, 20.
30. Jennings, *Christian Imagination*, 21.
31. Jennings, *Christian Imagination*, 23.
32. Jennings, *Christian Imagination*, 23.

exist on the negative side of sexual ethics. Thus, the body of the woman who bears the mark of sex work (i.e., the fallen woman) merits all manner of violence and punishment like the slave body. Jennings challenges reconciliation in order to cultivate a theology of liberation of the oppressed from their bondage and the oppressors from their false idols. As Barth describes it, reconciliation tears down, builds up, and transvalues all images and idols essential to the perpetuation of social exclusion, ethical privilege, and all forms of trafficking by opening humanity beyond literalized images and the desire they produce. Through this theology, reconciliation emerges as a unique gathering together of humans into a community.

In order to fully account for Barth's theology of reconciliation, one must understand his engagement with covenant and creation as preludes to reconciliation. In creation, according to Barth, God creates the stage upon which God will perform God's acts of reconciliation.[33] Barth marries covenant to creation, which requires an understanding of intimacy that assumes both in their deployment. Creation is the external basis of the covenant, and the covenant is the internal basis of creation. This dictum means that the internal logic of God's creation contains a promise already anticipated in its very existence. For example, Barth uses the example of the tree of life central to the garden as the expression of God's desire that humanity might live with God.[34] This covenant as the internal basis of creation means that God desires creation's flourishing as if it were God. God does not merely create and then leave creation to itself. God desires an intimacy and constancy in creation. Barth offers a poignant picture of the intimacy envisioned in creation and covenant. Barth uses matrimonial images to convey the intimacy of the Hebrew covenant:

> Its whole witness to God's covenant is shot through by the knowledge that this centre where it is broken and despised, and persists only in this form, is not the whole story, and that it has its frontiers in a very different beginning and end, where *Yahweh* and His people are together and are one flesh.[35]

The intimacy for creation envisioned by God is akin to the intimacy of marriage where two become one flesh. Such is the origin and end of the covenant, the desire of God to be humanity's God and humanity, God's people.

Reconciliation, then, fulfills this covenant by gathering the creation community even as humanity falls away from God's covenant. In other

---

33. Barth, *Church Dogmatics III.1*, 41, 43.
34. Barth, *Church Dogmatics III.1*, 255–60.
35. Barth, *Church Dogmatics III.1*, 310.

words, God fulfills the covenant. Barth argues that one must go to the cross to see the full measure of this rebellion by humanity and commitment to humanity by God. On the cross, one sees the rejection of God as the "True Witness."[36] The True Witness, namely Christ, is the touchstone that reveals the untruthfulness of human sin.[37] The God who confronts humanity is the one "Slain and Crucified of Golgotha."[38] Here is the lynched man for the world to see, and God confronts the sinful man out of the person of the Son. God comes as the True Witness to this rebellious world, and as a result, suffers in the world humans have remade according to social capital, code, and their favorite idols.[39]

The way of the Son of God into this far country means that Christ is the rejected one, the impure, the one that contaminates and disgusts those who hear and see him. He is the cursed one who hangs on a tree (Gal 3:13), who touches lepers (Matt 8:3), who dwells with adulterers and tax collectors (John 8:1–11; Luke 19:1–10), and who breaks religious code to heal (John 5:1–18). Christ is the true witness in this way as well, namely by revealing the emptiness of our moral disgust. It lacks the ability to bring life and neglects the realities obscured by disgust. God's way into the far country confronts and opens the literalized images to transcendence in God by illuminating the humanity obscured by code and disgust, which represent iconoclasms of temptation. Therefore, even as the faithful witness suffers, one still sees the intimacy with the covenant God desires. God is *pro nobis*. Barth recognizes that the center of Christian dogmatics is this indicative of reconciliation.[40] Even in Christ's suffering and crucifixion, God is with and for humanity *as God*. As such, the God of reconciliation is the one *pro nobis* who fulfills the broken covenant to draw humanity back to God and to one another.

Nevertheless, God's fulfillment is mercy. Even though humanity breaks this covenant, God takes the full responsibility of the covenant on Godself to fulfill. As Barth writes, Christ is "the Good Samaritan who shows mercy" on us.[41] The fact that God takes the responsibility upon Godself to fulfill the covenant gestures to grace as God's central posture.[42] Barth defines the covenant as grace: "the free and utterly unmerited self-obligation of God

---

36. For more on the True Witness, see Barth, *Church Dogmatics IV.3.2*, 1–63.
37. Barth, *Church Dogmatics IV.3.2*, 5–6, 10.
38. Barth, *Church Dogmatics IV.3.2*, 10.
39. Barth, *Church Dogmatics IV.3.2*, 21, 29.
40. Barth, *Church Dogmatics IV.1*, 1.
41. Barth, *Church Dogmatics IV.3.2*, 47.
42. Barth, *Church Dogmatics IV.1*, 22–23.

to the human race which has completely fallen away from him."[43] Grace marries reconciliation and covenant. Grace is dialectically an unmerited act performed for humanity by the Wholly Other God to bring humanity into covenant.

The fulfillment of the covenant in reconciliation does not negate the covenant made to Israel, and Barth rejects such supersessionist perspectives. Instead, the new covenant and reconciliation of all humanity find its grounding purpose in the covenant made to Israel. The covenant with Israel inaugurated the intimacy between God and all nations on earth. Israel was the chosen vessel for this work, but she strayed from that vocation. Therefore, God gives a new covenant. Humanity, which falls away from God, will be restored by giving a new heart. Furthermore, as is written in Jeremiah 31, in correspondence to this new covenant, God will be their God, and they will be God's people (Jer 31:33). As such, Barth compares the giving of the new heart to the circumcision of the heart in Deuteronomy 30:6.[44] The new covenant expresses an effectual grace that enables belief, first to Israel, then to all the people. Not only does God fulfill the covenant with Israel, but God also fulfills Israel's mission to the nations. Neither the nations nor Israel will be forgotten in this divine reconciliation.[45] Instead, the closed circle will open to a "wider circle [that] also encloses them."[46] The wider circle represents an iconoclasm of fidelity at the heart of Barth's theology. Reconciliation opens the literal image of community to transformation.

To this end, one can detect how covenant and iconoclasm appear in Barth's account of reconciliation. Through an extensive exegetical exploration of the covenant in the Hebrew Scriptures, Barth utilizes the new covenant in Jeremiah 31 as a point of departure for reconciliation. Jeremiah 31 promises a new fleshy heart inscribed with God's Law in the new covenant. As Barth indicates, the promise of the fleshy heart is the "free, but effective grace of God."[47] Barth's purpose in this emphasis on grace is that the incarnation is the giving of grace to enable Christians to obey and follow. Barth argues that reconciliation is God fulfilling God's promises to Israel in the covenant. God is only the God of the covenant, and the grace of that

---

43. Barth, *Church Dogmatics IV.1*, 24.
44. Barth, *Church Dogmatics IV.1*, 29.
45. Barth, *Church Dogmatics IV.1*, 28.
46. Barth, *Church Dogmatics IV.1*, 31.
47. Barth, *Church Dogmatics IV.1*, 31.

covenant cannot be recalled.[48] One does not earn reconciliation with God, but rather God works in profoundly undeserved ways toward humanity.[49]

Barth provocatively uses an images to describe the incarnation as a means to describe the movement of God toward an unworthy world. The first image is the path of incarnation as "the Way of the Son of God into the Far Country." On this way into the far country, God draws humanity into the triune life while remaining God.[50] As such, God invades a world hostile to God as one who is both human and divine.[51] God invades not only to come to what is hostile to God and God's own but to interrupt the vicious cycle of violence to make humanity's guilt and the reality of sin God's own.[52]

An important image of reconciliation appears at this juncture, namely Christ as the Judge judged in our place. Barth's theology of the cross aids the development of a counter-theology for Christian sexual ethics by iconoclastically resisting images that lead to coercion, oppression, and social exclusion. In his dialectical framework, Barth illuminates the frailty of our judgements. Only God can judge, and human judgments only perpetuate the crucifixion of the Son. Barth's theology of the cross dialectically defames through judgment images that humans code for the sake of social exclusion. But we need not fear when facing this judge, because when one appears there they are

> not in front of the throne of some most high, unknown cosmic judge like that whom some heathens invented in fear and trembling! No: in front of that one who has loved us from eternity and then in his birth in the stable of Bethlehem and in his death on the cross of Golgotha and who has drawn us to him only out of kindness! In front of that one in which God drew the covenant with us human beings and kept it faithfully and fulfilled it! This will be our judge.[53]

One cannot turn the cross into a weapon for oppression because the cross exemplifies that "God's revelation is not in our power, and therefore not at our command."[54] Judgment from God is gracious in this way because God

---

48. Barth, *Church Dogmatics IV.1*, 40–42.
49. Barth, *Church Dogmatics IV.1*, 65–66.
50. Barth, *Church Dogmatics IV.1*, 151.
51. Barth, *Church Dogmatics IV.1*, 5.
52. Barth, *Church Dogmatics IV.1*, 167.
53. Karl Barth, "Sermon 'Vor dem Richterstuhl Christi' on 2 Corinthians 5:10 of 24 February 1963," in *Predigten 1954–1967*, 231, quoted in Tietz, "Standing on the Boundary," 176–77.
54. Barth, *Church Dogmatics II.1*, 66.

understands our pain and trials. It is not like a purity code. One can use it falsely, but the true cross of Christ stands in radical iconoclastic condemnation of such use by removing our control the presumption of our chosen idols, purity codes, and the social exclusions entailed in both.

The cross of Christ violates the presumption of social exclusion by encouraging the priority toward reconciliation. In the language of code fetishizing, piety and God's blessing flow directly from an individual's ability to make autonomous choices, follow the law, or perform other legalistic requirements. According to the Kantian agent, privilege exists precisely at the site of this ability. However, Barth presents the law not to privilege any in-group over others. The law still commands humanity and condemns it through judgment. This sinful state is undoubtedly a tragic state and, to quote Paul, "who will rescue me from this body of death?" (Rom 7:24, NRSV). However, humans cannot exist in a relationship of privilege to the law. Instead, the law claims every person as an equal co-conspirator with sin.

The only one who can enter under the judgment of the law and take the total weight of its judgment can free humanity from this miserable state, even Barabbas.[55] Barth locates humanity in relationship to patterns of sin and death with Barabbas. Humans are not those who justly adhere to the law, but are justly condemned by it. Humanity can only replicate the temptation of sin to divide and define the difference between good and evil as a possession to wield against their neighbor.[56] In short, humanity sins when they try to be the judge.[57] The stronghold of judgment is our desire and the basis of social exclusion. Humanity as judge does not even spare God in its judgment. Therefore, God enters into human judgment as the Judge in order to break the image and open it anew to receive not only the neighbor but God as well. As such, social exclusion arises from the root of sin, namely through the desire to choose between good and evil. Humanity cannot stand as judge, only God is Judge and commands. The creation of moral communities of those included and excluded thus emerges from the place of the original sin.

Into this situation of sin and stronghold comes the cross and resurrection, which compromises our stronghold and "destroys it," again providing an indicative account of reconciliation that performs an iconoclasm of fidelity.[58] Jesus is "very man and very God" and "has taken the place of

---

55. Barth, *Church Dogmatics IV.1*, 224.
56. Barth, *Church Dogmatics IV.1*, 225.
57. Barth, *Church Dogmatics IV.1*, 225.
58. Barth, *Church Dogmatics IV.1*, 225.

every [person]. [Christ] has penetrated to that place where every [person] is in [their] inner being supremely by and from [themselves]."[59] In this way, Christ dispossesses every human from their right to judge. The person's "knowledge of good and evil is no longer of any value. [They are] no longer judge. Jesus Christ is judge."[60] This judgment dispossesses humanity from the circles of purity that they draw for themselves to exclude by existing at its center and bearing the fullness of its judgment. Christ destroys this circle by submitting to its judgment through crucifixion. This act is God's most profound form of solidarity with humanity and the source of reconciliation.

Barth's account of reconciliation includes the logic of salvation to break bracketed human disgust narratives of Christ's saving work. In his Good Friday Sermon "The Criminals With Him," Barth argues that the criminals crucified with him on the cross form a unique solidarity with him and form the first true Christian community.[61] Only through examining the way that God in Christ sits in solidarity with these criminals can one glimpse the true scope of salvation from sin. This community cannot escape the justifying, salvific work of Christ that Christians celebrate on Easter. To know the cross means accepting a profound claim: *Christ was condemned as a criminal.* He was judged, arrested, imprisoned, and sentenced to death.[62] Here Barth's theology of the cross includes Christ's calling to the excluded by standing with them. He "bears the wickedness" of these criminals as his own.[63] This wickedness is done to him and those with whom he hangs in solidarity on the cross. Those condemned with Jesus, excluded by the crowds, are included in the cross. Christ's solidarity with the criminal does not reify and affirm their exclusion, but rather calls it to account. Christ, "like them, was condemned and crucified as a lawbreaker, a criminal."[64] From here, God reconciles by judging not only the criminal's sin but the crowd's sin as their judge, reflecting it to all humanity on the cross to call humanity to repentance, and putting that same sin to death. The empty tomb is a monument to our failure to replace God with our idols. The cross opens judgment to a reality beyond it. God defames the literal desire to be judged as good against another who is evil. It is from here that God alone saves without humanity.[65] Human action thus does not achieve what only God can do. Their actions

---

59. Barth, *Church Dogmatics IV.1*, 225.
60. Barth, *Church Dogmatics IV.1*, 225.
61. Barth, "Criminals With Him," 76–77.
62. Barth, "Criminals With Him," 76.
63. Barth, "Criminals With Him," 80.
64. Barth, "Criminals With Him," 81.
65. Barth, "Criminals With Him," 79.

are good for nothing, their virtues do not perfect.⁶⁶ In short, God is the Judge against anyone who might wield the power of judgment to remind humanity that the desire to achieve goodness results in the sin exhibited at Golgotha.

Golgotha as reconciliation does not purify exclusion, but rather sanctifies a union between God and humanity by bearing away the sin placed upon him. Christ bears it away to take it to death, thereby defaming it (Gal 3:13).⁶⁷ The exclusion that defines the division must be abandoned and the purity codes must be defamed. The criminals and those who put them to death are two sides of the same redemption. God reconciles both, but God stands in solidarity on the cross with all those condemned as criminals who face the unjust death of social exclusion. The images of Mary/Eve, the Whore of Babylon, the fallen woman, the prostitute, the trafficked, the pure and impure, the violated and the rejected—Jesus hangs on the cross with them. Jesus, by defeating sin through bearing it to himself, is both the punishment for humanity and punished by humanity's judgments. He puts to death the reality of death and all systems of justification that mobilize the powers of death to their end. Jesus stands with the crucified of the world as one who hangs there next to them. Thus, Barth helpfully articulates an iconoclasm of fidelity that rejects false community and false piety to open humanity to transcendent sources. By dying as an impure criminal and being raised as God's exalted Son, Christ draws true community outside the stronghold of pure and impure in order to summon humanity to respond. Christ's exclusion sanctifies a new space not to graft the outsiders into the stronghold but to destroy and create a new intimacy, a new reconciliation.

In this analysis, the cross cannot be a cheap moralism. The cross is iconoclasm and indicative. It destroys false images of God (iconoclasm) and the reconciles humanity to God (indicative); it motivates a new seeing, a new aesthetic not formed by purity and impurity, but rather a new intimacy between neighbors near and distant. This desire competes with the original sin to judge for ourselves inclusion and exclusion by craving intimacy, not exclusion. Here the starting place for theology and ethics thinks from the place of the excluded to challenge and examine privilege. All ethics and theology must think from this place, which is the iconoclastic indicative.

---

66. See Jacques Ellul's emphasis on Christian ethics without means. Specifically refer to his use of Barth in Ellul, *To Will & To Do: An Introduction to Christian Ethics Volume II*, 86–95.

67. Barth, *Church Dogmatics IV.4*, 56.

Excursus: Hans Urs von Balthasar on Barth's Theology of the Cross

In order to illustrate this iconoclastic image feature of Barth's theology, I turn to an interpreter of Barth's cross. Hans Urs von Balthasar is a Swiss Catholic theologian who deserves a place in twentieth-century theology as a peer of Barth more than a mere interpreter. Nevertheless, Balthasar offers keen insight into the aesthetic quality of Barth's theology of the cross as unrepresented in the world of images. Balthasar continues a trend in Barth's theology that the cross is iconoclastic. The cross images the unbearable, ugly nature of the world, and it serves as a medium to display the harsh nature of the sin in the world that destroys and excludes even God. However, according to Balthasar, Barth extends even this part of the world's fallenness into the very life of God. As Balthasar writes, the cross "embraces the most abysmal ugliness of sin and hell under the condescension of divine life, which has brought even sin and hell into that divine art for which there is no human analogue."[68] In his own way, Balthasar's interpretation of Barth moves the cross away from a colonial capture that justifies imperial violence. Instead, the cross turns the theological aesthetic of colonialism on its head. Zurara, and the colonial, must stare into the horror of the cross and see the body discarded there. The cross embraces "everything else which a worldly aesthetics (even of a realistic kind) discards as no longer bearable."[69] The colonial, here, serves as *the* worldly aesthetic by locating only a privileged group inside the suffering of God as a way to liberation. However, on the contrary, the cross locates beauty inside the crucifixion to challenge and destroy the false images of colonial imagination. The cross is iconoclastic as it is indicatively present in destruction and reconciliation. In this aesthetic key, reconciliation does not assimilate to bind to death but unites in intimacy people around a new center of belonging. Only *this* kind of social intimacy destroys the structures of social exclusion, and its supporting buttresses so that a new kind of moral community can emerge.

Barth's theology of the cross challenges the aesthetics of communal purity and social exclusion. When humans cast others into hell, the cross binds to that reality with the excluded to reveal their utter beauty and thus destroy the sinful system. The strongholds of purity and social exclusion mock the reality of faith, which is the reality of Jesus Christ. As Barth writes, "faith has already been done by the One whom I follow in my faith, even before I believe, even if I no longer believe, in such a way that He is always, as Heb 12:2 puts it, the originator and completer . . . of our faith."[70]

68. Balthasar, *Glory of the Lord*, 1, 124.
69. Balthasar, *Glory of the Lord*, 1, 124.
70. Barth, *Church Dogmatics II.2*, 48–49.

To make such a point concerning the cross is not masochistic to sanctify maltreatment, as Zurara does. Instead, God makes a new abode in the cross with those outside the structures of purity. An iconoclasm of fidelity must shift outside the narratives of purity so essential to evangelical purity ethics to another holiness, another beauty.

Resurrecting Bodies: Karl Barth's Theology of the Resurrection of Jesus Christ

In Barth's description of reconciliation, the final word on sin is not the death of Christ but the resurrection. The crucifixion of Christ brings death to sin and separation from God, but the resurrection destroys by giving a new life *beyond* death offered to all humanity.[71] The resurrection of Jesus is the *beyondness* on the far side of the cross in Barth's theology. Barth writes, "His raising, His resurrection, His new life, confirmed His death. It was God's answer to it, and to that extent its revelation and declaration."[72] The resurrection, in short, reveals God's defeat of death.[73]

In the resurrection, Christ not only defeats death but returns to the Father and brings humanity with him. Barth writes, "It was God who went into the far country, and it is man who returns home."[74] The creation here is a new intimacy with God on the far side of the cross. Jesus goes into the far country, a creation hostile to God, and experiences the death of the innocence chewed up and trampled down. However, in going into the far country, Christ in his person intercepts ancient kinship networks and reorients them through Christ's resurrected body. The resurrection then serves as the point of departure that reveals all theology. As Barth writes, "If there is any Christian-theological axiom it is this: *Jesus Christ is risen, he is risen indeed!*"[75] This central confession is the content of the Christian faith and gestures to the central identity of Jesus.

The resurrection is not merely rising from the dead but rather that which is *beyond* crucifixion, an iconoclasm of fidelity. Christ first appears to the disciples in a way similar to his life with them in order to couple the knowledge of Christ's earthly life and crucifixion to the resurrection as an "act of God ... underlying their whole knowledge of Jesus Christ."[76] The res-

---

71. See Barth, *Church Dogmatics* IV.1, 288–92.
72. Barth, *Church Dogmatics*, IV.1, 299.
73. Barth, *Church Dogmatics*, IV.1, 294–96.
74. Barth, *Church Dogmatics* IV.2, 19.
75. Barth, *Church Dogmatics* IV.3, 43. Emphasis original.
76. Barth, *Church Dogmatics* IV.1, 296.

urrection is the revelation and provides thoroughly an *a posteriori* account to see the earthly life of Jesus to which "the whole New Testament thinks and speaks . . . and to understand it we must be prepared to think with it in the light of this event."[77] The resurrection is not an illumination logically sequential in history, but rather the light by which one discerns the whole of the witness to Christ.

The resurrection thus witnesses to a specific free act of God that locates reconciliation on an eschatological trajectory. Among Barth's description of the resurrection is that it represents God's sovereign act to not only gesture beyond the crucifixion, but to humanity. Christ is risen and thus so will humanity rise. The Son receives the resurrection from the Father as a passive gift as a part of the reconciling work of the Son on the cross. However, the cross is not alone but rather joined to the resurrection in the sovereignty of God. Christ is *pro nobis* and God the Father, in the resurrection of Jesus, acts on the ones included in Christ's *pro nobis*. The resurrection is God's sovereign "Yes" to humanity to the "No" of death. In the resurrection of Jesus, life opens beyond the grave. In short, reconciliation occurs precisely at this point when the Yes opens beyond the No, which is Barth's dialectic of iconoclasm.

The resurrection of Jesus, as Barth understands, is the awakening of the judgment on humanity that oppresses and kills to maintain its purity.[78] Resurrection, like the cross, is an act of justice for both the sinner and the sinned against. In the latter, Christ stands in solidarity with the sin hurled against margins; in the former, Christ frees from sin's oppression that leads to oppression. God's answer to the injustice of the cross is the resurrection. It is a "verdict" on humanity to claim it back from the powers of death: to heal, liberate, and save. As such, it fulfills the emphasis on the empty cross through a Yes to intimacy with God and a No to separation. The power of the resurrection thus speaks against all human participation in the No, all rejection and exclusion, and instead reveals in the stronghold of death an empty cross and an empty tomb.

Everlasting Life: Karl Barth's Theology of the Resurrection from the Dead

The final No to separation and Yes to intimacy occurs only in the resurrection of the dead.[79] This element of Barth's theology is, admittedly, underde-

---

77. Barth, *Church Dogmatics IV.1*, 292.

78. Barth, *Church Dogmatics IV.1*, 292.

79. On the importance of the resurrection of Christ in history, see Barth, *Church*

veloped in the *Church Dogmatics*. However, Barth briefly gestures toward this in the *Dogmatics* and in earlier work such as *The Resurrection of the Dead*. This latter text articulates one of Barth's most sustained exegetical accounts of Christian hope. Though this moves us from the realm of Christian reconciliation to redemption, the constructive tension between those two moments remains a significant one.

Barth approaches the text of 1 Corinthians as an apostolic text, namely, as John Webster claims, that the "origin and context of the text is God's communicative presence, before which both Paul and the contemporary interpreter stand."[80] Barth focuses primarily on the paradoxical hope of the resurrection of the dead in his exegesis. As Barth argues, the Corinthians, and all humanity, live in ignorance of death. Though this seems impossible, Paul illustrates that the Corinthian's self-sufficient religiosity prevents acknowledgment of their finitude, which leads to their iconoclasm of temptation. Much like humans with a propensity to purity code fetish, Paul reminds the Corinthians that their state is finite and needs correction. In other words, the division of pure and impure do not save. The "religious vivacity of the Corinthians" insists on wisdom without needing the resurrection of the dead to which their lives *should* be oriented.[81] Paul reminds them, and Barth reminds his contemporaries, that the best efforts of finite human religiosity amount to the same end: death. Here, Barth points to a paradoxical hope in Pauline theology: hope occurs positively and negatively, negative in the dizzying confrontation with death, and positive in hope beyond death. The cross of Jesus already presents such a defeat. However, the Corinthians fail to see the importance of hope in their lives.

Paul presents the Corinthians with the hope of the resurrection inside the paradox of death and life. "The recollection of death," as Barth writes, "is so important, so urgent, so disturbing, so actual because it is in fact really the tidings of the resurrection behind it, the recollection of the *life*, of our life that we are not living and that yet is our life."[82] The reminder that we shall die points to the limit of finitude, but Paul uses this to point to hope. Summarizing Paul's emphasis on the resurrection of the dead, Barth writes,

> The dead: that is what we are. The risen: that is what we are not. But precisely for this reason the resurrection of the dead involves that that which *we are not* is equivalent with that which *we are*: the dead living, time eternity, the being truth, things real.

Dogmatics IV.1, 292–93.

80. Webster, *Barth's Earlier Theology*, 71.

81. Barth, *Resurrection of the Dead*, 20.

82. Barth, *Resurrection of the Dead*, 109.

All this is not given except in hope, and therefore this identity is not to be put into effect. [83]

Time and eternity, death and hope all swirl around the same narrative of resurrection of the dead. The present is not the future and thus not final. Christ's resurrection secures the general resurrection against the reality of death and our idolatry to our own finitude. The Corinthians cannot live as if they received the fullness of the resurrection because this life will end and cannot be literalized. Humanity is not yet what it will be, not yet fulfilled, but the reality of Christ's resurrection and the hope of the general resurrection leaves it in tension. "We are," as Barth writes, "still living this life, as yet, we, indeed, only know time; it is the 'not yet' which separates us from the resurrection."[84] The not yet of our lives is the reminder of hope, and it is a warning to the religiosity of the Corinthians that their current life is not enough. Divisions of pure and impure are not enough. The not yet is the reminder of finitude and the not yet reality that far surpasses and condemns it. Much like the resurrection that creates the negative space of the empty tomb, humanity hopes and waits for the resurrection.

That hope is not the continuation of time but its end. "*This* end," as Barth writes, "the end of our sins, which can only end when history ends, and *this* beginning, the beginning of a new life, which can only begin when and where a new world begins."[85] The empty cross is God's triumph over sin, death, and oppression. However, many still suffer under the powers that Christ has defeated, but Barth identifies that "Paul speaks of it not in the imperative or the optative but in the *indicative* mood."[86] There is a "new thing" at the heart of this eschatological hope to which those under the threat of death must cling.[87] It is a reality that bears on the present condition of death. The resurrection of the dead is an iconoclasm of fidelity that finds the crosses in our midst to bring history's victims down from their crosses into resurrected life, making a way into that which is beyond the literalized desire imposed by others in *their* crosses. It is the final freedom from the oppression of sin, but it is not moralism. The resurrection of the dead orders reality not according to sinful humanity but orders it rightly to God. As it stands, hope is a reality beyond death that moves the Corinthians' audience and the contemporary one. Hope thus breaks open the limits of history, or, as Barth states, "we are living the life limited by that horizon, we are

83. Barth, *Resurrection of the Dead*, 108–9.
84. Barth, *Resurrection of the Dead*, 151.
85. Barth, *Resurrection of the Dead*, 134. Emphasis original.
86. Barth, *Resurrection of the Dead*, 28.
87. Barth, *Resurrection of the Dead*, 28.

living in time for eternity, we are living in the hope of the resurrection."[88] The newness is the resurrection of the dead and no doubt the culmination of reconciliation.

Without the crucifixion, the resurrection of Christ, and the resurrection of the dead, there would not be reconciliation. Reconciliation is a fellowship between God and humanity created by God through the incarnation, crucifixion, and resurrection of Jesus as a free act that will culminate in the resurrection of the dead. As such, reconciliation depends on the cross and resurrection to participate in the indicative's iconoclastic power. The motivating image of Barth's theology of the cross comes as the Judge judged in our place and the indicative challenges moral judgment as one who comes for us and takes our place. Furthermore, the resurrection as the sovereign power beyond the cross that brings human efforts to naught orders reality to a newness of grace only witnessed by the disciples and that for which the church yearns in hope. The inner texture of reconciliation pulsates with mutually cooperative indicatives, which indicates that at no point, all the way down, does Barth envision a theological ethic based on a required code and exclusion. Instead, the very fabric of existence unites humanity to a new beauty and intimacy that transcends literalized desire, calling all to respond in testimony.

CONCLUSION: NEW IMAGES

In conclusion, a new theological vision of sex and the body must precede the ethics of sexuality. The current purity model is diseased, and its images are idolatrous. According to the social exclusion model, each person wants to remain the judge so that they might be judged as good on their own. Such a graceless account of ethics moves humanity into places of deep depravity and idolatry. A theological vision for sexuality must find new pathways of imagination that vivify new practices of intimacy not bound to codes. In short, a full iconoclasm that blasphemes the theological and moral order of the social exclusion model must emerge. The response to reconciliation is a call to act as if humanity were God, but as one summoned to a new kind of community. Barth's account of reconciliation makes an iconoclastic switch to think from the place of the excluded (i.e., the crucified) in order to reimagine sexuality.

---

88. Barth, *Resurrection of the Dead*, 151.

4

Iconoclastic Sex

Sexual Ethics from the Margins

INTRODUCTION

CODES SERVE AS A form of naked imperatives that construct rules and images that work in tandem with our purity/disgust reflex. In the chapter 2, the code fetish unmasked does damage. This insight emerges through the individuals surveyed. However, each also confesses and gropes for a different future for their lives, sexuality included, that arises from encounters with God and the holy that radically change their perspective. That sexual ethics is not primarily about the rehearsal of an abstract code, but divine revelation and experience, shifts the moral ontology of sexual ethics from code to command. In this chapter, I argue that the shape of sexual ethics must adopt a receptive posture toward the divine command in its indicative presentation through divine revelation, resulting in empowerment and action through testimony and the cultivation of affections into virtue. This method proposes a moral life for survivors, those still in the web, people who have never experienced the web, and all of us to the ends of mutuality. The previous chapter offered a clearing of the brush to begin again, not from a place of naked imperative but indicative.

As such, this chapter will explore the moral contours of such a reality that keeps intimacy as a central feature of any sexual ethics. In short, it will be to explore the claim already articulated by Ted Smith when he writes that the

> accent on the indicative of divine reconciliation, though, allows us to imagine the presence of God in a very different way. God is present not where the world lives up to some imperatives that God has given but in the fact of free responses . . . For the presence of God does not depend on relations of identity. On the contrary, to say that God is gracious is to say that God remains present to creatures and institutions that are *not* identical to God.[1]

Therefore, ethics does not propose a particular alignment with law or identity as the means to embody reconciliation. Instead, ethics is the cultivation of free response *in light of* the encounter with God *in reconciliation*. As such, the social logic moves the moral life toward reception rather than exclusion.

In order to do this, I remain in Barth's theological project. As will be shown, Barth's command ethics are not naked imperatives but the presence of a moral ontology that encourages crisis and free response. Such a response is not a natural theology of disgust. Instead, ethics comes by way of disruption and reorientation. Barth's theology will then be the basis for an ethics of testimony that simultaneously empowers the agent to act within a moral framework not possible in the former model of coding and images. The move to testimony empowers all equally and does not define who can act morally, which cultivates virtues and dispositions that make sexual ethics possible. The bases of grace, iconoclasm, and covenant will remain central to guiding the selection of virtues of justice, love, truthfulness, and humility. These virtues and bases will guide the provisional ethics covered in the following chapter.

PART I: BARTH'S ETHICS OF COMMAND

Reconciliation cannot dissolve into a cute moralism or code fetishism but must continually grow and encircle believers. Moral thinking takes shape as a witness and testimony to the indicative of reconciliation. Barth's vision of the moral life rests on commands arising from indicatives that never close off into social exclusion. Barth challenges Christians to *hear* the command in the indicative mood, not as a specific code, but rather as a free response empowered by the indicative. Reconciliation cultivates a multiplicity of Christian lives and bids each specifically into the community without collapsing into relativism.[2] It creates freedom and permissions guided by the command of God. The consistent measure of its morality lies entirely in its

---

1. Smith, *Weird John Brown*, 120–21. Emphasis original.
2. Barth, *Church Dogmatics IV.3.2*, 182–83.

source in the indicative, which is God's reality to be known, experienced, and worshiped. Nevertheless, this indicative is a living Word, which cannot be collapsed and captured, but always escapes containment. The circle is drawn for us, and the posture is always to receive reconciliation, the commands, and virtues necessary for life.

To this end, Karl Barth offers a theological description of commands to lead the reader's attention away from code prescriptions, which lean toward an ethic of social exclusion, and back toward God. For Barth, ethics is a form of testimony that acknowledges and affirms the work of God in Christ for humanity (*pro nobis*). Commands are not codes in Barth's theology. As David Clough argues, when approaching Barth's theology of command, we must "set aside almost everything we associate with divine command ethics."[3] Barth illustrates the difference between command and code while revealing the preference for the former in three distinct ways. First, a code is a command that severed itself from its source, namely the very nature of God. To experience God means to experience a command. God's presence is "the answer to the ethical question, the supremely critical question concerning the good in and over every so-called good in human actions and modes of action."[4] As such, humanity is determined in every situation and context to be witnesses *for* God.[5] The opening indicative of the commandments is given to Israel, "I am the Lord your God, who brought you out of the land of Egypt, out of the house of slavery; you shall have no other gods before me" (Exod 20:2–3, NRSV). This passage succinctly depicts the indicative of their election with compelling moral activity necessarily entailed. The indicative encourages the deepest, free moral response opened in an iconoclasm of fidelity to God. God stands at the center of Israel's identity and thus humanity's life. Because God is *their* God, they will be *God's* people.

Election to covenant with God becomes a central conviction of the moral life because it is the basis of command. As Barth continues, "The divine election is . . . the determination of [humanity]—[their] determination to this service, this commission, this office of witness. It is [humanity] who is determined in this way. Therefore . . . [humanity] is certainly not a mere thing . . . but a *person*."[6] Thus, the election of humanity determines them for service and obedience that flows directly from the very being of God, who elects humanity to be God's people and who elects Godself to be their God. Election requires liberation and freedom in a non-representable way for humans. Therefore, the moral life is not the adherence to codes

---

3. Clough, *Ethics in Crisis*, xiv.
4. Barth, *Church Dogmatics II.2*, 7.
5. Barth, *Church Dogmatics II.2*, 2.
6. Barth, *Church Dogmatics II.2*, 2.

absent God, but rather a human determination in response to the indicative of God's revelation through their election.

Second, and directly related to the previous point, Barth helps resist the exegesis present in the social exclusion model. The moral imperatives present in Scripture are not codes or principles to be lifted and applied, but commands. Barth terms any search for codes "biblicism," which mirrors code fetishism. The precise nature of biblical command does not negate their authority in times different than their own; their concreteness merely names the contextual authority necessary to understand the commands.[7] The commands are not codes because they are not abstract from the present, contemporary encounter with the will of God. If the goal of Christian ethics were merely to find commands and lift them out of one world into another, Christians would commit the sin of "casuistry," which Barth defines as the attempt to abstract codes from their context in Scripture and source in God.[8] Casuistry is the claiming, deploying, and attempted mastery of God's commands isolated for oneself and one's possession, thereby turning them into a code in which they judge all proper performance. Mastery fails the test of faithfulness to an indicative and instead mistakes the command of God for "a universal rule, an empty form, or rather a tissue of such rules and forms."[9] As such, casuistry is not the command of God. Instead, God's command is a specific and divine "Yes" that the human creature must recognize. Humans do not find sanctification by their strength and power but instead in God's electing, covenantal faithfulness. Herein lies the stark contrast between command and code; God's command must be obeyed so that humanity might turn away from their ability to achieve, and the code is an achievement. The command does not grant election but rather asks the faithful to respond to it.

Third, the command of God is specific and contextual while not collapsing into a code. Barth envisions a receptive account of human ethics that relies on God's very self to receive. In this way, the commands remain tethered to God and specific to the person as they receive this indicative. Barth's command ethics makes command a moral ontology to encounter rather than a possession for entry into God's social network. If the command arises from God's very self and is not the subject of an abstract code from Scripture, then it is equally specific to each creature as they stand before God. The command is the divine "Yes" to each person's specificity so that they might be sanctified, and it is a command to each creature bound to code fetishes.

---

7. Barth, *Ethics*, 80.
8. See Barth, *Church Dogmatics III.4*, 5–8.
9. Barth, *Church Dogmatics III.4*, 9.

To avoid code fetishes, one cannot abstract the command as a separate feature from the very life of God in Barth's theological ethics. Instead, the command is indicative. Its shape is beautiful, and the response is not the fulfillment of an imperative but a witness to the reality itself. In short, God commands himself in the activities God enacts for humanity. Because God has done certain things for humanity, grace urges humanity to take them up as gifts and perpetuate them in their lives. One need only approach the triadic nature of Barth's command ethics to see that the command is not a universal principle. This triadic structure of the command of God is God as Creator, Reconciler, and Redeemer, which locates creation, reconciliation, and redemption as the ontological basis of human action. As such, it conflicts with code fetishism and the imperative mood. The triadic structure iconoclastically confronts the literalized images and any contrary ideological image that might captivate God's creatures. As such, Barth's theological ethics takes shape precisely as witness and testimony rather than a command abstracted from God's life.

Barth's command ethics is unique and does not follow many traditional accounts of command theory in ethics. It is not dependent upon prescribed rational content available to Christians without the necessity of faith, though it does possess rational content, but rather emerges from the creating, reconciling, and redeeming covenant in which humanity finds itself. The command arises, by way of analogy, from the saving work of God's fidelity. In order to fully see the constructive work beyond what it negates, namely code, one must appreciate the various elements of moral formation Barth envisions.

Barth emphasizes two different aspects of the command of God. The first is general ethics, which deals with the encounter between humanity and God as covenant partners. Barth writes, "that God gives His command, that He gives Himself to be our Commander . . . [means that the addressee] is brought into that confrontation and fellowship with Jesus Christ."[10] The relationship is covenantal in that the encounter is personal, and the human must receive God as commander and respond to the command. Like reconciliation, the covenant as the basis of command means that ethics is a living shape moving literalized desire to a transcendent source.[11] It is prayer and supplication, knowing one must ask, seek, and not possess.[12] In short, God gives Godself for humanity and gives commands to humanity within a covenant relationship with humanity.

---

10. Barth, *Church Dogmatics II.2*, 38.
11. Sonderegger, *Systematic Theology Volume 2*, 278.
12. Barth, *Church Dogmatics II.2*, 132–59.

In addition to general ethics, Barth provides decisive special ethics. General ethics begins with the fact that God gives Godself to humanity as its commander, but special ethics begins the process of actualizing command in an individual context. The rhythm of God's trinitarian command (creation, reconciliation, redemption) provides the general context from which specific ethics will emerge. As Barth writes, God's triune work in creation, reconciliation, and redemption "have in view the institution, preservation, and execution of the covenant of grace, for partnership in which He has predestined and called man."[13] The covenant as the general context of ethics meets the sharpening of God's acts that determine our specific responses to the world around us. Whatever one does in ethical activity must confirm in human action God's work. Christ already fulfills all elements of God's creating, reconciling, and redeeming work, but this work serves as our commission. Human activity takes shape as iconoclasm of fidelity in response to God's work. In other words, as Barth understands, "God who has created man and enabled and commissioned him to do his own work is the God who is gracious to man in Jesus Christ."[14] The command is specific to the individual's circumstances and encounters with the living God, but the resulting actions will align with the internal logic of God's initiating, gracious activity.

Having established the covenant as the grounding of command, Barth moves into the formal conditions of his command ethics. Though humanity cannot treat past commands as the literal command to lift from the text and abstracted from God as a specific activity, there is a consistency in God's command. Barth's command ethics, in this way, possesses many similarities to Kant's moral philosophy. Barth writes that "the universally valid command of God applies to me and affects me in a very definite way cannot be taken to imply that I can treat it as conditioned by the peculiar factors of my personal situation; that I can secure and fortify myself against its universal validity as it certainly applies to me too."[15] Barth does qualify the ethical command to those who are "covenant-partners with God and therefore placed under the divine command."[16] Thus, like Kant, Barth foresees the person in the same situation bound to the formal command "I do." To be clear, Barth, unlike Kant, does not propose neutrality in command ethics. Instead, it is the covenant that serves as the basis of command. The one who commands is the one who has already created, reconciled, and redeemed humanity to the end. It is this God we face with our activity. Therefore, even

---

13. Barth, *Church Dogmatics III.1*, 43.
14. Barth, *Church Dogmatics III.4*, 49.
15. Barth, *Church Dogmatics II.2*, 144.
16. Barth, *Church Dogmatics II.2*, 144.

when one encounters moral luck or injury or any systemic issues that would disrupt moral thinking, God lovingly takes this into account. The one who commands is not unaware of our trials nor unsympathetic to our pain. The command given in grace meets the need of our suffering. This command is proper for the individual and all those facing systemic evils. Thus, the covenant is freedom because it is to God that we are finally accountable.

The formal requirements of command ethics lead to material commitments as well. This formal aspect is a complex element of Barth's command ethics but a helpful and necessary nuance for those seeking clear discernment. Here Barth deals with the various prescriptions in the Decalogue and the Sermon on the Mount. Barth privileges these two passages, but also many of the prescriptions found in the Pauline and New Testament corpus. What do we do with these commands? The commandments characterize the arena in which the limits of God's command occur. Barth writes that the command "must not violate these prescribed limits."[17] In short, they help us recognize the command given in the encounter with God and how to discern what is God and what is not. However, these contextual commands do not merely exist as codes or universal moral norms awaiting actualization. Instead, Barth proposes something far more complex, which requires theological leg work. One must engage the Scripture to orient oneself to the contextual commands to hear well. Even though the command in the Bible is not synonymous with the one we receive in the encounter with God, it does shape humans into well informed hearers. This preparation does not mean that God will only ever command the same—there will be cases where a new command emerges from the encounter. However, through the formation of contextual commands, one knows how to listen.

Excursus: Clarifying the Radicality of Grace and Dialectic of Barth's Römerbrief

Before transitioning to virtue, I wish to dwell for a moment longer on the disruptive nature of Barth's ethics. One could read his command ethics and think he merely baptizes Kant's ethics, but this is not the case. To be clear, Barth does admit an appreciation for Kant, but he ultimately will not remain in Kant's debt. There are many reasons for this, most prominently that Kant cannot abide a lawgiver other than the self. However, I argue that the disrupting, strangely new world announced by the gospel proposes something far more radical than other forms of ethics in a self-correction against idol creation. When connected with Barth's deeply dialectical sympathies, ethics

---

17. Barth, *Church Dogmatics* II.2, 144.

must always be halted and disrupted by God's gracious initiative toward humanity. The virtues and ethics offered in the present work can never become static but provisional, in need of constant clarification and re-seeking the command of God. Judgment, as such, must be disrupted by God. The challenge, then, is to clarify the interrupting nature of Barth's ethics for both for the individual and the community.

Barth's dialectical hermeneutic of the moral life emerges from his classic work *Römerbrief (The Epistle to the Romans)*. The summarized hermeneutic is in Barth's opening to his interpretation of Romans 12. "The problem of ethics is presented once again (vi. 12–23, viii. 12, 13) as a great disturbance . . . for human behaviour must inevitably be disturbed by the thought of God."[18] The movement of ethics must face a disturbance of thought even though the encounter with God should include the reading of Scripture. However, ethics in command must disturb human thought with the thought of God, and this kind of ethics is "unsearchable."[19] God is Wholly Other and God's ways are not our ways. Ethics cannot be known as a priori knowledge. Thus, Barth proposes a dialectical form of thinking to preserve Christian ethics against the coding of ethical thinking today.

The disturbing element of ethics, according to the *Römerbrief*, arises from the defeat of false agency related to Adamic agency. Naturally, this discussion takes center stage in Barth's exegesis of Romans 6 and illustrates the central theological convictions of grace and resurrection. Barth writes, "Grace is the power of the resurrection."[20] Such power "disturbs" the tyranny of sin at work in our bodies and enables the impossible possibility of obedience to God. Returning to Romans 5, Barth draws from the lament of Paul "that before God no flesh is righteous" to illustrate the sheer hopelessness of humanity's situation before God.[21] Instead, the religion of the human heart as a human construct to earn or immolate God's goodness must be "catastrophically dissolved."[22] This disturbance of the human condition must ultimately prove the essential need for grace for humanity through the resurrection. As Barth moves into Romans 6, the necessary accentuation is the eruption of grace from the place of Adamic sovereignty's weakness, namely death. In short, Adam must die, along with human participation in Adam. Thus, the resurrection serves as grace at the place of Adam's weakness to disturb, overturn, and destroy any continuity between Adam and

---

18. Barth, *Epistle to the Romans*, 424.
19. Barth, *Epistle to the Romans*, 424.
20. Barth, *Epistle to the Romans*, 206.
21. Barth, *Epistle to the Romans*, 186.
22. Barth, *Epistle to the Romans*, 186.

the present humanity.[23] Only as those subject to the resurrection, which for Barth is thoroughgoingly eschatological, can humanity experience the impossible possibility of resurrection.

The disruptive nature of Barth's *Römerbrief* is undoubtedly no departure from the command ethics articulated in the *Church Dogmatics*. However, the purpose of the hermeneutic runs up against the idea that humans can expect God's command. Barth sees Scripture as preparation for humans for the specificity of actions commanded to them, and this does not appear in the *Römerbrief*. The approach of human knowledge as "system of ethics" is "dissolved" by the power of grace that enables the impossible possibility of obedience.[24] The constructive aspect of human thinking and doing participates in the "form of this world" in passing away to make way for its "transformation."[25] The only positive aspect of human activity is the action that "possesses ... a parabolic capacity, a tendency towards protest" of the sinful order.[26] It is positive in its negation. Thus, the event of grace that commands humanity resists our natural capacity to perceive the command. Therefore, the disruption afforded to humanity in their activity is a shattering of worlds, as Phil Ziegler writes, "contextualizing ethics in the 'strange new' world announced by the gospel of God" rather than contextualizing God in our old world.[27] In short, ethics can only disrupt the categories and systems of ethics available to humanity and it cannot create an absolute code ethics that replaces God. The disruptive element in ethics places humanity at a disadvantage because ethics takes the form of an activity that breaks expectations. It is still human, but it performs an impossible possibility that participates in world transformation, which protects the internal structures of the world.

Whatever can be stated about Barth's command ethics must engage these themes of disruption, grace, and resurrection. God disrupts and disturbs ethical thought in ways that challenge the fundamental basis of Christian ethics. Barth's work in the *Römerbrief* protects ethics from casuistry by disrupting humans' exact prescriptions and power in their Adamic state. The social exclusion model of sexual ethics relies on privileged positions

---

23. I appreciate how Phil Ziegler phrases this: "by its strictly asymmetrical contradiction of sin, grace works to 'disrupt,' 'revolutionise' and 'overthrow' any accommodation, equilibrium or coexistence between the old and the new, precisely in order that faith may stretch out towards' the sovereign reality of the new life in God." Ziegler, "Ethics and the Catastrophe of Grace," 340.)

24. Barth, *Epistle to the Romans*, 228.

25. Barth, *Epistle to the Romans*, 434.

26. Barth, *Epistle to the Romans*, 451.

27. Ziegler, "Ethics and the Catastrophe of Grace," 345.

and notions of purity. Disruption of grace "is the axe laid at the root of our own haphazard conceits."[28] Barth offers this warning to the privileged places of social exclusion: "To Christianity every human *high place,* every human position, every battle and controversy between men of this world, however sacred and inevitable the conflict may be, is no more than a parable."[29] Within this parable, Christians find the arresting opportunity to bear witness and testify to how God disrupts the high places and casts the mighty down from their thrones. In this way, ethics is not only disruption but decentering. To move from the place of privilege to those outside means decentering in testimony. Ethics is first and foremost a "recollection that God alone occupies the high place" and that human action only participates in that reality.[30] Concretely testimony and parable emerge in relationship to God. As Barth states, loving one's neighbor is a parable and testimony to the "Wholly Other."[31] Neighbor love becomes the concrete place where humans participate in the disrupting grace of God, wherein loving them means rebelling against the world's disorder.

Divine Excellence: A Slight Turn to Jonathan Edwards on Virtue

The hermeneutic of disruption orients Barth's ethics away from static code making, but Barth's ethics also point to the cultivation of virtue. This emphasis on formation in Barth brings up an exciting opportunity for reflection. If the command *forms* a particular kind of attention and hearing, then Barth displays virtue ethics *through* command. Barth's account of virtue relies heavily on command and reception, but the reception forms beyond mere concrete application of a command. Virtue still requires the formation of affections, but for Barth, virtue is not something humanity habituates. In order to draw out the peculiar form of virtue ethics displayed by Barth, I turn to theologian Jonathan Edwards, who conceives a similar virtue ethics. Reading Edwards in light of Barth exposes something obscured in Barth's thought, namely the affections and their training through the revelation of God. Such a shift challenges a misunderstanding that God speaks abstractly. Rather, in Edwards, one glimpses a theological reading of virtue as training moral senses that complements Barth's theology.

The training of moral sensibility begins in conversion. Like Barth, Edwards is suspicious of natural capacities to pursue virtue and ethics

---

28. Barth, *Epistle to the Romans,* 466.
29. Barth, *Epistle to the Romans,* 466.
30. Barth, *Epistle to the Romans,* 444.
31. Barth, *Epistle to the Romans,* 452.

due to sin. Therefore, conversion is an essential starting point that creates "new dispositions" in the believer's heart.[32] Thus, conversion, as Elizabeth Cochran summarizes, "is an event that changes human nature such that natural faculties can be exercised in new ways."[33] This opens up human capacities iconoclastically to the transcendent in a way that leads to their transformation. Edwards, like Barth, recognizes that ethics is not chiefly concerned with decisions but with capacities. Grace, in conversion, renews the capacity to pursue virtue. To be clear, this renewing of capacities is not a set of "new faculties."[34] Instead, the Spirit of God acts upon our existent faculties to pursue virtue.

After the renewing of affections, the virtues one pursues, as in Barth's theological ethics, reside in the character of God. The formation of affections is where Edwards most aligns with Barth and distances himself from habituation. Virtue is properly an excellence that belongs to God, not humanity. As such Barth and Edwards profess a dialectical virtue ethics. Nevertheless, through intervention, God gives these virtues for us to inhabit. However, the question remains: if the goods are inhabitable yet not achieved through habituation, how does one inhabit them? The answer is, yet again, found in conversion. Through conversion and regeneration in the power of the Holy Spirit, God enables humans to participate in the true virtue of God. "Grace," as Cochran argues, "does not operate only at the first moment of conversion, but it continues to transform our natures."[35] Only God can exhibit true virtue, but humans can participate in this beauty of divine life through their coordinated virtues.

The way that humans participate in God's beauty and excellence lies in the activity of God, namely God's saving work. This emphasis, as with Barth's command, illustrates that the divine agency of God enables our participation in virtue. As Edwards writes, through the "communication of God's holiness . . . the creature partakes of God's own moral excellence, which is properly the beauty of the divine nature."[36] This "divine emanation" empowers the agent to know true virtue and that this true virtue should be loved above all other human pursuits.[37] This virtue is the *telos* of human nature, but humans lack the natural capacity to work toward this end. Therefore, the emanation of divine holiness provides us with the ends (*telos*) of human life and the means to pursue those ends. Grace continually

---

32. Edwards, *Religious Affections*, 206.
33. Cochran, *Receptive Human Virtues*, 107.
34. Edwards, *Religious Affections*, 206.
35. Cochran, *Receptive Human Virtues*, 109.
36. Edwards, *Ethical Writings*, 442.
37. Cochran, *Receptive Human Virtues*, 49.

transforms and sanctifies the affections to love God as true virtue. This ordering of desire moves humanity into the right relationship with God, oneself, and one's neighbor. Edwards, as does Barth, notes that humanity entirely depends upon God to discern true virtue. However, unlike Barth, Edwards understands that some aspect of God's virtue speaks to a natural capacity already in the created order. Furthermore, God shapes human affections through command towards these ends of creation and causes them to be accountable. Even though sin distorts human agency, it does not destroy it.

In sum, Edwards, coupled with Barth, offers a virtue ethics against code ethics. The command sends humanity into crisis, toward freedom in order to cultivate new affections and virtues to inhabit. Barth's theological ethics is dialectical. One does not discover virtue through habituation in Barth but rather the encounter that leaves its mark much as a crater to a bomb.[38] This is due to his rejection of natural theology. Purity culture, code fetishes, and iconoclasms of temptation are all forms of natural theology wherein certain images or practices correspond directly to God. Barth troubles the ability to identify external natural goodness even in a fragment as it appears in Edwards. Furthermore, Barth's theological ethics is not primarily but only secondarily a virtue ethic. The command encounter is continually necessary for every new action and decision. The affections need transformation in Barth, but this transformation is to hear the command more clearly. However, Barth does share an appreciation for a human agency with Edwards. Barth locates agency in covenant, whereas Edwards accounts for it in regret and accountability. For Barth, the covenant is the entire ground of creaturely existence and changes our accountability structure to a gracious commander rather than external factors. It is the one to whom the creature knows in covenant that judges their actions and their loves. However, Barth's ethics is far more radical and disruptive than Edwards's virtue can provide alone.

PART II: FROM COMMAND TO TESTIMONY

If Barth's ethics requires testimony as a parabolic witness to God, then it is the correct moral posture to divine command. Testimony empowers all kinds of disciple-agents to act because God is utterly immanent to all. A testimony is an attempt to articulate an event in one's life. As Anna Carter Florence argues, testimony is "both a narration of events and a confession of belief: we tell what we have seen and heard, and we confess what we

---

38. Barth, *Epistle to the Romans*, 29.

believe about it."³⁹ This definition encompasses the empowering nature of testimony in Christian worship and the vulnerability in the words that often arise from places of brokenness and pain. Testimony is a reception, a conversion, and a witness to something new. The role of testimony concerning ethics requires exploring Ted Smith's claim that command "invites faithful, free responses, which become testimonies to God's great indicative of reconciliation."⁴⁰ Testimony is a continual reenactment of God's unnatural grafting of a strange community together. The reconciliation of many stories into a new intimacy rerouted through Christ's body. Furthermore, the intimacy of the breaking open of community leads to an iconoclasm of fidelity tied to the saving activity of God rather than to idols of social exclusion. Testimony changes the nature of the community by challenging the images central to its subsistence.

Barth's Ethics of Witness: Testimony

The command ethics of Barth, coupled with the virtue ethics of Edwards, requires one final connection back to the indicative and iconoclasms of fidelity. Again, Barth's ethics of command is not a code, but a morally formative indicative that shapes the hearer into virtuous response. However, the responses are not scripted, but entirely free. Ethics, for Barth, is more akin to a permission. Ethics is responsible, yet not a call to literalized desires.⁴¹ Thus, through response and testimony a freedom and playfulness emerges in ethics through the way it disrupts, reorients, and charts new paths. The way Barth expresses this freedom is witness. Witness is a testimony to the command and, thus, reforms the affections to desire God more fundamentally than other structures and codes of meaning. Witness is, thus, the central ethical response to the command.

The free response first suggested by Ted Smith and developed in Barth's account of witness comes against human propensity to totality. One could see the centrality of witness in Barth's thought or the necessity of encounter to instrumentalize and use voices, namely to assimilate them into a collective whole. Such assimilation requires that certain voices become mute in light of certain codes. For example, purity codes only make room for the pure. Thus, ethics, as Kant implicitly argues, is only for some individuals. As Adkins beautifully illustrated, some do not fit the code "pre-morally" and only serve as the negative pole in a system of goodness. In such a totalizing

---

39. Florence, *Preaching as Testimony*, xiii.
40. Smith, *Weird John Brown*, 119.
41. For more on Barth's language of permission see Barth, *Zwei Vorträge*, 3–10.

ethical system, the operation of, as Barth terms it, a "universal collective whole" emerges as a creaturely attempt to define every creature's place perfectly.[42]

Barth, rather than elevating a particular creature, argues that the providential weaving together of the multitude is for the love and rule of each individual.[43] Each person has their own "independent significance and validity" that cannot be instrumentalized but "[attains] its own individual ends, and in this way the common end of all individuals."[44] Barth, in this way, illustrates the radical difference between the universal and the kingdom. In the former, individuals are instrumentalized to realize a creaturely perfection. In the latter, the whole only comes to fulfillment as all reach their individual, specific fulfillment. The common end is not for the privileged to fully thrive at the expense of others, justifying removing others for the sake of temptation, but humans only reach the end together, a truly saving solidarity. Barth concludes, "[God] loves and rules them, therefore, in their inter-dependence, their mutual association. But on this account He does not love and rule them any less but to the highest degree possible in their particularity and singularity."[45] This account of providence maintains a distinction and unity beyond the polarizing instrumentalizing on one hand or autonomous individuality on the other. It is a profound community ordered and organized by God that honors community and particularity together without losing either in transition. When the church gathers to hear the testimonies of the faithful, they come together to see God's care in each other collectively. To participate in God's love requires this kind of coordinated care, this kind of reconciliation. To live into the command of God the Reconciler is to love precisely in this love, namely the recognition that we need God and one another, or, as Rowan Williams writes, citing a Russian friend, "we all go to heaven in each other's pockets."[46] In the Barthian sense, to grow in love is to testify and witness.

Providence makes possible the ability to hear and receive testimony as a individual's encounter of the command while also creating the conditions whereby the community itself will respond to voices in the community. Witness and testimony function almost interchangeably in Barth's theology, but Barth is very suspicious of any centering on subjective experience. Jesus is the one true witness in Barth's theology.[47] However, Christ is not alone in

42. Barth, *Church Dogmatics III.3*, 177.
43. Barth, *Church Dogmatics III.3*, 178.
44. Barth, *Church Dogmatics III.3*, 178.
45. Barth, *Church Dogmatics III.3*, 178.
46. Williams, "Beyond Goodness," 162.
47. Barth, *Church Dogmatics IV.3.2*, 11.

this witnessing capacity, as humans join in witnessing.[48] As in all responses to God's command, Barth envisions testimony with the "normative description in the imperatives of the Sermon on the Mount or the admonitions of the apostolic Epistles."[49] Though the Scripture tempers expectations, the weight of testimony lies in God's reconciliation of the world not in terms of personal activity but in the reality that bears upon them. As Barth writes, "Christian ethos does not allow itself to be understood as an end in itself. It is not a first thing, but follows from what Jesus Christ and Christians, what He who commands and they who obey, are in themselves and in their mutual relationship prior to their command obedience."[50] Testimony, thus, is the free response of which the Christian has multiple, particular avenues of freedom available to her.[51] God is the final Judge in all particular, free responses to the command.[52]

God as the final Judge also leads to liberation. Ethics as witness empowers the recipient of the command to live a life coordinated to their liberation.[53] God judges (i.e., the Judge judged in our place) to set free and reconcile. The liberation of reconciliation makes humanity a living witness through the articulation and embodiment of their freedom.[54] In other words, the one testifying enacts their freedom through the embodiment and articulation of surprisingly new activities and vocations. This testimony, to be clear, is not about the subjective element but only considers the subjective secondary to the reality of reconciliation with God and the community as per God's providence. As such, the free response of witnesses is participating in the supreme good and the sovereign Lord.[55]

In sum, Barth's ethics of command calls for a response in testimony and witness. The ethics of command is not about coding the actions appropriate to specific character traits and making them a part of the universal collective. Instead, it is the openness to which the liberated human can and must respond. It is empowering to receive such a command because it awakens capacities for ethics. Since these vocations and testimonies vary in expression, they cannot be prescribed in advance but instead emerge through the encounter with God's command. The command thus releases from bondage and empowers new actions corresponding to the new reality arising from a

---

48. Barth, *Church Dogmatics IV.3.2*, 185, 202–3.
49. Barth, *Church Dogmatics IV.3.2*, 186.
50. Barth, *Church Dogmatics IV.3.2*, 188.
51. Barth, *Church Dogmatics IV.3.2*, 182–83.
52. Barth, *Church Dogmatics IV.3.2*, 183.
53. Barth, *Church Dogmatics IV.3.2*, 183.
54. Barth, *Church Dogmatics IV.3.2*, 202–3, 221–22.
55. Barth, *Church Dogmatics IV.3.2*, 191, 235.

person's life. Ethics is, in short, a response to a command that creates a new reality particular to the individual who testifies through their words and deeds. Thus, testimony is the enacting of an iconoclasm of fidelity because it is the opening of the human to name what is not of themselves and the new transforming activity opened beyond their immanent lives.

A Brief History and Theology of Testimony

Barth is not the first to think through the implication of testimony. In this section, we think with and beyond Barth to listen for the command among those marginalized in sexual ethics. The new ethics thinks with Barth in the emphasis on free response and witness as the reflex to divine command and beyond Barth in locating authority in a preferential option for the poor and marginalized. It is from here that we can renew moral energies and form ourselves to hear the command so clear to these voices. Furthermore, these testimonies are a new means of certainty that replace the propensity to code ethics that tempts humans to measure their goodness against one another. The positive testimonies of God's transformation and the negative testimonies of the church's failure must both be told. They both form certainty for moral formation and a new sexual ethics that arise from mutuality. Thinking from these voices will be a venture into a far country and will result in a new voice and framework for sexual ethics.

Testimony is an essential feature of worship that defines reality for the faithful and shifts the attention from dominant systems of power to other places. As such, it forms an alternative epistemic framework for theology and ethics. Though testimony often appears very subjective, it nevertheless bears a different kind of certitude. As Old Testament scholar Walter Brueggemann argues, testimony forms a unique identity exhibited in the people of God in Scripture.[56] As the distinctive speech of God's children mobilized toward God, testimony serves to locate humanity's way of knowing outside of the places of privilege where the social exclusion model traditionally lies.

Biblical scholar Walter Brueggemann helps illustrate this epistemic shift through an appeal to the legal courtroom. In a trial, a jury considers testimonies as a means to access an event they (i.e., the jury) did not witness. The testimony is a public presentation that "constitutes reality."[57] As Brueggemann writes, "it causes to be, in the courtroom, what was not until this utterance. In this sense, the utterance leads reality in the courtroom, so

---

56. Brueggemann, *Theology of the Old Testament*, 120.
57. Brueggemann, *Theology of the Old Testament*, 121.

that the reality to which the testimony is made depends completely on the utterance."[58] When the court reaches a verdict, the testimonies presented in the courtroom participate in a new reality through the judgment of guilt or innocence. Brueggemann argues that testimonies are essential in the witness of Scripture. For example, testimony in the context of Israel does not reach a new legal reality; instead, "testimony becomes revelation."[59] Testimony participates in these events through their bearing witness and joins the community together through the truthfulness of its witness and iconoclastically opens it to receive from beyond itself. The testimony becomes revelation in this way as it discloses the reality of God as actions of love make known in the reconciliation of God.

Brueggemann's analysis of testimony as revelation-affirming speech mirrors much of what J. L. Austin terms "performative utterances." Austin argues that one does not merely describe reality in a performative utterance but aims to accomplish something as well.[60] A speech act depends on shared stories and recognition held by the speaker and community, which is its power. However, Brueggemann's presentation of the testimony moves speech beyond the shared conventions of the hearers to serve a more potent form of speech act. Testimony thus is radically disruptive in this way, with the ability to posit a new reality that simultaneously draws on conventions of the community (i.e., covenant) but yet exceeds them through the elimination of the limits often held by hearers of the testimony. As such, testimony presents a new reality governed by a new imagination that decenters privilege and old ways of knowing and certitude.

The power of testimony at the heart of Scripture extends into the testimonies present in liturgical contexts. Testimony originates as a kind of preaching and proclamation that draws from ancient Hebrew contexts. However, the proclamation of testimony still enlivens the testimonies of individuals who share their encounters with the living God.

Testimony, then, performs an essential iconoclasm of fidelity in the lives of those who testify. The testimony deconstructs the images that often place power and purity in the hands of an in-group against others. The new certainty offered in testimony requires that the community listen to divine command presented in others to cultivate the corresponding virtues to inhabit the command. As Florence argues, the deconstruction process "permits us to uncover the masked priorities and power dynamics of a text that may warp its authority structures, and so create ingrown systems that

---

58. Brueggemann, *Theology of the Old Testament*, 121.
59. Brueggemann, *Theology of the Old Testament*, 121.
60. Austin, *How to Do Things with Words*, 108–9.

lead to oppression and suffering."[61] In short, it names the power that often determines the family resemblance by which Christians determine social acceptance or exclusion. Furthermore, testimony destroys the borders of purity that seek to preserve goodness for oneself as a possession by breaking open the enclaves to a vision of others outside its walls. As such, testimony sends the community into a wilderness pilgrimage away from the logic of purity and goodness that it claims for its safety. Testimony does not pull those outside the boundaries of purity inside but rather destroys the border walls themselves as it empowers from the outside.

PART II: TESTIMONY AND TRAFFICKING

The individual and communal aspects of testimony help complete a shift gestured to in this work, namely the place of privilege from which Christian sexual ethics thinks. As stated in chapter 1, the place of privilege is a largely Kantian subject free to choose disinterestedly from myriad choices. This place is primarily a fiction to trafficking survivors while they were in their trafficked situation and even for those subjected to harsh purity codes. Testimony moves the moral center of Christian ethics from the image that holds it captive. Testimony successfully empowers the marginalized individual's voices by bringing them into the center of deliberation. In testimony, the survivor speaks of their trauma and experiences. Whether the individual is Christian or not, these testimonies give a voice to those made invisible by the systems of ethics that do not consider their fate. Ethics cannot remain in the tenor of purity that drives out those who no longer bear its image through toxic violence. The testimony pierces through the veil of this system of goodness to lay its depravity bare.

Furthermore, testimony sets a new course for the survivor of both purity codes and trafficking by showing the new actions and judgments made possible by God's reconciling work. Though many are not Christian in this study, it matters to hear testimonies of all kinds from these places that lack privilege as a means to reorient moral thinking about sexuality. The community and the one who testifies share space through solidarity within one another so that the disempowered become empowered and the privileged surrender their privilege.

To fulfill this shift in privilege, I offer features of testimony that impact the one who testifies and that impact the broader community. The testimony shapes the individual to empower and enables a new place of thinking that must correspond to a new certitude and reality. Ethics, thus,

61. Florence, *Preaching as Testimony*, xv.

is no longer centering code purity into its matrix but empowerment and liturgical enmeshment in the multitude. In the web of trafficking, we find many factors that contribute to the perpetuation of trafficking. Combatting the web requires visualizing the systems and structures that harm and dehumanize. Testimony enables the visualization of the web even as it attests to God's indicative presence, which includes a new activity not enclosed in the former web. Thus, I argue that the community must practice testimony as a liturgical element of its life to center these stories alongside God's story.

Empowerment

When God meets in command, the response in action is a unique testimony as it confronts each individual and empowers them. As Adkins pointed out, the issue in much of anti-trafficking work is the definition of who is and is not an agent. Testimony removes that hierarchy to empower the agency in those positioned as less. This aspect of testimony is nuanced because it involves liberation and vulnerability. Cheryl Sanders helps illustrate the empowering capability of testimony through an examination of slave narratives. In the United States domestic context, the slave narrative was a scandal to the narrative of white supremacy at the heart of slave holding. The narratives written by Fredrick Douglass, Harriet Jacobs, and many others challenged certain narratives of social exclusion based on racial purity at the heart of systemic racism. Slavery was very disempowering, so the autobiographies served to empower the disempowered.

In these slave autobiographies, Sanders argues that the presence of testimony as an early religious experience of enslaved people led to their dismantling of the yoke of racial systems that held them in place. The testimonies first attest to a person's conversion, which, as Sanders identifies, means a "turning away from sin and wrongfulness and turning toward God and righteousness."[62] In this case, it is not only the sinful patterns of one's life but the ability to turn from the sins placed upon oneself. This shift is significant because many white enslavers used Christianity to domesticate their slaves. However, the liberating message of the gospel untethered from white supremacy encouraged enslaved people to see themselves not as less but as more in God's eyes.[63]

The "testimonies" of the enslaved people resisted the stereotypes usually reserved for them. Instead, the encounter with the living God, the one who burns and shines with light everlasting, enabled enslaved people

62. Sanders, *Empowerment Ethics*, 11.
63. Sanders, *Empowerment Ethics*, 13.

to see themselves sharing space with this God. Sanders continues that few enslaved people "acquiesce[d] in the notion that God willed their bondage and subservience to whites. Instead, the enslaved people embraced the dynamic gospel of freedom that was preached, taught, and practiced in the quarters."[64] In short, their conversion and the testimony of enslaved people led fellow enslaved people to navigate their enslavement. Testimony led some to wait passively and others to rise and fight, but their faith and testimony led them to choose their course of action.

In the same way, survivors of trafficking testify to their liberation and movement against the social exclusion models. In a culture that will only finally recognize survivors as unclean, fallen women, the testimony of survivors speaks to the same kind of turning from sinful exclusion. The survivor does not need the community to make room because that ideal only reinscribes social exclusion and hierarchy in a new way. Instead, the testimony reflects a radical inclusion in the life of God. This inclusion is not a making room but rather a grafting in through conversion. The fire of the great fugue burns away the space in the Christian community that sees according to the logic of social conversion. The fire that burns away the exclusion also vivifies and enlivens. It empowers those disempowered by the web of violence, addiction, and oppression that holds survivors excluded.

Love Feast: The Liturgy of Testimony

Testimonies are not merely for oneself, though they do empower the individual. Testimonies are also public records and public accounts, as in Brueggemann's courtroom analogy. The testimonies offered through the study must guide the community to a new ethical posture. So even though testimony serves an individual need, namely empowerment of capacities toward moral life. This is how Barth describes ethics, which leaves little room for collaboration. However, it is not just the individual nourished by the testimony, nor is the individual the only one shaped by it. Testimony, especially in the US domestic church, serves a liturgical function in many places of worship.

One such example of testimony's liturgical function arises from the early days of the US domestic Christian denomination, the Church of the Nazarene. In its early days, congregants in the First Nazarene Church in Los Angeles, California, celebrated a service known as a love feast. Readers familiar with the Wesleyan heritage will recognize the place of love feast in Christian worship. Nazarene love feasts were services that contained many

---

64. Sanders, *Empowerment Ethics*, 13.

typical aspects of a standard Sunday worship service but also included, according to Dirk Ellis, "as many testimonies as time permitted."[65] The leader of the Nazarene movement, Phineas F. Breese, valued the love feast, which began as a Christmas celebration but morphed into a bimonthly service of celebration and thanksgiving. These events primarily aimed to declare through testimony the goodness and triumph of God's love to encourage the conversion and sanctification of the attendees. The service became a staple of the movement's communal life and remained so throughout Breese's life. The service appeared in local gatherings, camp meetings, and revival services as the Nazarene Church spread increasingly eastward.

The importance of the service was the change ignited in the lives of those who listened and testified.[66] The testimony not merely of the subjective element, but also the work of God, manifests in a way to shape others to seek God in the encounter. In other words, the testimonies liturgically celebrate the commands of God that lead humanity to salvation. The question of the communal role of testimony is not a subjection of the individual to the communal. Quite the contrary, upon receiving the testimony, the community recognizes its need for change and formation. The testimony serves as a destabilizing witness that reorients the community away from sin to God's command. As such, the testimony does not organize the community around the individual but around the revealing God witnessed in testimony that nonetheless changes the community's priorities and the borders that formerly stood in place.

Testimony: Grace, Iconoclasm, and Covenant

Both Sanders and the Church of the Nazarene illustrate well the role of testimony in empowerment and shaping a community toward proper ends. Testimony contextualizes the work of God in the community to empower the one testifying and also help the community see the good work of God in the community here and now. An aspect of the study performed for this present work included a space for this kind of contextualizing witnessing to empower these women's voices as the means to locate the indicative of reconciliation for theological ethics of sex. Without this testimony, one only aims in the dark at what kind of ethics might confront the purity fixation and code fetishism that dominates much of sexual ethics. The purpose, liturgically, of hearing these testimonies forms the community to receive not only the one bearing the testimony, but also the account of the moral life

---

65. Ellis, *Holy Fire Fell*, 189.
66. *Nazarene Messenger*, "Sabbath July 6th," 7, quoted in Ellis, *Holy Fire Fell*, 189–90.

they offer. As Barth attests, ethics is a type of witness to the indicative of God. These testimonies name the indicatives that open a pathway beyond the immanent experiences previously known to them. I highlight three areas of testimony that offer new images of the moral life that replace concepts such as code, purity, and even social capital. These three images are not new codes, but rather indicatives and images that shape a moral imagination to cultivate the possibility for a free response in codes.

Grace

I first turn to a theology of grace that motivates sexual desire inside of God's desire for humanity. I begin with the stories of hope that led me to this theological concept and how it manifests solidarity from reconciliation. Two survivors, Tracy and Darla, described moments in their childhood when they could escape the abuse experienced at home by sneaking away to a local church. These women came from different areas and sneaked away to different churches, but each place shared a similar feature: a kindness that these young girls did not find at home. Tracy describes that she would quietly get ready on Sunday mornings, walk down to the corner of her street, and wait for the church bus to pick up the children in her neighborhood. She notes the disparity between home and church by simply stating it was her one escape and that she always liked being there. Similarly, Darla, who also snuck away to church many cold Sunday mornings, speaks more explicitly about the kindness she found at church. The church was Darla's "safe place" because the pastor and congregation "just embraced me. Yeah, just like, love on me when I would go to the church and always take us to like camp to get us out." Darla describes a kindness that translated into material safety for her. In the cases of Tracy and Darla, the church served as a place where their dignity was recognized and affirmed. Though neither girl ever shared their abuse with the church as children, as many do not at this age, they found a place that met them and loved them where they were.

The kindness described by Darla and Tracy is grace that arises from a specific kind of theological grammar for an unmerited favor from God to humanity. Rowan Williams describes grace best when he writes, "Grace for the Christian believer is a transformation that depends in large part on knowing yourself to be seen in a certain way: as significant, as wanted."[67] The kindness shown to Darla and Tracy manifests a recognition of something sacred in each one, that they are not merely objects of abuse but rather worthy of love. At these churches, the young girls learned a new rhythm that

---

67. Williams, "Body's Grace," 59.

would stick with them for a lifetime, a rhythm of grace. It is the rhythm and pattern of a God who travels to a far country and wanders about in the dust of a people that first starts the drum beat of a loving kindness to us that must extend to others. The people reconciled to this God learn to see with different eyes not according to a code or social capital, but to the Judge judged in our place. This God, when incarnate, goes to the place of the criminal, not the most socially or religiously pure, as the site of divine reconciliation to defame a system predicated on social exclusion. In this space, God speaks to the outcast today: you will be with me in paradise (Luke 23:43). The most excluded will find the most inclusion. In short, it is reconciliation through defamation and judgment of our exclusionary habits.

The rhythm of grace extends beyond childhood. As Darla recounts, the pastor who showed her kindness as a child was also the leader of her celebrate recovery group after she exited the matrix of trafficking, addiction, and imprisonment. The rhythm of grace is steady and enduring in the face of the ungraciousness of the world and gives to those who have not received or earned. Bobo, another participant, speaks of this kind of grace from a different ministry that provided transitional housing for those leaving rehab and prison. She described the grace she received through a phone call from this ministry director. In order to be eligible for housing one must complete a certain number of check-ins. Bobo was not able to meet the expectations due to her accelerated release and could not find housing due to the CO-VID-19 pandemic. The program director called and Bobo assumed that she would deliver bad news. However, the director invited her to come stay in their housing program, only asking: "Is this where you want to come?" Bobo responded "yes," and the program director merely responded, "Okay . . . then I'll be there [to pick you up from prison]." Bobo, who at the time of her interview was in the middle of her longest stretch of sobriety, is a product of the grace shown to her by this program. One cannot overstate the importance of grace in understanding this new community. Grace is an unmerited favor. In every participant, merit and achievement were the means to access community. Grace begets mutuality and mutuality leads to healing without expulsion based on missteps baring the way to healing. Bobo found in this new community an acceptance not predicated on achievement or merit, but unconditioned. The lifesaving communities found by all participants must mirror this approach. When asked what the difference this director and organization provided, she powerfully states that it showed "love of Jesus like, completely 100 percent . . . It didn't matter anything that I've done wrong in my life . . . it didn't matter. That wasn't who I was. I could [experience freedom and I learned] that I matter, that I was enough, [and I was given the opportunity] to really like ground those [ideas] in . . . for the first time in my life." The love of Jesus who dances into creation and within the triune life expresses grace to all humanity and reconciles humanity to the triune life. Participating in the ministry of reconciliation requires grace and so our sexual lives must follow suit. Reconciliation in this way cannot mean assimilation because it empowers every person to speak and live in God's gracious care. As such, there is a responsibility to pass on that which was given to each person (1 Cor 11:22–23), namely, to be gracious and kind.

To be clear, Bobo, Darla, and Tracy do not merely receive grace, but freely give it. As articulated at the end of chapter 2, solidarity without mutuality robs people of their dignity. Rescue work, which dominates the popular imagination, does not honor the complex dignity of the individuals it seeks to "save" because it robs them of their ability to be other than victims. Alternatively, the approach that heals is one that encourages mutuality, which also clearly represents grace. God's grace sheds the love of God abroad in our hearts, which enables humans to know that they are loved and wanted by God. Furthermore, grace inspires humanity to love God and grow in grace through love for nonhuman creatures, self, and their neighbors. Grace encourages this profound affirmation of the relational *imago Dei* in each human. As Williams continues, the entire drama of grace is that "God desires us, *as if we were God*, as if we were that unconditional response to God's giving that God's self makes in the life of the Trinity."[68] Grace is that divine initiative within which humans respond to God in love that affirms and enkindles love for God, self, and others. A gracious desire is one in which the agent knows they are wanted and desired in a way comparable to God's love, which is holy love. It is not objectifying or violent but seeks the gracious affirmation of the other. Furthermore, this grace also elicits a response, namely the loving, gracious desire of the other in return. Much like responsible grace to God's love, gracious longing enkindles this loving affection for self and others, eliciting a loving response for self and others. Relationally it must affirm the other, not destroy or objectify. This gracious response means that one's desire for another must treat the other as an "occasion of joy."[69] Stacy, the final survivor of trafficking interviewed in this study reveals how grace that elicits love and healing in her turns to heal others. Stacy reflects one how she felt during her addiction and years of trafficking and the change she now knows.

> I wouldn't have no self-worth. I would feel less than less and lower than lower. And I just love being who I am today. Yeah, love it. You know, because anybody can call and say "hey, can I

---

68. Williams, "Body's Grace," 59.
69. Williams, "Body's Grace," 59.

borrow such and such?" If I have it [I say,] "Yes. Sure you can." You know? I like helping people. I don't like it. I love it. It's [the] best feeling ever. You know, I'm not taking from somebody but I'm giving to somebody. And that's totally a different area for me. Being flipped on its head the way things used to be.

Grace is not only received but transforms dispositions into graciousness toward oneself and others. Grace cannot be possessed but moves to every place. In short, upon being reconciled by the Judge judged in our place, humans now participate in the ministry of reconciliation (2 Cor 5:18–20).

The language of grace utilized in these women's stories should inform sexual ethics. Sexual desire, in the order of grace, orders desire according to shared solidarity with the neighbor in their goodness. This grammar of grace illustrates that privileged relationships are not the places to begin in sexual ethics. Gracious sex is not first about the *kinds* of relationships often cited as the consummate end of sexual ethics. Furthermore, neither is sex primarily about sex acts or pleasure alone. As Rowan Williams argues, "sexual union is not delivered from moral danger and ambiguity by satisfying a formal socioreligious criterion. Decisions about sexual lifestyle, to repeat, are about how much we want our bodily selves to mean, rather than what emotional needs we're meeting or what laws we're satisfying."[70] Gracious sex is about the bodily meaning that God intends for humanity expressed in reconciliation. Sex is a longing that finds fulfillment in seeking the neighbor not as a sexual object but as one created *imago Dei*. It does not deny that we have sexual attractions and drives, nor does it condemn them. To believe in the reconciling work of God means that our full humanity and desires all find restoration in the relational solidarity that God intends. Gracious sex recognizes that our sexual desires can only be an affirmation of an already present goodness in the other person whom themselves are deeply loved by God. Therefore, one can learn about sexual desire from the relationally committed and the celibate because both affirm and embody the truth that sex acts do not earn an individual their created goodness. Gracious sex is not predicated on evil tempers that establish hierarchies of violence that destroy the body but grows from holy tempers that desire to affirm the creature's place in the economy of God's love.

In sum, grace is a core concept of healing for survivors—a grace that not only heals the person but encourages mutuality must emerge as a crucial theological posture in sexual ethics. Grace thus embraces community with a whole host of people seeking mutuality, relationship, and healing. One's goodness is not predicated on code, but on a graciousness already given

---

70. Williams, "Body's Grace," 64.

in their humanity. Through the lens of grace, sexual ethics can clearly see issues of moral injury and moral luck that prevent code ethics from viewing the complexity of sexuality. Only this way can we be free of our idols and participate in God's gracious call to saving solidarity.

Iconoclasm

Grace is the first theme and a necessary posture to receive the gift of saving solidarity, but the grace that emerges from reconciliation carries with it the indicative power of iconoclasm. As such, iconoclasm emerges as an important second feature of sexual ethics. The idols of social and sexual capital that dictates a hierarchy of appropriate and inappropriate bodies to divide between Mary and Eve must be defamed. New pathways emerge from this defamation, rerouting our understanding of goodness from purity codes and to the crucified, defamed body of Christ. Defaming systems of goodness will lead humanity to a place of solidarity against totalizing structures while also liberating humanity from idols of selfhood grounded in death-dealing structures.

Iconoclasm emerges as a theme in the study of participants in trafficking and purity culture who experience a lack of worth when compared to other, more pure images of sexual subjects. In survivors of trafficking, the women expressed that the sexual activity in their trafficking experiences left them feeling disgusted. As Stacy shared, "I felt like a piece of crap [after sex]." This feeling, when internalized, becomes moral injury, and accepts ill treatment as a necessary consequence of their "evil" state. This theme of disgust also emerges in our study of purity culture. Twyla, a participant in the purity culture side of the study, states quite clearly that sex or sexual thoughts risked impurity and being "dirty for the rest of my life." The policing and shame of those in the Christian community who fail the purity paradigm is debilitating. To recall Terry, this impurity and dirtiness extends even to those who experience sexual abuse and assault. The only challenge to this image came through new communities who formed new images in the subject. Thus, the language of purity codes underwent iconoclasm.

Carnes argues that iconoclasm defames certain structures of meaning; such theological work opens a possibility for life previously held captive by a restrictive literalized images. The image of Mary, Eve, and purity all cultivate what we termed a social exclusion model of sexual ethics. As such the very doctrine of reconciliation as presented by Barth performs an iconoclasm of fidelity. As God reconciles the world to Godself through the incarnation, crucifixion, and resurrection, separation from God is ended.

The Judge stands with the excluded and impure on the cross and takes this separation to the grave and defeats through a new intimacy enacted in the resurrection. One must see how even God's judgement on sin, as envisioned by Barth, transforms isolation into hope. When appearing before God, one arrives not before a harsh judge but one who comes in cradle and crucifixion to draw close to humanity. The judgment executed in the last days will be one that draws close rather than separates. The destruction is the image of oneself as separate and unloved. No image of God or humanity can serve as a metric that includes some while excluding others.

Covenant

The hunger for belonging arises from human relationality and thus the multitude. In the multitude one must account for different language structures and experiences. The multitude as a community of difference draws humans ever deeper into the love of God through exercising desire. The multitude relies on varying language structures that cultivate nuanced participation in the love of God. The difference does not threaten community but deepens its reach through the ability to express the love of God via this variety. Covenant, theologically, must exist in this openness to receive the multitude, or else covenant becomes a means of social exclusion. Thus, the covenant is an exercise in fidelity able to receive the neighbor.

Theologically the history of covenant and sexuality is a complicated one. In recent years, the covenant language supports the legal institutions of marriage and its troubled legacy, including racism, sexism, and violence. Covenant is not a legal agreement, but rather, as Hak Joon Lee writes, "God's organizing principle to de-organize an old community and re-create a new, just community."[71] As such, the human filial covenant cannot be separated from God's covenant to organize a just, whole community.

The theme of covenant is a predominant feature of those healing from sexual trauma both physical and spiritual. Focusing primarily on those under the influence of purity code realism, sex was a taboo difficult even for those who only grew up believing in the impurity of sex. Purity is, for these women, a type of sexual capital to exchange to their future husband. As Terry comments, "I already thought like my body belonged to my future husband." However, for quite a few women in this study, covenantal love served to rehabilitate one's sense of self and sex. The sexual capital model of sexual ethics turns sex acts into a means of control and manipulation. It is the responsibility of young women, in purity culture, to maintain purity

---

71. Lee, *Christian Ethics*, 53.

for a future husband. As Regina recalls the expectations placed on her as a young woman not to engage in sexuality in any form even to the detriment of knowing her own anatomy: "if you didn't follow all of these [rules] then you would have to . . . answer to your partner. And like, that almost made you worse of a partner. Because you were like impure, like your body had been used like a commodity . . . So that could like make or break a relationship if someone had found out that you had sex before becoming married." All sex, thus, was merely a means to be fit for or controlled by another.

Covenantal love is different. It is a love between partners that participates in and expects the other's flourishing. Terry offers a profound description of covenantal love:

> I was able to see that like intimacy, even if it's just like kissing or holding hands isn't about like control, or about assessing the value of another person . . . it's simply about loving that person. And when your value hangs on intimacy, and whether you've done it or not, it's a control factor . . . And so when I started to break that down, like seeing how much like he loved me, I loved him that it was like, we didn't love each other because we were physical. We were physical because we love each other, you know, and that grows and blossoms and continues to grow. And it's not always perfect, and sometimes it doesn't go right and it's fine. We love each other.

Covenant is, as Lee argues, a disruption to old ways of organizing relationships and opens them up to new transformations. The slow, patient love between Terry and her husband broke down the old way of sexual capital and enlivened a way of intimacy that grows and blossoms despite perceived imperfections. Terry also clarifies an important feature of covenant, namely mutuality. The commitment to Terry also includes a desire for mutual efficacy. Love did not grow out of the exchange of sexual capital for love, but love was a gift that cultivated the conditions for physical intimacy. The loving commitment comes first and physical intimacy second. This does not collapse covenant back into code and purity, thus losing Terry's insight. Rather, covenant is not a commodity to be exchanged, but a commitment to the needs, desires, and future of another.

The practice of covenant must be prudent not to become a code fetish. The only way to do this is to ground the covenant not in marriage but God's creative activity. Barth's theology of covenant emerges in the context of creation through his famous dictum: covenant is the internal basis of creation and creation the external basis of covenant.[72] Both creation and

---

72. Barth, *Church Dogmatics* III.1, 93–324.

covenant require one another and exist in the same space as an outpouring of the divine fire.[73] Covenant, thus, forms the telos of all of creation.[74] The ordering and de-organizing of creation according to God's love draws it to intimacy with God and reorganizes it around just relationships. These relationships are gracious and iconoclastic in the ways already described. However, the nature of covenant intimately connects to the sacred character of human relationships and seeks to honor the sacred life one finds there. The covenantal nature of sexuality is not merely a justification for marriage but deep resistance to social capital. Covenant is the liberation of human relationships from the metrics of sexual capital, and instead, is the consistent affirmation of human dignity in the face of exploitation. Covenantal sex participates in the telos of creation not through its participation in marriage but rather in its participation of the God who brings creation to life through the vivifying presence of the triune God.

Covenantal love between romantic partners was not the only means of covenantal love that led to healing. A community of covenant also aids the defamation of sexual capital through a commitment to a person in community, leading away from the capitalistic exchanges that one normally associates with sex. Rather, sex emerges not from an exchange that is either wanted or unwanted but a deep commitment to the flourishing of another. Darla, a survivor of trafficking, attests to just this point. She speaks of a pastor present to her as a child who spoke good things into her life as a child and even as an adult led her celebrate hope recovery group. This pastor, she states, illustrates a consistent presence of grace that mirrors covenant. As a lost child suffering abuse and even as a recovering addict, he loved her. In this way, love was a promise made by this pastor that was kept over time. This pastor illustrates the rhythm of grace necessary to show God's love to individuals of all kinds and backgrounds. Furthermore, through the changes and shifts in life, this love is consistent and cultivates mutuality. It illustrates that one can experience love exactly where they are and experience healthy relationships.

Darla, when confronted with the possibility of a sexual relationship, affirms that it is the love of a community of covenant that helps her think through a healthy sexual relationship. This is not a strict, purity culture realism, but a different realism that patterns sexual practices after the telos of her life. Darla believed due to her life on the street that her body meant "nothing." However, through the encouragement of her community and her potential spouse she learned that sex can be good. She admits that the sex she now has with her husband is not "everything," but it is "oneness" and "a

---

73. Barth, *Church Dogmatics III.1*, 95.
74. Barth, *Church Dogmatics III.1*, 96.

good thing now." Covenant begets intimacy because once one knows that their life and body matter not according to metrics of sexual capital but according to a love that blossoms and grows, so that sexuality finds its place as good.

If we commit to the idea that Christian sexual ethics is not first and foremost about sex acts or relationships but the meaning of bodily life, then the communication of grace to Darla does not require sex. To recall Terry, love does not require physical intimacy but places physical intimacy in line with other practices that promote long-term flourishing. To understand sex means understanding grace. In essence, it requires one who can see the value of a body without first possessing the desire or want to have sex with it. Only this can best communicate grace to a body. Covenant is not an anachronistic code applied here, but rather represents a deep desire of all participants. It is the kind of love that stays and is committed despite sexual performance. Some of our participants found this and others did not. However, it is a crucial testimony to the kind of love most valued by participants in this study. Sex, thus, is a response, in Christian sexual ethics, to the superabundance of God's love for humanity.

PART III: FROM TESTIMONY TO VIRTUE

The preceding analysis primarily serves to clear the stigmas of sexual ethics by refocusing moral imagination around the themes of testimony. The shift signaled here removes one's sexual history or capital as the literalized desire and exclusive measurement of one's moral worth in the community. The movement from indicative to testimony shifts ethical thought from a place of toxic goodness to testimony, leading to empowerment and community. The proceeding sexual ethics will, with the lessons learned, help agents and communities embody a different kind of moral life capable of mutuality and solidarity. It is not new in the sense of never existing but orients sexual ethics through a different matrix that does not perpetuate social exclusion. The shapes and textures of command lead to new pathways of embodiment.

If the command opens humanity to receive, it also shapes and forms a specific character capable of hearing. Command ethics moves the testimony-receiving community into the moral logic bound by receptive moral ontology. The command is God's interaction with the world, but humanity is not merely passive. In receiving the command, like in beauty, a new habitus emerges that can be exercised in character formation. Thus, as Barth and Edwards presuppose, virtue ethics is a necessary companion to command ethics. Douglas Campbell helpfully summarizes the connection between virtue ethics and command ethics to show how virtue and command go hand in hand. He writes that unless

> the rightness of certain actions hasn't entered our imaginative world yet, we won't be able to conceptualize what God is asking ... [Command] ethics, putting things more technically, requires an underlying *language* and *grammar* of ethics to be intelligible and function at all. [Commands] ultimately make sense only in terms of stories, and so only a deep grounding in the story of Jesus will open up any possibility of a mediation of the ways of Jesus as God communicates with us in later navigational situations.[75]

Virtue ethics and command ethics "interpenetrate and reinforce one another."[76] Virtue, therefore, is essential not only as a means to inhabit the character of divine speech but also informs how one hears the command. "The more virtue," as Campbell urges, "the more obedience (which is correlate to [commands]); and the more obedience, the more virtue."[77] Command, then, is not a single code universal but rather the invitation to the living shape of Christian ethics.

Virtue Ethics: Sexuality

The virtues necessary for a healthy sexual ethic find themselves through the practice of reception and receiving specific virtues. In this way, the shift in ethics is not to ask, "what is the good that I must do," but rather, "what *is* good?" Christian ethics must ask, with Bonhoeffer, "what is the will of God?"[78] A rule, when divorced from the will of God, attempts to stand on its own and becomes a code. Bonhoeffer identifies any attempt to single out a code that displays my own "being good" as an abstraction from the will of God. The question of ethics is not one of moral selfishness but a moral ontology. Again, the question is not how the agent becomes good but what *is* good. As such, the code must secure its efficacy against competing for goods as the source of ultimate reality. In short, codes urge there is only one way for humans to become good, which Bonhoeffer understands as the wrong question—shifting to the moral ontology of ethics forces an iconoclasm of fidelity in moral activity. If the indicative is reconciliation, then the activity must destroy and upbuild in that indicative reflex toward solidarity and

---

75. Campbell, *Pauline Dogmatics*, 552.
76. Campbell, *Pauline Dogmatics*, 552.
77. Campbell, *Pauline Dogmatics*, 552.
78. Bonhoeffer, *Ethics*, 47.

mutuality. As with testimony, it cannot prescribe activities in advance; else it collapses back into the coding. Testimony cultivates a love of the individual flourishing and communal belonging that God desires, but the cultivation of virtue helps humanity practice that flourishing and community now and listen to God's command.

Virtue ethics emerges from a contemplation, in the Aristotelian tradition, of the ends toward which our actions gesture. Virtue, in this tradition, is acquired human excellence achieved through habits and practices taken up throughout a lifetime. Many who argue for virtue ethics do so with this project in mind. However, the kind of virtue offered here, as in Barth and Edwards, defines itself as the emulation of the excellence found in God. Virtue then becomes a command through insisting on a specific kind of life for the believer. Though there are not two exclusive camps for virtue ethics, the two traditions just articulated construct virtue differently. In the latter category, the one offered by Barth and Edwards, one receives the actions and excellence of the moral life. The central conviction of both is an ethic that focuses on whom humans want to be rather than what they do alone. The purpose of reflecting on virtue does not collapse ethics back into unhealthy purity. Instead, it situates the desire to be a community within an alignment to that excellence. Ethics conditioned by a social responsibility in the life of God places a matrix of excellence before the individual within which they must act. Virtue, then, as the formation of command, will help translate the command of God into communal life.

Virtue is an important category to resist the principled approach of social exclusion. One does not begin with personal preference or an eternal set of truths that guide exegesis, ethics, and theology. Instead, one identifies the excellence required of one who inhabits their role. As philosopher Alasdair MacIntyre understands, this is the purpose of virtue ethics. He writes,

> To identify an occurrence as an action is in the paradigmatic instances to identify it under a type of description which enables us to see that occurrence as flowing intelligibly from a human agent's intentions, motives, passions, and purposes. It is therefore to understand an action as something for which someone is accountable, about which it is always appropriate to ask the agent for an intelligible account.[79]

Virtue thus provides the accountability necessary to understand one's actions. The virtue ethics tradition must constantly face the disruption *of* divine command and must be accountable *to* the command.

---

79. MacIntyre, *After Virtue*, 209.

Before turning to these ethics, I will first unpack the centrality of virtue to for sexual ethics to resist code and place disciple-agents in a better position to hear command. Sexual ethics is fraught with issues pertaining to its prescriptions. Allen Verhey and Stanley Hauerwas argue that a central issue related to sexual ethics is the tendency to overcorrect. Sexual ethics is at once too prescriptive and, in response, too permissive. Christianity certainly possesses overly negative prescriptions, but the point that Verhey and Hauerwas make is that correcting the negative aspects tends to miss how sexuality can be dangerous.[80] Sex is not innately dangerous, but as we have followed in this study, it can be violent and violating for some. To assume that sex begins from a place of safety for all perpetuates the privilege of the social exclusion model. Sexual ethics does not first postulate a correct technique or code of sexuality that must be fulfilled. Living sexually in this world can occur as "technical experts or as whole (and vulnerable) persons, as pleasure seekers or covenant makers and covenant keepers."[81] A virtue-centered approach to sexual ethics raises the question of the persons one wants to be so that any choices of sexual activity might align with humanity's chief good.

Practical reason must gravitate around the three testimonies of grace, iconoclasm, and covenant. These three construct a vector for sexual ethics. The prudential weighing in response to these testimonies motivates reason toward the right ends of humanity. The right ends do not merely arise from the very excellence of God, who commands as God acts. The three testimonies, as previously stated, materialize through the intimacy and solidarity-inducing work of reconciliation wherein God restores humanity to everlasting covenant with God, creation, and one another. Thus, the prudential weighing of human ends must occur inside the indicative of reconciliation, and these three testimonies shape toward those ends. Through this formation, a practical reason emerges, but the virtues, like Barth's account of the theological virtues, guide the disciple from the reality of reconciliation to concrete actions.

Traditionally, chastity is the central virtue for discussing sexuality and practical reason. However, recent studies illustrate that chastity alone does not serve a robust understanding of the type of character desired in sexuality. As Jean Porter rightly recognizes, chastity is a species of temperance, a cardinal virtue that aids the agent fulfill their proper ends, and temperance concerns proper moderation.[82] However, this is not merely about the refraining or repressing of desire. Rather, temperance urges that the agent

80. Hauerwas and Verhey, "From Conduct to Character," 13–14.
81. Hauerwas and Verhey, "From Conduct to Character," 15.
82. Porter, "Chastity as Virtue," 287.

"spontaneously desires that which is in accord with her genuine good, comprehensively understood, and does not desire what is inconsistent with that good."[83] Formed in response to the end of intimacy with God and neighbor, the disciple finds a desire formed that reflexively draws them more deeply into the indicative of God's reconciliation. Nevertheless, temperance through chastity enables the ability to will one's proper ends with clarity and insight.

The virtue of temperance is not just an individual agent's concern for their good but also the good of their neighbors. Sexuality is not a singular act; it always involves others who require our good work. Therefore, temperance and chastity cannot remain alone in the prudential weighing of action. As Porter argues, the agent must "also incorporate some reference to the claims of others and the demands of the community as a whole."[84] Sexual acts involve at least two parties directly, and several more indirectly as sexual acts involve a community of people. As Stanley Hauerwas states quite clearly, sexuality does implicitly offer an account of politics and the common good, namely how we think others should be treated and loved.[85] The shift to virtue helpfully locates that ethics is not only about whom the agent or disciple wants to be but the entire shape of the community. This means that the agent and the community must be mindful of the demands of other virtues, such as justice.

Thus, the reality found in grace, iconoclasm, and covenant relies on a constellation of virtues that helpfully ground these three testimonies in specific kinds of activity. The testimonies present the moral compulsion for action, but those actions are not codes. Instead, they are commands from God to do good to all people (Galatians 6:10). These commands through testimony lack the code-like structure that cultivates idolatry of a particular form of life and specific actions. The commands form and shape in virtue so that specific actions proceed from the commands but are open enough to encapsulate a variety of witnesses and testimonies, as Barth allows, while still creating recognizable patterns of behavior under similar recognizable patterns of virtue. The constellation of indicatively shaped virtue allows for a developed practical reason that enables the disciple-agent to weigh clashing goods prudently. As James Keenan argues, one "cannot propose heuristic guides that prefabricate solutions with the material data is still forthcoming. We need virtues that go beyond protecting the single good of [any one virtue or indicative] and that allow us to interpret in each instance which of the

---

83. Porter, "Chastity as Virtue," 287.
84. Porter, "Chastity as Virtue," 291.
85. See Hauerwas, *Community of Character*, 176–79.

primary virtues ought to be in play."[86] These virtues should ensure the right relationships and the proper realization of human flourishing in God.[87] These virtues must empower the agent to act while also cultivating regard for others. To this end, I propose four virtues (justice, love, truthfulness, and humility) that enable an appropriate constellation for the recognition and enactment of these new testimonies. In each virtue, the practical reason necessary to judge actions appropriate to the virtue will occur in conversation with the testimonies of grace, iconoclasm, and covenant. The virtues will also consider complementary virtues that *thicken* virtue to consider the movement to those who lack privilege and prevent social exclusion while also naming goodness capable of drawing in those outside the boundaries of sexual ethics, redrawing them around the reception of Christ's excellence. As in the significant shift to receptive moral ontology, virtue must cultivate a posture to receive empowering ends in God and the neighbor's good.

Justice (with Mercy)

I begin with justice to honor its centrality in speaking to conditions of human trafficking. By placing justice at the beginning of sexual virtue, we force sexual ethics to recognize that love and chastity do not prefigure morally appropriate sexual activity alone. As Margaret Farley writes, "love is the problem in ethics, not the solution . . . we know that not all of our loves are good, though they are loves. There are wise loves and foolish, good loves and bad, true loves and mistaken loves."[88] The role of justice in sexual ethics must helpfully question the love worthy of pursuit and the absolute excellence in the God that meets humanity.

The formal definition of justice that occupies a central place in theology and philosophy is to render what is due to another. This formal definition is the basis of all kinds of justice (e.g., retributive, distributive). However, the formal nature of this definition betrays a weakness in the concept of justice, namely that the nature of "what is due" lacks concrete specification. As Margaret Farley writes, "there can be—in the name of justice—systems in which slavery is endorsed, certain groups of persons are marginalized, and women and men are 'legitimately' treated unequally."[89] The social exclusion model champions such forms of justice, which emerge when ethics is

---

86. Keenan, "Virtue Ethics and Sexual Ethics," 126.
87. Keenan, "Virtue Ethics and Sexual Ethics," 126.
88. Farley, *Just Love*, 196–97.
89. Farley, *Just Love*, 208.

a code according to which ethics only proceeds from one form of life over and against others.

To be clear, "justice" is on display in the life of Jesus. When Jesus announced the inauguration of the kingdom, he did so under the proclamation of the Year of the Lord's Favor depicted in Isaiah (Luke 4:18–19). The Jubilee proclaimed the release of the captives and recovery of sight to the blind. As André Trocmé persuasively argues, the "power of salvation is such that it brings with it acts of liberation."[90] Trocmé sees liberation operating in two ways. The primary way is the liberation of those from unjust systems, which attends to Jesus' original message of salvation that ties spiritual realities to material ones. Trocmé continues,

> compassion for the poor precedes the acquisition of treasure in heaven. What matters primarily to God is the lot of the poor. It is for them that the rich young ruler must sell his possessions; doing so *is* the treasure. To practice compassion is to reestablish the poor in the condition God willed for everyone. God will, one day, entirely reestablish the poor, with or without the help of the rich.[91]

God desires the restoration of the despoiled and this is an end privileged among other ends. The other side of this salvation is also the salvation of the wealthy from their possessions. Salvation is liberation and justice by judging systems as sinful and freeing humanity from their captivity. The security and meaning that the rich find in their possessions must be found in God, relieving the material conditions that beget poverty. This liberation extends to various aspects of the Christian life, but it is most evident here. Thus, liberation is a crucial piece of Christ's call to justice and a chief means of recognizing the presence of justice.

The renewal of justice in the Christian tradition is a needed return today. God liberates and reconciles humanity for the creation of just community. In the later twentieth and early twenty-first centuries, American evangelicalism suffered and continues to suffer a great suspicion of the term *justice*, though this attitude stemmed from earlier issues in the movement. David Gushee helpfully recognizes that much of this confusion arises from the misunderstanding and translation of the Greek word *dikaiosune* in the Christian Scripture as a spiritual form of piety rather than through its material connection to the Hebrew account of justice.[92] This impact is devastating as it leaves Christianity lacking virtue. The result is the injection of other

---

90. Trocmé, *Jesus and the Nonviolent Revolution*, 39.
91. Trocmé, *Jesus and the Nonviolent Revolution*, 39.
92. Gushee, *Introducing Christian Ethics*, 124–25.

norms into the Scriptures themselves.[93] If any group needed an iconoclasm of its idols, it is Christianity. One can see this in the social exclusion model by taking specific standards of humanity and privileges alien to Scripture's just, liberating message.

The shape of justice must rely on another virtue, namely mercy. James Keenan clarifies the critical role that mercy plays in executing justice. He writes that mercy "does not temper justice as so many believe; rather, mercy prompts us to see that justice applies to all, especially those most frequently without justice, those abandoned to the chaos of the margins."[94] Thus, mercy organizes thinking about deploying justice to particular people in particular places. As St. Thomas Aquinas argues, mercy is a virtue in the intellectual appetite's dissatisfaction with evil and its presence among our neighbors.[95] In this way, Thomas argues that mercy takes precedence over other virtues "for it belongs to mercy to be bountiful to others, and, what is more, to succor others in their wants, which pertains chiefly to one who stands above."[96] In this way, mercy pertains most specifically to how God shows mercy to God's creatures. Since it indicates the rational appetite's ability to find evil unappealing, it can simultaneously recognize the various ways of implication while offering grace to the one most impacted by evil. The invitation to mercy is a material means to resist toxic goodness by participating in the God who becomes flesh.

Love (Fidelity)

Though justice is an all too important virtue for sexual ethics to correct and embrace love, love also remains a central virtue on its own. In a moral ontology of reception, love is the ability to receive well. Love is not alone a feeling, but an activity. This is not a rejection of romantic love but contextualizing it within the more extensive actions that flow intelligibly from the virtue. "Love," as Farley writes, "is spontaneously receptive but not a passive reaction; it is active in response constituted in the union, shaped by perceptions and understandings, and engaging of myself in affirmation of what I love."[97] Love as a romantic idealism alone can neglect the formative aspect of its

---

93. See Gushee's discussion of white American evangelicalism in Gushee, *Introducing Christian Ethics*, 125.

94. Keenan, "Virtue Ethics and Sexual Ethics," 128.

95. Thomas Aquinas, *Summa Theologica*, Pts. II-II, Q 30, Art. 3. Answer.

96. Thomas Aquinas, *Summa Theologica*, Pts. II-II, Q 30, Art. 4. Answer.

97. Farley, *Just Love*, 203.

purposes. Virtue must be central in sexual ethics to create the conditions whereby humans form into persons capable of sexual love.

Love is a central virtue for sexuality because it requires a shift in thinking from ourselves to something else. As Iris Murdoch writes, love "shifts the center of the world from ourselves to another place."[98] Love in this way is an occasion that inspires "'unselfing' wherein the lover learns to see, cherish, and respect what is not [themselves]."[99] Ethics thus requires love to shape the affections toward the Good and motivates subsequent appropriately good actions toward the neighbor. Murdoch insists the will cannot lead to a moral transformation; only love and attraction to beauty can positively transform. This clarification reveals the necessity of the Beautiful and the Good beyond being. Only when one is drawn beyond the literalized desires and fetishes for the other can one learn a new way to see the everyday realities that confront the individual.

The virtue of love creates a disposition to gracious response in sex. "Loving," as Farley writes, "involves placing one's *affective self-affirmation in affective affirmation of the beloved.*"[100] Here is best expressed the graciousness of love. Grace for the disciple-agent, as Rowan Williams stipulates, is the knowledge that one is desired and wanted. Sexual activity is only good insofar as it coordinates to the testimonies. Humans express a desire for others as a central element of sexual ethics, namely that within and without sex, another is desired in the way one longs to be. As Farley understands, desire is both for oneself and another. Any healthy sexual ethic will involve the interplay of appropriate self-love and other regard.[101] However, desire cannot be literalized to objectification. We do not desire merely to fulfill pleasure. Though pleasure can and should be sought in sex for its own sake, it cannot be pursued at the expense of the beloved. Instead, grace is the affirmation of the dignity and needs of the beloved and the neighbor for *their* own sake. Each is beloved, and each is precious and sacred. This grace extends beyond potential sexual partners to all people to find the worth of another separate from their ability to provide pleasure or satisfaction for the individual.

It is within this gracious aspect of love that pleasure must be understood. It is personally good because it is a bodily pleasure that itself is good. Christians since Augustine have misguidedly associated pleasure with evil, but it is an aspect of bodily life that is good. As Karen Peterson-Iyer writes, "sexual pleasure is not unlike a cool drink on a warm day or a hot soak for

---

98. Murdoch, *Sovereignty of the Good*, 17.
99. Murdoch, *Sovereignty of the Good*, 17.
100. Farley, *Just Love*, 201. Emphasis original.
101. Farley, *Just Love*, 205–6.

aching muscles."[102] Though it is not the only good to be sought, it can, without careful guidance by virtue, lead to an overly developed individualism that leads to objectification and abuse. It is proper for its own sake but also understood as a part of the virtuous life.[103] The pleasure that occurs through sexual activity can communicate a more profound desire and good, namely the ability to communicate their good and the love and good of another.[104] Pleasure, as a means of love through the communication of desire, can aid in deepening love and trust between individuals and communities.

Like justice, the communal commitment of love requires an appreciation of fidelity as a crucial aid in love. Justice is the impartiality of action for one another, and love also knows impartiality as it forms itself according to neighbor love. Traditionally the distinction between preferential love and non-preferential love troubles Christian theology. For example, Søren Kierkegaard argues that Christians must eliminate "the distinction of preferential love so that you can love the neighbor."[105] However, when considered within the constellation of virtues, such as justice, love requires an expression that can hold non-preferential and preferential love in tension. Though Kierkegaard broadens love beyond mere preferential love, these relationships do exist. One must form preferential relationships so that they do not eliminate the possibility of non-preferential relationships. The need for honest preferential relationships opens the possibility to love without social capital, privilege, competition, and exclusion. As Keenan argues, fidelity "is the virtue that nurtures and sustains the bonds of those special relationships that humans enjoy whether by blood, marriage, love, citizenship, or sacrament. If justice rests on impartiality and universality, then fidelity rests on partiality and particularity."[106] The problem that partiality raises is the sheer number of commitments required of us. If our neighbor, as Kierkegaard argues, places a demand on us through the command to neighbor love and, as Keenan argues, humans must negotiate claims of partiality, then a large number of demands already exist. Fidelity helps humanity negotiate this field of commitments by knowing when to leave or stay in our commitments, relationships, and actions.[107]

I argue that the practical reason for discerning commitments to non-preferential relationships can arise from virtuous preferential love. As Kate

102. Peterson-Iyer, *Reenvisioning Sexual Ethics*, 37.
103. Peterson-Iyer, *Reenvisioning Sexual Ethics*, 36.
104. Peterson-Iyer, *Reenvisioning Sexual Ethics*, 37.
105. Kierkegaard, *Works of Love*, 61.
106. Keenan, "Virtue Ethics and Sexual Ethics," 127.
107. See Ward, *Wealth Virtue, and Moral Luck*, 63–66.

Ward argues, "in fidelity, we are emotionally present in doing our acts out of love."[108] Fidelity, then, is the ability to see the concrete reality of a person as justice requires and receive the neighbor or beloved as they are.[109] As a person formed in fidelity, one can visualize the commitments in one's life, weigh them, and act prudentially in those relationships for their flourishing and the disciple-agent's flourishing. The relationship of fidelity enables the virtues of care and commitment capable of communicating the graciousness necessary to love others in general. In short, preferential love can cultivate the virtue of love and, thus, enable its excellence in non-preferential relationships as a reflex of that formation.

To this end, love also directs specific attention to the beloved. Farley writes, "if I love someone as my spouse when the other is espoused to someone else, it means I do not take account of the other's commitments, which are part of his or her concrete reality; I falsify the nature of the relationship between us."[110] Thus, we state that fidelity helps negotiate not only individuals but communities of people. Fidelity helps us recognize the embedded systems of interconnected relationships of all humanity. To love is to make correct judgments about this system and to see each person within their concrete reality, which includes these broader systems. Love, thus, is a covenant to oneself and one's neighbors. Love as covenant participates in the covenant as the internal basis of all creation. If covenant forms justice to liberate, the covenant forms love in mutuality for the creation of new relationships and alternative communities of love.[111] Thus, covenant serves as a commitment to the well-being of others and is love in a true form. As fidelity shows, one must be present in acts of love and commit to the flourishing of others. Without this covenant to and mutuality with another, there is no love.

Truthfulness

Most Christian sexual ethics relies crucially on the justice-love dialectic. However, in this dialectic, the claims of justice and love can compete with one another; thus, the justice-love dialectic requires other virtues to help negotiate the claims of each. We have already explored the tension between

108. Ward, *Wealth Virtue, and Moral Luck*, 64.
109. Ward, *Wealth Virtue, and Moral Luck*, 64.
110. Farley, *Just Love*, 201.
111. This model of covenant arises from the recent work of Hak Joon Lee. He sees covenant as a dialectic movement from liberation, relationship, and new, alternative communities. See Lee, *Christian Ethics*, 53.

partial and non-partial love, but the problem becomes further complexified when justice and love do not envision similar actions. For example, what does one do when a person's love conflicts with the justice owed to a person wronged by the beloved? To this end, I argue for two virtues to help negotiate these competing claims.

The first virtue is truthfulness. In a world of fake news and conspiracy theories that spread through viral social media posts, truth no longer possesses meaning. However, truth and the corresponding virtue of truthfulness must reemerge as a central practice of the faith community. As David Gushee argues, most engagements with truth or truthfulness revolve around the acceptability of lying.[112] However, truth is more than a technical morality about fulfilling specific codes. That the gospel speaks of the followers of Jesus as bearers of truth recognizes that it is a necessary feature of the Christian community. Citing Ephesians 4:25–32, Gushee recognizes the role that truth-telling plays in the formation of community. The absence of truth leads to the destruction of community while the presence of truth and truth-telling creates a community where each is "members of one another" (Eph 4:25, NRSV). Truth enables the ability to make and keep promises that serve as the basis of any covenant. Truthfulness "is that part of the covenant that binds members of the church with Christ and one another in a shared commitment to nurture truthful character and to tell the truth to one another."[113] In other words, the ability to speak the truth and also be *recognized* as a truthful person is the basis of trust. If the disciple-agent or even the community of Christians will ever be trusted, then it must be able to speak the truth and keep it. In everything from the ability to make a covenant with an intimate partner to the community's proclamation of "good news," the ability to tell the truth remains a central feature of its ability to be trusted.

Since the basis of truth-telling and certainty in Christian speech arises from testimony, the central aspect of truth is its iconoclastic function. Testimony serves as a means to cut through the deceit and lies of sin to hear and speak the truth about oneself and receive others into the community. However, truth as testimony can also disrupt idolatry. Recall that the lack of a grammar of justice inhibits the community's public life and, thus, causes them to interpret Christian public life in light of other interests. The result, in many cases, is that Christian speech becomes tempered by interests alien to the truthfulness of the gospel to maintain power or its position. Thus, truth only serves the end of maintaining position and only appears

---

112. Gushee, *Introducing Christian Ethics*, 94.
113. Gushee, *Introducing Christian Ethics*, 99.

as technology in service of power. Iconoclasm can name this apparatus of power in its fullness to reorient "informational processes, systems, and contents" to the covenantal nature of truth-telling in the internal make-up of the community and the external. It should be "expected" that the testimony of the community is truthful.[114] In other words, the moral unction, to tell the truth, should exist even when it condemns the disciple-agent.

Humility (with Sacredness)

The second virtue that helps negotiate justice and love is humility. Notably, humility is a deeply misunderstood virtue and one that needs recovery. Humility is deeply iconoclastic in its connection to the cross. The destruction of the moral order through indicative not only initiates new practices (i.e., taking down the crucified from their crosses) but also cultivates particular virtues inherent in the new creation. The virtues only emerge in the aftermath of the category-breaking invasion of Christ into the cosmos that brings every practical reason to the ground. Since it is category-breaking, this indicative gives imperatives, not merely for concrete and specific actions fulfilled in commands, but also virtues to be developed. When understood correctly, humility forms the moral imagination around human beings, empowering and critical.

First, humility is a virtue of empowerment. Josef Pieper writes that humility "is [a human's] estimation of [themselves] according to truth."[115] Pieper's insistence on truth matters here because the truth is not an excuse for self-deprecation. Instead, in truth is first an emphasis on one's self-worth in the eyes of God. Pieper continues that a failure of humility, namely sin, turns from the truth of creaturely goodness toward some transient good.[116] In its correct understanding, humility is a mirror of God's humility. God comes to earth in lowly human nature to heal us from the sin of pride. However, this is not merely a call to abasement. Drawing from the work of Augustine, Kate Ward argues that humility understood through God's humility leads to redemption and "promotes, instead of detracting from, intrinsic human worth."[117] The activity of redemption and God's path to bring it about reveals the immense worth of humanity. It is, as theologian Kathryn Tanner describes, "non-idolatrous self-esteem."[118] The purpose of

---

114. Gushee, *Introducing Christian Ethics*, 103.

115. Pieper, *Four Cardinal Virtues*, 189.

116. Pieper, *Four Cardinal Virtues*, 191.

117. Ward, *Wealth, Virtue, and Moral Luck*, 66.

118. Kathryn Tanner, *Politics of God*, quoted in Ward, *Wealth, Virtue, and Moral Luck*, 68.

this humility is to see the truth in all situations of our relationship with God. Too often, this is exclusively self-abasement in the Christian tradition. Nevertheless, if humans must turn from pride to seeing themselves correctly, there is a coordinate turn from self-abasement. Transient things, such as social capital, can be a reason for abasement or, as Ward argues, "small-souledness."[119] Therefore, humility requires an essential companion virtue of magnanimity in which the individual sees their better qualities in themselves and others. Following Ward, Pieper, Augustine, and Tanner, those transient things must also be held in deep suspicion.

This turn from transient things helps aid an embodied critique of code fetishes. "Humility," as Ward argues, "helps us moderate our desires for 'high things' and form a truthful view of our own capacities."[120] Virtue, the formation of desires and loves, forms one's affections in particular ways. Humility trains the affections, not in a desire that thinks greater of humanity through the pursuit of purity, but also does not think less of its humanity or neighbors in a lack of purity. Ward writes, "humility requires that we realistically assess the qualities we have that are 'of God' and the qualities of our neighbor that are of God. In humility, we can acknowledge superior qualities of our neighbor when we find them."[121] One does not realistically look at humanity through their possession of capital but rather the ones of God. This realistic look always at the cross as a lens because each is a guest of the crucified. In humility, we see each value according to the great work of redemption as each human is the subject of God's redemption. Therefore, no transient thing, such as capital, can serve as a more significant metric to measure humanity than God's humble sharing of our humanity in the incarnation and cross. To turn from such a gracious welcome of humanity would be a sin.

The humble one's ability to recognize their worth is a welcoming grace, and this grace encounters each differently according to their measure. The proud should be humbled, but the lowly lifted up. Thus, an essential element of humility is an appropriate awareness of sacredness or human dignity. Sacredness, as indicated in Barth, is the affirmation that Christ shows us in creation, reconciliation, and redemption. In all cases, in humility, one is never debased but aware of the sacredness of human life. Sex aims at affirming human dignity and the sacredness of life. The importance of sacredness is that in the immorality central to human trafficking lies the attempt to destroy the sacred in another. Many women who experience trafficking express a history of domestic violence and assault. The importance of the

---

119. Ward, *Wealth, Virtue, and Moral Luck*, 67.
120. Ward, *Wealth, Virtue, and Moral Luck*, 67.
121. Ward, *Wealth, Virtue, and Moral Luck*, 67.

insistence on humility as human dignity and sacredness in sexual ethics is not for the sake of a false sense of purity wherein violating a purity code results in the making of a Horcrux that irrevocably damages the soul.[122] Instead, it merely states that the violence inherent in domestic violence, sexual assault, trafficking, and other forms of sexual violence attempts to squelch individuals' awareness of their human dignity and sacredness.

The "sacredness of life" language has become an empty, meaningless phrase in American political discourse due to the hypocritically narrow lens through which many US domestic conservatives use the term. However, the term *sacredness* need not be avoided or dismissed; instead, it remains a crucial aspect of ethics. David Gushee writes, "when believers ascribe sacredness to human life, we do so because we believe that we have received divine revelation that God has ascribed such sacred worth to life."[123] This sacred nature of humanity is not a possession but a gift given in their creation through a dynamic relationship with God. This gracious connection between humanity and the covenant between God and humanity to keep this connection makes creation generally and the creature specifically precious to God.

Humility is the virtue that grants access to this fundamental recognition of sacredness intimate to every person. The inhumane way that people treat one another makes recognition of sacredness difficult. The sacredness inside the people who experience trafficking often flickers against the overwhelming brutality of those who manipulate and violate their humanity. However, humility offers a morsel of good news: God desires that humans know themselves to be precious, dignified, and sacred beyond measure. In short, each must know that God loves them exactly as they are. This is the basis of human sexuality, namely that, as Peterson-Iyer writes, "each life is sacred, and the social order itself must function to support and benefit the well-being of each person as well as to invite the *full* participation of both persons and groups."[124] Dignity is the creation of mutuality as the equality of sacredness as a necessary feature of sexual encounters. In short, individuals come to sexual acts as equals in sacredness. Furthermore, this is the basis of full participation, and the dignity appertaining to it creates conditions of the whole, just sexuality. Peterson-Iyer continues, "mutuality and equal

---

122. A Horcrux is a magical device described in the final volume of the fictional Harry Potter book series. It is created through killing another person who causes a rip in the soul. This analogy attempts to exemplify the way that evangelicalism traditionally talks about sex before marriage. This theme emerged the study through Terry's interview.

123. Gushee, *Introducing Christian Ethics*, 108.

124. Peterson-Iyer, *Reenvisioning Sexual Ethics*, 24–25.

regard ask that we open ourselves to the genuine value and insights of the other as well as allow the other to impact our own deeper identities and sensibilities."[125] Humility, as access to the sacredness of our humanity, results in the space within which sexuality can become a means to uplift and encourage the best within each person. Sex must remain gracious because it nurtures that sacredness and does not extinguish it.

Without belaboring the point of the sexual virtues, it is worth noting the way the virtues shift the disciple agent from a place of social exclusion to intimacy. In all of these virtues, no codes or sexual capital emerge as proper prerequisites for inclusion in the community. Intimacy, it should be noted as well, is not merely about sexual acts, and the one who desires a life of celibacy draws from these virtues. To recall Jacques Ellul, the problem in ethics lies in a technical approach that thinks merely of the technique of an act as fulfilling moral norms. In the virtue approach, the acts must align with their true and proper ends. Therefore, the celibate is equally in need of the virtues as the sexually active. The purpose of the virtues is not merely a sexual technique but rather to align the meaning of sexual practices with virtue itself.

CONCLUSION

This chapter provided an account of moral theology that is at once theologically grounded but also morally directed to the reality of trafficking. Divine command ethics is not casuistry but the presence of God that energizes moral sensibilities. Inevitably people respond to this divine presence that is at once a testimony to the presence of God and moral activity. The repetition of the encounter and testimony-making practice sets the Christian community on the path to cultivating the appropriate virtues for sexual ethics. Uncovered in this process is a call to reject the idols of purity and privilege and instead pick up the call to other-regard and responsibility to oneself and one's neighbor. This only happens through formation, and these virtues guide specific actions. Testimony forms the one who receives it and they become better placed to resist the tyranny of trafficking.

What remains is an account of sexual ethics that makes sense of the command and the virtues cultivated in the command. They will be provisional but directed toward the reality of trafficking and the code ethics that shift the material expression of ethics from exclusion to intimacy. In short, the provisional ethics will develop the receptive moral ontology inherent in divine command's virtue-making work.

125. Peterson-Iyer, *Reenvisioning Sexual Ethics*, 44.

5

Love Never Fails

Provisional Sexual Ethics

INTRODUCTION: FROM SEXUAL VIRTUE TO SEXUAL ETHICS

THE CONTENT OF THE present chapter fits the description of what one expects in a book on sexual ethics, and it presents in the most explicit form the sexual ethics and practices I envision for iconoclastic sex. Though it should be clear by now, this chapter cannot occur without the previous four. There needs to be a thick description of the problem, the reception of testimony, a new theological trajectory with a dialectical tension, and the centralizing of new virtues. After this challenging work, we proceed with the provisional ethics of the iconoclastic sex offered.

The provisional nature of sexual ethics occurs within the current situation of sexual ethics, which exists in tension with a desire for a less restrictive sexual ethic coming out of the sexual revolution and the redoubling of a fundamentalist resurgence around sexual ethics. For those who call for a less restrictive sexual ethic, consent is the exclusive qualification that must be met. To be clear, consent is fundamental and foundational for any sexual ethic, but it is not enough. "Sex," as Amia Srinivasan comments on this shift in sexual ethics, "is no longer morally problematic or unproblematic; it is instead merely wanted or unwanted. In this sense, the norms of sex are like the norms of capitalist free exchange."[1] Though provisional, the ethics pro-

---

1. Srinivasan, *Right to Sex*, 82.

posed below attempts to construct a world that responds to the testimonies of the women in this study, namely by mobilizing their voice and virtue to construct a better world. As such, Christian sexual ethics must commit to the realism of its own position. The claim that sexual ethics hinges on a prerequisite of merely wanted or unwanted activity neglects the fact that sex forms a particular kind of community that can share in certain attitudes that lead either to flourishing or abuse. Consent, thus, cannot be the only metric for sex, but rather sexual ethics must insist on consent in cooperation with the virtues that form the ability to give and receive. In other words, sexual ethics, as this study argues, must consider mutuality as a top priority. These virtues and activities are not merely limited to consent but cultivate positive activity that leads toward flourishing for all in the community.

Finally, I want to clarify up front that the ethics provided here are provisional based on the kinds of activities that correctly inhabit the above virtues and account for the testimonies provided. I use the word *provisional* in order to highlight two things. First, I wish to highlight the continual need for the encounter with God. The command must remain crucial and central to the work of Christian ethics. However, Christian ethics must consider the contexts of the command and the corresponding testimony as certainty. The context I work with is the study of survivors. The command forms and shapes those who encounter not only God but the testimony of these women. Therefore, each section will begin with a brief reference to the study and why these traditional areas of sexual ethics speak to the lives of those studied. To recall, a central claim of this work is that the way that humans conduct their sexual lives impacts broader individuals. In this way, sexuality already includes a politics. I will end each section with a conclusion on how the proposed moral activity addresses those caught in the web of trafficking and purity. The moral witness response must coalesce with the testimony of the women who experience trafficking. Even for the women who do not profess the Christian faith, their testimony is a new kind of certainty in God's kingdom governance against the tyranny of sinful code ethics. Formed in their encounter with God, each responds to each and receives each in virtuous response. In this way, sexual ethics is not merely about what one does in sexual relationships but the communities that exist *because* of our sexual ethics. Again, virtue is not primarily about what we do but who we are. The only question is: whom do we want to be?

PART I: SEX IN A WORLD OF TRAFFICKING AND PURITY

I begin the ethics portion of this work with a reflection on sexual acts in general. What constitutes good sex? This question arises from the conviction already signaled by Rowan Williams that one must know why sex matters at all before prescribing the relationships most appropriate to that goodness. As already stated, the ethics offered below are provisional to fully accommodate the need for an ongoing encounter with the command of God. The posture precedes the prescription of sexual ethics. I offer below ethics profoundly tethered to the testimonies of the survivors of trafficking and purity culture. Furthermore, it forms thinking *with* the testimonies to think *from* the place of victims of code fetishes.

Focusing first on sexual acts helps recognize the purpose of sex itself. Below, I couch sexual activity within the three testimony-images offered by the women in the study. The women offer an account of sex both apophatically and cataphatically through naming those realities that affirm or deny their dignity. Furthermore, the constructive language of grace, iconoclasm, and covenant inform the specific rationality for the goodness of sex. I attach to them examples of each embodied in sexual activity or a specific sexual act. These are not new codes. For example, I link grace to singleness. Such a connection does not mean that only those who commit to singleness can perform gracious sexuality. Quite the contrary, I only offer this connection because this form of embodiment *can* illustrate this testimony well. As already indicated by the survey itself, the women in this study struggled to find their value apart from their body, that sex should be pleasurable, and what constitutes good sexuality. These three optics serve as the testimony of the women in our study and they answer the concerns that they raised.

Grace: Singleness

Grace grounds all sexual ethics. To recall Williams, grace for the believer is a transformation that depends on knowing oneself to be seen in a certain way, as significant and wanted. Before identifying the appropriate relationships, one must reflect on why sex matters in the first place. Grace is essential for all sexual ethics to resist the purity/impurity dialectic that prevents the inclusion of all people in the beloved community. Purity culture, like the buyer in trafficking, values a body according to its lack of sex. In short, one's value, or sacredness, is tied to something else. Grace erases this metric, enabling a new mode of relating where each creaturely reality one meets does not need to fill a function or capacity for human dignity or sacredness. Grace already declares, as Barth argues, that God is for this person. Thus, grace speaks to the intrinsic desirability of others. To be clear, this does not suggest a lack of fidelity or relationships of preferential love, nor does it suggest that others should be reduced to objects of pleasure. To do either would be to swing sexuality to opposing extremes of objectification. Grace is thus a language that thinks of reconciliation as the aim of all creation. If so, each creature finds themselves in a well of deep desire and not merely as objects of calculation.

A language of grace rather than objectification gives a thickened sense of sexual activity. Sex does not merely mean the following of a code but rather the utilizing of moral imagination. Anything less would be risking objectification. For some ethicists, objectification is a necessary feature of sex. It is irrational and reduces the other to an object of one's code fulfillment or desire. In this sense, sex is merely a fulfillment of codes toward the end of fitting a specific image. It is good if sex looks and feels a certain way. For example, sex between two married purity code-following virgins is good because it fulfills a purity code image. To be clear, this does not mean that two people experiencing sex for the first time in the confines of marriage is wrong or not preferable; I merely indicate the functional nature of codes through this example. It means placing a high premium on those recognized as "pure" or image-fitting. This premium is so high that it justifies the maltreatment of those who do not align with its image. The coding to an image aligns with the latter sense of objectification that utilizes another for one's pleasure, or in Kant's moral terms, using a person as a means to an end. This latter sense is the reason for Kant's suspicion of the viability of sexual ethics. The purpose of sex, in this respect, is a pleasure for the subjective party and, according to Kant, cannot be moral. Each must be objected to each. Therefore, coding to an image in order to find an object that will bring the most pleasure is the goal. In this sense, specific images guide sexual ethics rather than grace.

In order to cleanse moral energies, a hermeneutic of sexual ethics can help envision sexuality free of objectification for the other. To make singleness a central hermetic of sexual relationships does not deny sexual desire. Instead, it declares sexual desire as firmly gracious. In other words, sex does not define the body's goodness. Grace already names the body's belovedness before sexuality ever touches it. Sex is not necessary but entirely gratuitous to the grace already given to the body. Thus, it takes an optic of singleness to locate sex as something entirely unnecessary to find how it can *be* good.

A crucial aspect of grace and singleness lies in cultivating a social imagination free of sexual objectification and cultivating healthy sexual desire. Grace possesses an entire language wherein one prioritizes the neighbor's health and needs before any sexual activity occurs. Furthermore, the neighbor's dignity exists regardless of any sexual experience or utility presented to the single person. Singleness is a vocation entirely of its own that approaches sex from its provisional place.

To this end, the graciousness of sex requires that the disciple-agent practice humility. Humility forms disciple-agents according to their value without cultivating subjective supremacy. Humility enables one to receive the neighbor outside the logic of objectification and into their spaces of need. The neighbor is not an object, nor must they *earn* their value. Grace confronts every human reality with care. Therefore, the humble person recognizes that the neighbor's value is not a reality discerned primarily by the disciple-agent.

Grace also leads sexual ethics to the cultivation of love. Love requires unselfing and thinking from another place. To love another involves attention to the concrete reality and a practice that promotes their good and even pleasure. Love requires mutuality and the cultivation of the *neighbor's* agency. This posture reverses the code fetish model wherein one meets specific images to be loved. Grace challenges such assumptions and begins with a different base, namely that the individual matters before, during, and after any sexual activity. Love, even as it seeks the pleasure of another, acts toward the neighbor, the beloved, in a way that aligns actions with the sacredness at the heart of every person as creatures of God. The actions that affirm the dignity of another are loving. These actions are not merely done to another but performed in concert with that other person's mutuality. Thus, there is a clear standard by which one can discern loving from unloving actions. In short, love encourages flourishing. This loving attention cannot be something one earns, but only that which is given and received.

Though grace does lead humanity into morally appropriately sexual relationships, it is also a means of self-care. Grace means humbly knowing oneself to be loved and desired. Sexual ethics cannot be so other-regarding that it neglects the care and love for the disciple-agent lest they make an object of themselves. Grace requires mutuality *and* reciprocity. After all, grace for the believer is the knowledge of oneself as wanted, desired, and loved.

The testimony of grace helpfully locates the goodness of sex within the matrix of belonging and care central to communities able to resist trafficking. The images of sexual activity that lead to social exclusion cultivate an atmosphere of trafficking in two ways. First, it creates possibilities of exclusion. Second, it turns others into objects. Notice the difficulty with which survivors note the images that guide social exclusion. The fallen woman, the Whore of Babylon, and addict become the cipher through which their bodies must fit. Even in violating pasts, the presence or absence of sexuality is the only metric by which the social exclusion model can welcome belonging. Furthermore, purchasing or participating in systems of trafficking is profoundly ungracious. It does not love insofar as it can no longer contribute to the flourishing of the person caught in the web. It is unjust because it cannot look at the concrete reality of another. It lacks humility because it only serves the buyer's ends insofar as the neighbor becomes an object of pleasure in itself and denies their sacredness. Contributing to trafficking directly through purchasing or indirectly by excluding those who would be vulnerable to the web trafficking is ungracious. The promise of iconoclastic sex is the ability to be gracious in the face of difference and differing experiences. It exists in concert, iconoclastically, with the deep well of intimacy formed in reconciliation as solidarity privileging a loving community over purity. Its goodness grows ontically from the site of Christ's love for the world to bring about a beloved community. In other words, the community can only resist the lure of trafficking as it learns to participate in God's welcoming grace.

Iconoclasm: Pleasure

Iconoclasm is an extension of grace. The moral imagination suffers malformation when suffused with idolatrous images. These images divide between lovable bodies based on possession of sexual codes or evil bodies coded as impure. Furthermore, these idolatrous images sometimes warrant unimaginable violence to bodies that do not fit their coding. Coding thus emerges as a natural theology that moves ethical thought in direct opposition to the command of God. No one comes to goodness or the love of God by right. An iconoclasm of fidelity holds to this perspective to subvert the tendency of individuals and communities to create hierarchies of those worthy and unworthy of love.

The central promise in sexual ethics given by iconoclasm is the transvaluation of the idols of sexual ethics—specifically, the idols of code contagion that begets toxic goodness and the privileged place from which sexual ethics operates typically. Iconoclasm shifts thinking from the places of those traditionally excluded, which requires the virtue of justice. In sexual ethics, justice binds humans to one another in a way that accounts for the concrete reality and "due" afforded to the neighbor both in their present condition and future potential. Only through attention to this human reality can one render what is due to this person.

Grace, through love, already invites that one must make this epistemological shift. However, justice-shaped iconoclasms of fidelity address larger systems of injustice by cleaving to the justice that is God's liberation as expressed in the life of Jesus. Iconoclasm must also shape the community with distinct yet coordinated actions to grace. Sex, when approached with iconoclasm, not only shows other bodies that they are beloved and sacred but that the structural shape of the community must form itself to allow for the flourishing of people. Iconoclasm more accurately describes the destruction necessary for sexual ethics because iconoclasm destroys idolatrous structuring.

Iconoclasms must follow the pattern of iconoclasms of fidelity, which destroys necessary barriers in four distinct ways to cleave to the indicative. First, iconoclasms of fidelity do not sit idly by in the face of injustice in the community. Truth must speak to domestic abuse, pedophilia, and other forms of sexual violence. To allow or commit to these activities is not only ungracious but unjust. The direction of iconoclasms of fidelity must observe careful precision. Even as the beloved community takes imaginative presidency over desires for personal piety and injustice, it must adhere to an even more intimate vision of community. As the stories of trafficking indicate, those who suffer do so at the hands of permitting systems of rape, domestic violence, and exploitation.

Furthermore, the cycle of toxic goodness excludes the structure of pure and impure. As the bearers of sin, the latter must experience according to code contagion punishment to illustrate communal purity. Justice iconoclastically destroys the idols of social exclusion and engages the community in taking down the crucified from their crosses. The direct fidelity to the cross must heed the crucified among us. To think from the place of the crucified not only helps those suffering under unjust treatment but takes a hammer to the structure itself.

The question of iconoclasms of fidelity further strengthens itself when combined with humanity; in the context of iconoclasm, humility swings like a double-edged sword. It destroys the idol's image while clearing room for the individual to flourish. To be clear, every person must experience both sides of humility. However, in systems where one in-group experiences privilege to the detriment and exclusion of others, this group must experience more of the humble lowliness of humility. The one who suffers must experience their humanity's humble loftiness and sacredness. In short, justice resembles equity when thickened by humility.

Second, sexual ethics does not collapse into technique. Thus, iconoclasm destroys certain idols that sex must serve specific functions. Such idols include the assumption that sex must always create pleasure for one party over the other, individuals must possess the perfect body, or that sex serves the ends of procreation alone. The iconoclasm of fidelity as a base of iconoclastic sex cultivates intimacy in those who participate. Like singleness, iconoclasm requires a broad understanding of sexuality, not merely as acts to perform toward the perfection of pleasure. Iconoclasm is not a technique. To be clear, pleasure is essential in sex, but it is not alone important. Sex must cultivate intimacy with another, one's community, and God. Sex as the sharing between two individuals of the sacred, precious character of another does not require specific images. For example, the idolization of the orgasm is not the mark of good sex, though it can enhance it. Sexuality can and should encourage intimacy, which means that good sex does not always culminate in an orgasm so long as it enables intimacy. Intimacy is about connection, which involves sharing life to cultivate fidelity bonds in ways that raise awareness of each person's goodness.

Furthermore, intimacy begets trust to honor the vulnerability implicit in sexuality. Neither technique nor body-shape dominates sexual ethics, but the cultivation of virtue under the command of God. It is more important that sex be loving and just rather than end in orgasm because virtue connects humans to the good of their neighbor while also enabling participation in God.

To this end, pleasure is a stigma in many Christian communities. The feeling of sexual pleasure, since at least the time of Augustine, scares many faithful into a false fear of sin. Pleasure is an end to pursue, but like virtue, it matters the end at which it arrives. The end cannot be literalized. The pleasure that cultivates intimacy is different from pleasure that cultivates selfishness. Both give pleasure as ends, but the latter is the basis of sexual violence and the former the basis of intimate connection. As such, pleasure can be pursued as an end but only inside the larger rubric of virtue and intimacy. In short, the one formed in virtue can pursue pleasure as an end because that person possesses the necessary affections and formation to give and receive pleasure without turning the neighbor into a means to an end. Intimate sex can and should be pleasurable for its own sake, but pleasure for its own sake must avoid the risk of merely satisfying one party's desires or doing so to harm the other. Iconoclasms of fidelity ordered toward intimacy weed out the differences between these two kinds of pleasure.

One does not need to possess a certain kind of body to cultivate intimate sex or experience pleasure. Images of sexualized bodies pervade culture and cultivate an idol of those worthy of sex. In short, the idol of good sex also presents certain bodies as more sexually able than others. Iconoclasm reasserts that bodies of all kinds can communicate this kind of care to one another, which relieves the pressure on certain bodies that merely become objects of sexual fantasy while empowering others traditionally excluded. Iconoclasm intensely interrogates the existence of bodies caught in a matrix bearing sexual objectification vis-à-vis a cultural standard. As model and social media influencer Emily Ratajkowski writes about her experience with her body and sexuality, "In many ways, I have been undeniably rewarded by capitalizing on my sexuality... But in other, less overt ways, I've felt objectified and limited by my position in the world as a so-called sex symbol."[2] Ratajkowski helpfully names the internal impact of narratives of empowerment through objectification. If nothing else, Ratajkowski describes back to a culture that her empowerment is more nuanced than merely feeling confident in one's skin, and it is not "true empowerment."[3] She details several instances that the empowerment afforded to her through her modeling must be submitted to the satisfaction of the "male gaze."[4] As she recognizes, she does feel powerful and confident in her body, but she also feels that her empowerment is not her own because it is through another. The feeling of diminishment or loss of empowerment considering the weight placed on her as an image cultivates a vicious expression of sexual ethics that even extends beyond Ratajkowski. She can profit from her body even though she does not possess the image of sexuality that she exemplifies. Furthermore, those who do not exemplify it often go to extreme measures through body mutilations, dangerous surgeries, and dietary expectations to mirror the profitable bodies even though such empowerment would only be through another. These bodies participate in the sexual capital that seemingly causes buyers the most significant amount of pleasure and sexual satisfaction.

To defame the image of the perfect body means liberation for all because there is no longer an image to capture, attain, or destroy bodies. In short, sexual capital pillages people's lives and creates false expectations. Bodies, thus, iconoclastically must not participate in a literalized image for exchange. The search for bodies that most appropriately align with an image of sexual profitability creates a trafficking market. To code in this way perpetuates a system, but recognizing this must not result in the condemnation of those trying to survive in a system. What must be defamed is the *economy* upon which bodies are bought and sold. Sex must not be an achievement of bodily perfection. Instead, it is the rejection of it. Iconoclasm moves sex from the proper fulfillment of an abstract ideal such as the "sexiness" of a body or its performative abilities. Instead, iconoclasm moves sex back into its proper place as that which cultivates intimacy through pleasure and

2. Ratajkowski, *My Body*, 5.
3. Ratajkowski, *My Body*, 6.
4. Ratajkowski, *My Body*, 6.

trust. In short, all intimate sex should pursue pleasure for the sake of the other, which does not require a specific body or skill.

A word must be said about sexual disfunction and ableism. According to one National Library of Medicine researcher, roughly 43 percent of women and 31 percent of men suffer from sexual dysfunction.[5] This statistic excludes those who suffer from sexual disabilities. Sexual ethics, when pursued from a perspective of sexual ableism, neglects people with disabilities in dating, intimacy, and relationships. Iconoclasms of bodies and abilities are no more critical than for the individuals who struggle with one of these conditions. Their bodies are not unlovable or undesirable because they do not fit the image of ableist defined perfect bodies, which modern narratives of body positivity struggle to grasp. One must recall the hermeneutic of singleness that bolsters sexual ethics. Sex, sexual skill, or sexiness do not determine the value of a body but are only that which must align and affirm a dynamic of goodness already afforded to bodies in their sacredness. Sexuality is fundamentally a desire to be wanted and significant. This same desire can exist through other practices. Intimacy, to recall, is a form of trust and care that makes known a connection. Sexual desire exists among a matrix of actions that affirm the basic meaning of another person. Thus, a sexual ethic must include divergent cases within it, for they are persons of desire and significance.

Third, in many faith or secular communities, an ideal of sex is a prerequisite for the community. This myth is the first image to suffer the weight of iconoclasm. The image of purity or impurity that one uses to bar those from the community cannot last. The centrality of justice for iconoclasm is a coordinated faithfulness to a reality different than exclusion and moral perfection. The sanctified community is the only one that justly participates in God's liberation of the cosmos to bind to new relationships of meaning where those denied love might find similar liberation. Sexual history as a prerequisite for community prevents such binding. Thus, iconoclasms of fidelity hold fast to a community of reconciliation wherein the intimacy of reconciliation takes priority over purity, exclusion, and code fetish.

Lastly, the image of sex for the sole sake of procreation itself must suffer a correction through iconoclasm. Of course, sex can produce children and still is an essential ethical mode to discern. However, it cannot be the sole use of sexuality. Though many ethical systems of the past do not allow for a moral account of sex outside the production of children, there is no biblical warrant that sex is only for childbearing. Instead, when positively

---

5. Rosen, "Prevalence and Risk Factors of Sexual Dysfunction."

understood, sex is more often described as the pleasure of passion and desire directed toward one another. As Peterson-Iyer writes,

> pleasure moves us toward other, deeper goods: love and trust of one another, and even communion with God. In other words, while pleasure may be understood as premorally *good* because of the way it benefits human persons in a more immediate sense, it also serves human well-being in a more holistic way. That is, pleasure potentially points us inward, toward trusting, honoring, and caring for our own deepest selves, and concurrently outward, toward our larger, relational context.[6]

Pleasure is a more central end of sex when tied to intimacy because it is the unique way that those in sexual covenant honor the integrity, meaning, and value of the other.

To be clear, there is a place for childbearing inside the lens of iconoclastic sex. However, childbearing functions similar to pleasure as an end operating under a more extensive guide. Sex should be procreative, but the language of procreation as the bringing of life must broaden its traditional boundaries. Undoubtedly, sex that results in the birth of children fulfills this theme, but sex that affirms the dignity of the beloved is also procreative because it too creates and cultivates life. Procreative sex, iconoclastically understood, is humble because it builds up life in another. Iconoclasm allows ethics to serve those who cannot have children for one reason or another. Many suffer from infertility through no fault of their own and others risk their lives by doing so. Many suffer in silence under the desire to have children who simply cannot. With Hannah, the mother of Samuel, they cannot make their bodies do what their bodies simply cannot do (1 Samuel 1).

Nevertheless, barrenness does not mean their bodies cannot give life. In addition to Hannah, take, for example, the life of Sarah or even Elizabeth after her. Though it meant having a child as a gift for these women, others who follow them can still bring life to themselves and others. One could consider the countless other women who give life to those around them through various faithful acts not tied to childbearing. As the basis of pleasure in which individuals can trust another and their deepest selves, they can also cultivate the affections of virtue that enable them to bring life to others and affirm their human dignity. Though a small consolation to those who desire offspring, it is imperative that these individuals know that their lives are significant and that their sexual lives have meaning and purpose. If procreation does not observe these limits and possibilities, then bearing children merely becomes another type of sexual capital.

6. Peterson-Iyer, *Reenvisioning Sexual Ethics*, 37.

As I conclude the iconoclastic features of good sex, I add one more important feature of its base: truthfulness. Iconoclastic sex requires seeing through the lies of idolatry to name the truth. Iconoclasm destroys the image that posits a sexuality either entirely about pleasure or not about pleasure, or even that sexuality is about a kind of body that one must possess to reveal new truth to those caught in these extremes, which frees sex to the different ends of virtue that affirms the dignity in others. Truthfulness is the ability to see these ends, but also to name when sex does not fulfill these virtues. The ability to speak and hear the truth is a significant feature. Sexual ethics that cannot handle the truth cannot be moral and has no connection to the excellence of virtue found solely in God, who is truth. Sexual ethics must be willing to hear the testimony of others, receive it as truth, and respond accordingly.

It is important to note at this stage that sexual ethics cannot be relative. The good of sex finds certain norms already expressed on the bases of grace and iconoclasm. Sex must affirm the dignity of others, reveal their significance, and defame structures, be they institutions or social norms that limit, capture, or destroy the living, breathing people. The end toward which sexual ethics must direct its attention lies in eliminating sexual capital. The body's abilities, how it looks, or how it can produce do not determine the morality of sex. Sex is good in that it affirms the goodness of the body because sexual capacities and qualities do not *possess* goodness in themselves. Only by moving from goodness as a possession to goodness as loving affirmation can one move beyond the perils of sex that leads to sex trafficking. Such qualities as the only end of the individual to possess is the logic seized by traffickers. This overriding desire to possess or to idealize sex according to sure narratives of objectification underwrites an economy of sale. Instead, sex couched in the iconoclastic mode creates the conditions of an affirmation that requires attention to the individual's good present and future potential. The sexual exploitation of those caught in trafficking cannot do this. However, sexual ethics can go beyond merely the rejection of buying sex. Instead, the goal is to no longer contribute to social exclusion, commodification, or domestic violence that begets the conditions of trafficking. Utilizing the base of iconoclasm, sexual ethics must articulate a sexual ethic capable of resisting these tendencies. Thinking against the images and favoring iconoclastic sex resists the fundamental contributing factors to trafficking.

Covenant: Promise-Making

Covenant is encountered when moving to the final testimony of iconoclastic sex. Sex involves a complex matrix of meaning that can cause harm or bring life. Therefore, iconoclastic sex proposes covenantal promise-making and mutuality to assist the discernment of sexual activity so that one enters into sexual activity at the right time. Sex that cannot affirm the sacred character of an individual can cause harm, and domestic or sexual violence can lead to inward mistrust of the self.

Furthermore, even in just sexuality, attachments in sex occur through the development of trust and vulnerability. Covenant is the base that assures one enters into relationships at the right time, which does not eliminate the agency of a person, but brings agency into conversation with mutuality. Consent, a fundamental basis of any sexual encounter, requires a covenant-mutuality as the full expression of consensual sex. Consent does not stand alone and indeed cannot because without the basis upon which to hear and receive consent, consent can be manipulated and coerced. Covenant and mutuality are preferential but not exclusive in that the love practiced in preferential relationships must overflow. Covenant requires community, so it does not lapse from preferential love into socially exclusive love.

Covenantal love is the acknowledgment that the parties involved are ready for sex with each other—furthermore, covenant grounds sex in that it expresses justice as a central virtue. Just sex, as Farley already indicates, is an attention to a personal reality in order to render to that reality what is needed for flourishing. Just as friendship serves as preferential love, so too romantic love cultivates virtues of justice, love, humility, and truthfulness. The virtuous person performs a holistic posture of virtue in that they do not merely exercise these things at home. Craig Hovey illustrates this point very well when he points out how Aristotle argued that "virtues travel in herds." Hovey writes, "If we were to make a list of what makes a good roommate, it would probably be very similar to lists of what makes a good spouse, a good friend, a good employee, or a good employer. The virtues that are common to these lists are not just coincidences . . . virtues are 'transferable skills,' we might say."[7] In short, the disciple-agent's actions within preferential love cultivate coordinated practices of virtuous activity directed outside the preferential love into the world. Preferential love should not close off virtuous activity to the world. Sexual desire and practice cultivate a deeply rooted honoring of my sacredness and that of my neighbor.

---

7. Hovey, *Exploring Christian Ethics*, 84.

It is, therefore, most appropriate for sex to occur within covenantal relationships. The formation that one undergoes in covenant making and keeping cultivates the virtues necessary for sexual activity (i.e., just, loving, truthfulness, and humility), does not violate the dignity, and does not inhabit selfish practices. Covenantal love is, just as it indicates, a love that "unselfs," as Murdoch suggests, and sees the good of the neighbor in mutuality. In this way, covenants must occur between those capable of reciprocating, capable of unselfing equally. Both parties must possess equal autonomy and agency while also expressing love in mutuality. Covenantal love must take as its point of departure the covenant of God to humanity, which is not fulfilled reciprocally, and the covenants made possible *between* humans by God's covenant *to* humanity. This model helpfully locates grace and iconoclasm as essential features of iconoclastic sex.

The goal is not to repeat God's covenant as a lesser to a former but to think through a coordination of covenants within God's covenant that the disciple-agent can reasonably make due to this divine covenant. Take, for example, God's covenant to Adam and Eve. The covenant to them is an invitation to share in the creation with God and maintain the unique roles of caregivers to creation. Within this covenant, Adam and Eve can make covenants to one another as equal partners within the roles God gives to them. God's covenant, narratively speaking, precedes and grounds the covenant between Adam and Eve. Even in the creation account, Eve is a unique partner with Adam within creation. Thus, both experience the same promise and creation covenant with God, then experience the freedom to enter into covenantal bonds with one another. The fact that Eve's creation occurs after Adam's creation does not assume a level of subordination because they both share in the creaturely state to share space with God in the garden. Thus, this model provides a helpful narrative depiction of human covenantal love. The first humans must obey and follow God and, as such, possess the necessary equality to make covenants with one another and even pursue sexual bonds.

The kind of reciprocity acknowledged in this narrative structure in Genesis motivates an account of mutuality and autonomy important for promise-making and keeping. The covenantal bond motivates the ability to make and keep promises to one another. Covenant encourages mutuality in that Adam and Eve exist as unique creatures for one another that *can* fulfill covenantal bonds. The agency between these narrative humans is solid and mutual because both equally stand before God naked and unashamed (Gen 2:25) and even later in their punishment (Gen 3:22–24). This covenant between humans promises a place of respect for agency and mutuality to continue as an expression of covenantal fidelity. Justice, as already illustrated, requires this covenant. One must be able to commit, promise, and remain faithful to the present concrete reality of a person and their future flourishing. Covenant is, in short, a commitment to the sacredness of the person. Sex becomes a practice within a broader web of covenantal practices that illustrate this commitment to another person's sacredness. Sex, though of greater emotional and physical importance, sits alongside many mundane activities such as picking up the dry cleaning or whose hand you hold in hospice care. Such acts in service of one another create spaces for mutuality, but only as one's attention directs toward the individual reality of the person.

This directional attention must affirm a person's agency, and the more one can affirm the agency of another, the more mutuality occurs, which allows, as Peterson-Iyer argues, "that we open ourselves to the genuine value and insights of the other as well as allow the other to impact our own deeper identities and sensibilities."[8] Agency, which cultivates mutuality, mingles with the agency of another to affirm the other's dignity and hold them accountable for activity that does not live up to promises made. Agency moves the individuals into more profound personal freedom to enliven the promises made to one another. Like Adam and Eve, these two possess freedom before God and make promises to one another as creatures in that freedom. Thus, free agency leads to the deepest possible covenants wherein one can choose authentically.

The respect for agency, especially sexual agency, must be a reflex developed in the covenantal bond and the community. Sexual agency is essential to affirm even if, in the end, the others we encounter use their agency in ways outside the formations one encourages. As Peterson-Iyer writes, agency is a

> sort of freedom . . . more than simply a choice to dress provocatively, or not; to have sexual intercourse, or not . . . It includes profound affirmation of each person's capacity for self-determination, to choose not only her actions but also her ends, loves, and ultimately the meaning of her life. *This* sort of freedom roots itself in deep recognition of one's (and another's) dignity and self-worth, a dignity in Christian tradition embedded in the *imago Dei*.[9]

Peterson-Iyer stipulates that this account of agency must all consider the "larger cultural landscape" that possesses all kinds of peer pressure, expectations, privileges, and violence.[10] Peterson-Iyer elicits a language where individuals can recognize themselves as participating in constructing their actions. Though, theologically, humans cannot choose their ends but only

---

8. Peterson-Iyer, *Reenvisioning Sexual Ethics*, 44.
9. Peterson-Iyer, *Reenvisioning Sexual Ethics*, 70.
10. Peterson-Iyer, *Reenvisioning Sexual Ethics*, 70–71.

receive from God. Nevertheless, cultivating a community where individuals can exercise agency is a central task of a community. This community of agency again reminds us of the importance of testimony. Testimony requires a space wherein the encounter with God cultivates new energies, agency, freedom, and moral activity from God's very self. Making space for agency encourages encounters with God to *find* their true ends and receive the command specific to them. Thus, respect for an agency is a crucial part of all sexual ethics, but covenantal sex is the basis for enthusiastic consent. The covenant is the ongoing promise to act only in harmony with another's present and future good in mind to honor the dynamic reality of their sacredness, which includes their agency.

Promises to the agency of another require the consideration of consent, which is a fundamental requirement of all sexual ethics. To act toward the neighbor or beloved in a way that violates their consent is fundamentally wrong. However, consent is not enough to express agency. To recall Amia Srinivasan, the overwhelming focus on a language of consent shifts sex from a distinction of "problematic or unproblematic" to "merely wanted or unwanted."[11] An example for our study lies in sex for sale; the question, as Srinivasan argues, posed to sex for sale is whether the parties have agreed to terms on sex, not the conditions that give rise to the supply and demand wherein the majority of individuals selling are women, and the majority of individuals buying are men.[12] The point that Srinivasan critiques is if we collapse one's concept of sexual practice into preference, then we leave sexual desires uninterrogated.[13] Srinivasan draws on the example of a male professor accepting the advances of a young female student and thus pursuing a relationship with her. Srinivasan imagines a case where the student feels no fear in this relation. Nevertheless, she states that consent does not, in this case, touch on the more significant systematic issues surrounding the power dynamics at play here. She suggests that the professor breaks his covenant with his student, namely, instead of "sleeping with his student, this professor should have been—*teaching* her."[14] The fear of those who advocate for the consent paradigm is that the legislation of sexual desire limits choice, but as Srinivasan pushes back, "a practice which is consensual can also be systematically damaging" to those who practice it.[15] Thus, a larger rubric of

---

11. Srinivasan, *Right to Sex*, 82.
12. Srinivasan, *Right to Sex*, 82–83.
13. Srinivasan, *Right to Sex*, 84–86.
14. Srinivasan, *Right to Sex*, 128.
15. Srinivasan, *Right to Sex*, 147.

care, mutuality, and love must envelop consent, not discard it but give it the support needed to be free.

Naked consent free of a larger matrix of ethics leaves sex open to coercion. This does not mean consent is no longer an essential feature of sexual ethics. No action should be permitted without it. However, Srinivasan observes that consent cannot exist on its own. There must be an entire network of commitments in which consent can be given, withheld, and received without fear. Covenant and mutuality merely help individuals know when they are ready to enter into sexual activity *at the right time*. The virtues develop promises made and kept, and the attention paid to an individual occur over the spectrum of a relationship that allows for a deep knowledge of the individual, which is what Iris Murdoch identifies as the most profound expression of love.[16] Within this loving commitment, this covenant, one learns the rhythms of a person to be able to know when consent is given and retracted. Furthermore, one should know not only when consent is given and withdrawn but also that the grace to accept that the person's worth exists in a deeper, more fundamental place of sacredness. That sacredness does not diminish when the partner does not perform. Empowering the beloved through mutuality allows the space to give enthusiastic consent and only works through the cultivation of covenant, namely to coordinate consent with appropriate desires that promote and affirm the dignity of another in their sacredness. As such, covenant discourages any claim that one possesses a "right to sex" but instead that sex is a gift given in a relationship of mutuality and care.

Furthermore, covenant encourages the desire to continually check that consent remains and is not withdrawn because it is such a fragile permission and desire. As such, consent must be continually sought through the entire course of a sexual encounter and even a relationship. Therefore, I propose that covenant remains a central feature of sexual ethics. It names that one must fundamentally and finally have the good of another justly before one's vision so that pleasure is finally only pleasure insofar as the pleasure of the other is also sought in mutuality. It is a promise to one's neighbor and a faithfulness grounded in the very life of God. As such, sex can lead others to a deeper appreciation of themselves and cultivate the virtues of humility that build up a proper account of sexual relations not bound by social or sexual capital.

One final element of consent remains as it pertains to covenant, namely truthfulness. Consent must exist within a larger covenant framework, meaning that sex must cultivate the virtue of truthfulness. A feature of truth and truth-telling lies in the ability to speak the truth and hear the

---

16. Murdoch, *Sovereignty of the Good*, 27.

truth, which involves creating atmospheres wherein the truth can be shared without shame or condemnation. In this way, covenant encourages the cultivation of the virtue of truthfulness inside of preferential relationships to encourage the exercising of truthfulness elsewhere. Tragically, truthfulness lacks a fair hearing in many institutions, even the church, as the Southern Baptist Convention report on sexual violence or even the Roman Catholic child abuse scandals indicate. Many privilege the literalized desire of the institution over the harm it does. An institution that cannot speak the truth about abuse cannot share the truth of the gospel credibly. No news is good when couched in a platform that willingly and intentionally perpetuates sexual violence. To this end, truthfulness must become a central feature. The truth might cost the institution a public image, but the church must be willing to defame and defund images to cling to its message. Only when the church vigorously pursues a life of faithful, iconoclastic fidelity to the gospel and resists the posture of effective, institutional power and manipulation at all costs will the larger world potentially believe its promises. Until then, the covenant of God as given to the world and proclaimed by the church will only appear as a cruel joke. I believe such a shift is possible only when truthfulness emerges against our desire for purity.

Trafficking and Purity: What is the Purpose for Sex?

The reflections on grace, iconoclasm, and covenant answer the question: what is the meaning of sex? As indicated in the study, women in both purity culture and trafficking confess a great deal of abuse, shame, and broken promises. The purity culture tradition cannot correct these pains. As the study shows, they only perpetuate them because both survivors of trafficking and those who grew up under purity culture teaching express the same amount of stress and abuse. In each of these testimonies, a new imagination must emerge in place of the traditional purity culture that captivates not only in evangelical circles but also larger Christian culture of every confession and Western culture at large.[17] The desires of each participant is still a covenantal love. It includes desire for a place, community, and even romance that endures without a need to perform. Only a sexuality capable of being gracious despite any usefulness for sex, pleasurable for its own sake despite one's appearance or past, and that sex should be in a constellation of activities that promise to participate in the flourishing of the individual can form this new imagination. Furthermore, sex and a knowledge of the body

---

17. For an account of the larger cultural impact of purity beyond the church, see Jessica Valenti, *Purity Myth*.

is still a desire, but the places where sex, according to our participants, is most useful is in relationships where it is not the means by which they find worth or value. Sex is good, but it is not required for meaning. The relationships that encourage this last point are the ones that we promote.

PART II: TRAFFICKING AND SEX WORK

The previous sections named the good of sex itself as it confronts the testimonies and virtues of iconoclastic sex. However, sexuality is not the only element to consider; one must also explore the relationships in which sex occurs. The ethics of sex cultivate a practical reason for the disciple-agents to navigate the often difficult and complex nature of sexual intimacy while also establishing a community of character in which the conditions for sexual ethics can occur. Sexual ethics works for the survivor and other disciple-agents as they stand before God's providential work. The first set of relationships to explore are the myriad of relationships found adjacent to human trafficking, namely sex work. Trafficking participates in systems of sex work by force, coercion, or manipulation, but this is not to say that every sex worker is a victim of the same violence of trafficking. Nevertheless, profound similarities exist between sex work and trafficking, making it an essential relational pattern for consideration.

Sex Work Is Work

The first relational pattern for sex work lies in the sex work is work movement. This movement seeks the decriminalization of sex work in order to reduce violence enacted against sex workers and help cultivate the sex worker's flourishing. The question of sex work as a chosen field must encounter sexual virtues and testimonies. Is there a place for chosen sex work in a world of trafficking? Does the liberation of the survivor permit sex work as work? Analyzing this movement cannot lay unfair moral problems at the feet of the sex worker. The systemic issues in the world and the community's role in social exclusion of sex workers must also be considered. Sexual ethics must consider the reception of those with differing sexual experiences not as threats but as neighbors.

The first step in analyzing the sex work is work movement requires evaluating the claims of violence that come through criminalization. The conditions of criminalized sex work lead to an economic precarity that only perpetuates trafficking and prostitution.[18] Vitale provides an example of the

---

18. Vitale, *End of Policing*, 112.

police raid of a male escort site Rentboy.com, where workers advertised their services.[19] The result for the workers was not only criminal prosecution but also the loss of custody of children to the state, eviction by landlords, and other stigmas that prevented future job opportunities.[20] Thus, ongoing criminal activity is the only way to maintain economic subsistence. Though Vitale does not comment on trafficking at this point, the exact impact is true for survivors of trafficking in many cases where trafficking cannot be proven. For both chosen sex workers and the trafficked, the precarity resulting from criminalization impacts the stability of either party and encourages recidivism back into sex work. Thus, those who survive trafficking might engage in chosen sex work to find stability even though force through survival is no choice.

Strong proponents of the sex work is work movement rely on the above analysis to form their justification for decriminalization. According to proponents such as Thia Cooper and Kristian Braekkan, the "exchange of sex could occur fairly in a just economic system," free of criminal prosecution.[21] If the economic conditions, as these authors propose, were to change, the worker's relationships with the consumer would also change. The assumption is that the exchange of sex is morally neutral, and the purpose of the movement lies in making the exchange as just as possible.

The rallying cry, "sex work is work," calls for specific economic policies such as decriminalization to perpetuate the exchanges themselves, which is apparent in Cooper and Braekkan's defense of sex work when they compare the exchange of sex in sex work with the exchange for food and shelter (reproductive labor) for those in romantic relationships.[22] The comparison normalizes sex as a means of exchange and a means to profit. Furthermore, exchange, in this context, is less about the justness of the sexual act than the justness of the exchange itself, which Srinivasan indicates does not account for all the ethical questions in sex. The industry's interests, as feminist scholar Esperanza Fonseca understands, become fused with the interests of the sex worker and, thus, expand the market.[23] In this way, Fonseca pushes back against the claim made by Cooper and Braekkan that sex work should be paid for as a kind of sexual labor due to the harsh capitalism rampant in society. She writes that in response to this, capitalism

---

19. Vitale, *End of Policing*, 112.
20. Vitale, *End of Policing*, 119.
21. Cooper and Braekkan, "Analysis of the Sex in the Sex Trade," 146.
22. Cooper and Braekkan, "Analysis of the Sex in the Sex Trade," 148, 151–52.
23. Fonseca, "Problem with the Phrase 'Sex Work is Work.'"

is marked in part by the division between production and reproduction. Some claim that this division can be resolved via the expansion of domestic and sexual markets. Yet this contradiction cannot get resolved via domestic or sex markets, because those markets only create another form of the dual-exploitation of the woman. The commodification of her sexuality is not payment for work she already does, but the addition of a site of exploitation.[24]

Fonseca helpfully locates that the issue in sex work is the market structure itself. Thus, sex work is work is an attempt to preserve the market that does not prevent the violence it attempts to overcome. As Fonseca argues, the neoliberal cycle of exchange carries with it "a frequency of violence that cannot be reformed out of the sex trade."[25] The best that the sex work is work movement can do is create greater freedom within the structure of neoliberalism, with a more incredible submission to violence and coercion. It does not yet grasp freedom because it is still inside the structure and not empowering.

Sex work is work does not deliver women who practice sex work from the violence experienced in the trade. Legalizing sex work can reduce *some* violence experienced by sex workers and this must be examined. But as Fonseca argues, it only offers empty platitudes.[26] The freedom sex work is work seeks is not a freedom from violence, exploitation, and marginalization. One should be concerned with these elements of the sex worker's life, but a new kind of freedom must emerge. Indeed, there is an agency for one inside a system of biopower, but the system itself struggles to offer anything other than the choices that lead to exploitation of themselves or others. Sex work is work, then, is not the full rallying cry of care that it is presupposed. As Srinivasan again helpfully clarifies, this only inquires on the condition of exchange rather than the conditions of sex itself. However, this does not mean that society should continue to punish sex workers to the point of cultivating a cycle of insecurity void of commitments to their flourishing. I humbly argue that the moral posture in iconoclastic sex should be the care for those who still find themselves in the life of sex work but still recognize that sex work is *not* a good life due to this violence that cannot be reformed out it.[27] Therefore, one does not think of freedom in a capitalist guise but

---

24. Fonseca, "Problem with the Phrase 'Sex Work is Work.'"
25. Fonseca, "Problem with the Phrase 'Sex Work is Work.'"
26. Fonseca, "Problem with the Phrase 'Sex Work is Work.'"
27. I want to thank Micayla Wilson and Bailey Phillips for helping me clarify this point in the discussion of sex work.

instead seeks to dislocate it to find new freedom. The purpose, then, will be to find a new source of empowerment that does not honor this system, such as jobs with living wages and meaningful work that allows individuals to flourish and thrive.

To be clear, one cannot downplay the agency of those who choose sex work, and those not in the field should take the distinction between trafficking and sex work seriously. The heart of this distinction is how individuals exercise agency concerning their work. As Kate Ward highlights, some "disqualify sex work as work because it can be difficult, demeaning, and dangerous—in other words, because it does not appear to be *good* work."[28] The nature of purity and sex undoubtedly contributes to this idea, as does the violence that individuals experience in sex work. Good work, on the contrary, should be "fulfilling, non-exploitive, and enjoyable."[29] However, as Ward continues, many forms of work do not fit this definition, and sex work advocates only that sex work be considered along these other forms of work to create lines of advocacy.[30] The means of advocacy challenges traditional notions of empowerment. As Melissa Grant writes, "Sex workers must prove they have made an *empowered* choice, as if empowerment is some intangible state attained through self-perfection and not through a continuous and collective negotiation of power."[31] The agency of the sex worker nor the claim that sex work is bad work does not resolve the systemic issues at stake. Instead, it must place sex work as work to understand the broad matrix of economic factors that "constrain, entice and constitute the choices made by workers in the sex trades."[32] There are many kinds of work that also resemble harmful forms of work. To elevate sex work beyond them would be to argue that there are forms of work that are wrong and other forms of work that disempower.

If the goal is the equation of sex work to full empowerment, agency, and meaningful work, then as moral agents, sex workers must be respected to know this truth offered by philosopher Rey Chow when she explains, "*some humans have been cast as objects, while other humans have been given the privilege of becoming subjects.*"[33] The demand for sex workers will always exist, but one cannot seek to continue to create or participate in markets that perpetuate its existence. To be abundantly and perfectly clear, the sex

28. Ward, "Human and Alienating Work," 263. Emphasis original
29. Ward, "Human and Alienating Work," 263.
30. Ward, "Human and Alienating Work," 263–64.
31. Grant, *Playing the Whore*, 94.
32. Ward, "Human and Alienating Work," 265.
33. Chow, *Protestant Ethnic and the Spirit of Late Capitalism*, 2. Emphasis original.

worker is not responsible for trafficking. However, when the agreed exchange encourages exploitation through economic possession, this is not true freedom.[34] If there were no economy where buyers wanted sex, there would be no trafficking. The sex worker only participates in a system where buyers exist and in a system of sexism that would not be tolerated in any other sector. As such, the sex worker cannot end trafficking on their own.

Nevertheless, if one is in a freely chosen occupation, they cannot be alone in their decision. A new world of choice must be offered where agency can be exercised, healthy sexual desires and expressions sought, and lives can flourish outside these dangerous jobs. Even still, this section shows that the sex worker can have a role to play and not perpetuate this in their own lives. They cannot make this choice abstracted from structural changes that will make this decision possible for them. In short, if we call on sex workers to contribute to the end of trafficking by closing the market, they must not only receive bad choices. It is up to those purchasing to stop and cultivate a world of dignified work for all people. Therefore, no one party is responsible, but a complete moral conversion is needed, wherein the most vulnerable receive the most care.

Pornography

Solicitation is not the only form of sex work alongside trafficking. Pornography is an estimated 100-billion-dollar-a-year business globally, with a sizable amount of that business arising from the US domestic context.[35] A porn star is a sex worker in that the porn star utilizes their sexual capital (i.e., body, features, sexual acts) to make a profit. There is not merely one kind of porn star in that there are individuals who can control their product and those who do not. Thus, much of the distinctions in sex work versus trafficking exist in the production of pornography, though they can overlap.

In the interest of clarity, pornography needs a definition. Many fundamentalist and evangelical circles will assume that nudity of any kind is inherently pornographic. For the sake of this study, I agree with the definition proposed by researchers who claim that pornography lies in a dynamic exchange between content, producer intent, and consumer judgment.[36] Though an entire work can be written just on unpacking this, suffice it to

---

34. See Peterson-Iyer's excellent and nuanced account of agency and exploitation in *Reenvisioning Sexual Ethics*, 101–36.

35. Shor and Seida, "'Harder and Harder,'" 1.

36. See Ashton, McDonald, and Kirkman, "What does 'pornography' mean in the digital age?"

say that not merely one element can alone justify calling something pornography. The intent and content must align with the purpose of sexual arousal to serve another's pleasure. Though this, by definition, excludes the dissemination of sexually explicit material against the will of the subject contained within those materials, I include this within a definition of pornography not to defend it but expose it as an aspect of the systemic issues in pornography. For this work, I will focus on elements that directly pertain to trafficking that cultivate the violence, fraud, and coercion implicit in trafficking. Therefore, I explore three key elements: violence and degrading treatment of women in pornography, exploitation of women financially in pornography, and the markets created by pornography. In each instance, the content, intention, and consumption align to cultivate desires contrary to iconoclastic sex. I will conclude with another reflection on the bases and virtues of iconoclastic sex.

I begin with violence and the degrading treatment of women. Some researchers claim that in recent pornography, women suffer more overt violence and humiliating treatment than their male co-stars.[37] Though researchers debate whether the depiction has increased or not, these images and depictions of sex remain in the repository of pornography. These violent and demeaning acts can range from name-calling to physical violence such as punching and slapping, all the way to depicting sexual assault for a person's pleasure. This impact is widespread and malforms the consumer's imagination, but it also impacts the performer. In a recent documentary, *Hot Girls Wanted*, Rashida Jones explores the impact that pornography has on performers.[38] Though many, as with sex work in general, place choice as a central feature, it neglects the demeaning treatment women face. As one performer notes, upon attending a shoot, she does not know that the scene will be as violent as it is. She agrees to do the scene but leaves traumatized, stating that she was unsure if she could say no. The demand for increased violence in pornography creates the conditions where sex workers must choose to subject themselves to humiliating violence. In addition, the documentary notes the racial and gendered disparities that many performers face that only codify the privilege found elsewhere in sexual ethics.[39] Though the cynical reader will again fall back upon the performer choosing to do this, it is worth noting that in the documentary, many women interviewed arrive in the field under pretenses of modeling or acting.[40] Though the performers

---

37. Long, "Pornography is more than sexual fantasy."
38. Bauer and Gradus, dirs., *Hot Girls Wanted*.
39. See Monk-Turner and Purcell, "Sexual violence in pornography."
40. Bauer and Gradus, dirs., *Hot Girls Wanted*.

have more latitude to leave than those in trafficking, the presence of fraud exists in fundamental levels of pornography.

The presence of pornography in its content is violent and demeaning, the intention of those who produce the pornography is the creation of structural inequalities, and the consumer views this for pleasure—all comes under the critique of iconoclastic sex. The pornography in this dynamic cultivates the affections around harm.[41] Iconoclastic sex creates a more gracious sexuality per the grace and excellence of God, but pornography that demeans does the opposite, and it encourages the demeaning behavior to exist in the broader world too. Iconoclasm defames and defunds the images of sex that cultivate anything less than gracious sex, motivating it to justice and love.

To be clear, this is not the only kind of pornography. As other researchers note, some pornography attempts to showcase intimacy and care.[42] If pornography kindly showcases intimacy between others, is this appropriate? To this, I turn to an example offered by Ray Kurzweil, who thought about how technology enhances the ability for just sex to exist. Pornography, already a kind of technology available for sex, should be understood within Kurzweil's example. "Sex," as P. Travis Kroeker summarizes Kurzweil's understanding, "is merely the episodic manipulation of electronic data."[43] Thus a hyperrealistic form of pornography might solve the violence often found in realties like trafficking. Kroeker continues,

> [Kurzweil] imagines his fourth-grade son's ability to undress his fourth-grade teacher—and manipulate her in any way he desires—without affecting *her*; he imagines the ability to indulge many lovers at once, pleasuring himself by clicking on numerous sites and partners at the same time.[44]

Kurzweil, then, sees the final aim of pornography, namely the best use of media production and technology to cultivate private pleasure through the objectification of another to prevent larger injustice. Does such a reality cultivate virtue? Does the world improve through the ability of a fourth grader to do this? Furthermore, would the sharing of pornography, no matter the intimacy of the actors, for the sake of individual personal pleasure cultivate virtue? One cannot make promises to pornography or the individuals

---

41. The plethora of violent images in pornography cultivates a "genocide culture" that makes women's bodies the site of global violence. See Trzyna, *Pornography and Genocide*.

42. Shor and Seida, "'Harder and Harder'?," 5.

43. Kroeker, *Messianic Political Theology*, 178.

44. Kroeker, *Messianic Political Theology*, 178.

contained therein and pursue their good above all others. The access to such images and content only cultivates easy access to success without the need to cultivate justice, love, humility, or truthfulness. Sex must be the culmination of the series of actions that show the significance and sacredness of a body. This possibility of locating sex in a constellation of practices cannot occur in the production and consumption of pornography.

In addition to these structural issues, like all sex work, pornography creates a sex market. Many women who experience trafficking first do so through the distribution of a recording of an individual's sexual assault.[45] Those who experience trafficking have recorded their sexual exploitation distributed via third-party sites. For example, in 2020, a *New York Times* article detailed the sexual exploitation available for viewing on the pornography service Pornhub.[46] Various sources comment that individuals can easily access videos and images of women in trafficking relationships. Though a crackdown has begun on this site and others, they use these videos to make a profit and make little effort to differentiate between videos made and distributed with consent and those without consent. One cannot justly consume content from these sites, but they continue to inform and support pornography of this kind.

To this end, no account of pornography today can proceed without an account of the rise of social media sites such as OnlyFans that allows individuals in other professions and pornography producers to make pornography. Launched in 2016 by Tim Stokely, OnlyFans began as a means for content creators to share video clips and images of their work directly to fans. Initially, the site was not primarily for selling sexual content; however, in 2018, the company began to feature more explicit sexual content. The reality behind much of pornography (including OnlyFans), even though many in the industry claim it exists to promote a sex-positive purpose for pornography, is money. OnlyFans and other services serve the ends of what Alan Roxburgh calls "Modernity's Wager," namely to use one's assets to produce a financial gain.[47] OnlyFans allows users to produce their content and control the message it provides.

OnlyFans is more equitable than other forms of production. However, it still has its flaws. For example, in recent years, celebrities began using the platform to sell more sexually explicit images and content. Most famously among them was former Disney child star Bella Thorne. In most cases, the celebrities that joined the platform made massive amounts of money on

---

45. See MacKinnon, "Pornography as trafficking."
46. Kristof, "Children of Pornhub."
47. Branson and Roxburgh, *Leadership, God's Agency, & Disruptions*, 35–36.

the site. Thorne, for example, made one million dollars on her first day on the platform, which led to an explosion in sales on the site and exposure of OnlyFans to a broader audience. The only problem emerging from this occurrence was the sex workers on the site. The corporate structure of OnlyFans platformed celebrities, but the sex workers already on the site describe celebrity presence as one that draws attention and money away from their work. In short, many critics refer to Bella Thorne's actions as "gentrifying" OnlyFans.

Two tensions in OnlyFans should prompt theological and ethical reflection. First, sex workers critique celebrities like Thorne while missing their place on the hierarchy. As E. J. Dickson, a reporter for *Rolling Stone*, states in an interview on the documentary *OnlyFans: Selling Sexy*, "OnlyFans is not fully transparent about its ties to the adult industry because it wants to profit off of its sex worker user base while simultaneously making room for itself to grow further by attracting mainstream influencers."[48] Dickson no doubt names a lack of transparency in the site; however, this same recognition fails to see how the sex workers participate in a similar hierarchy where Bella Thorne exists at the top, sex workers on the site in the middle, and trafficked individuals at the bottom. The hierarchy creates a market where sex can be bought and sold. To recall Srinivasan, sex today is no more than a market of exchange. Like all markets, the macro-level informs the micro-level; thus, exploitation is a necessary condition of the market's power. To package sex as a product creates a demand that can only be satisfied through more excellent purchasing; as Augustine teaches in *Confessions*, vigorous sexual expression experiences significant atrophy that perpetuates the need for greater consumption. Absent the theological grounding of sex in the broader ethics of sexuality as a means to affirm and express the goodness of creaturely life, these markets thrive on diminishment and objectification. The creation of sexual markets normalizes the buying and selling of sex without much concern, like in the food industry, for the stories behind the product that one buys. OnlyFans, though not the fault of the individuals struggling for subsistence, participates in such a normalizing commodification.

Second, OnlyFans places economic profit as a central good that matters concerning sexuality. To be clear, this is not the only reason people make content on OnlyFans. Content creators acknowledge their desire to showcase their bodies' confidence and goodness. However, experts and sex workers on the platform justify content choices and presence through economic arguments more often than others. One example helpfully names the

---

48. E. J. Dickson in Baker, dir., *OnlyFans*.

concerns raised by such a posture. In addition to E. J. Dickson, the directors and producers of *OnlyFans: Selling Sexy,* shine a light on the kinds of modifications some women feel they must make to their bodies to earn the most money. Sex therapist and educator Shan Boodram discusses the rationale behind such a decision while a video of a young woman recovering from breast enhancement surgery plays in the background. Boodram states,

> Athletes go through extreme lengths to make their body perform in certain ways, as a sex worker, why should you be stigmatized for going through those exact same or similar lengths to make your body perform a certain way for optimal results? Personally, I think my litmus for it would be if I'm getting plastic surgery because it's a personal decision that I'm making because I want to get the best result from my body, the best results from the experience of sharing my body with the world and my business. That would be a place of empowerment.[49]

Boodram's quote shares the desire of many that sexual capital should be legitimized alongside other forms of capital, such as intellectual capital. To again share a concern about the economy, when preference is the measure, there exists no way to interrogate desires. Take, for example, the language of empowerment used by Boodram and Ratajkowski's experience. Empowerment through the shaping of oneself to the desires of another does not yield true empowerment. Furthermore, Grant argues that empowerment is a dynamic, not attainment through absolute market freedom.

Not only must the worker make changes to their body to codify themselves more perfectly into an economy of sexual capital for others to buy, but also for themselves. This capitulation, while economically advantageous, only exacerbates the code of the image and the economy upon which it is traded. Grace resists such a drastic change and claims that the body is significant no matter its shape, color, or abilities, not to condemn the worker but to cultivate a space where a new life can emerge transformed beyond literalized images and desires.

It should be clear that there is a double prescription to approach. Justice as the attention to an individual reality as they are now and who they will be in the future cannot fit inside the dissemination of pornography. The packaging of pornography is only so occasional and limited that it lacks a future-oriented approach because one cannot make promises to pornography. Furthermore, the way that pornography only supports the image-based perspective on sexuality runs counter to iconoclasm. The images of good sex presented in pornography narrow who is worthy or capable of good

---

49. Shan Boodram in Baker, dir., *OnlyFans*.

sex. To be clear, the iconoclastic approach to pornography cannot reify purity in such a way as to push future sex workers away from their beloved community. Instead, justice, through iconoclasm, must guide sexual ethics. Paying attention to the performer's individuality is not to find pleasure in the structures of injustice under which they struggle to survive. Instead, it is to cultivate a series of practices that enable an avenue to a different world and invite all to a different justice. Nevertheless, the conditions of the world must shift. Sex workers can impact the structures on their terms and find new expressions of sexuality that are loving, empowering, and gracious. In either case, humility must require that those who consume cannot purchase other bodies to own, and even those who sell must look and see the markets in which they participate. Only together, through the elimination of consumer and producer, can the market be destroyed.

Another reason for a critical lens in pornography is covenant. As already stated with the sex worker in general, one cannot make promises to the one who produces pornography beyond a one-time financial exchange. Even if these exchanges last long, promises require more extensive commitments of love and truthfulness to one another. The intimacy cultivated in the context of a constellation of promises to help another flourish cannot occur through a brief exchange. Instead, sex, and the virtues necessary to practice it, must come as the culmination of making and keeping promises. Medically, porn can destroy the intimacy between partners through the creation of sexual dysfunction (i.e., porn-induced erectile dysfunction) and the breaking of promises of fidelity. One cannot cultivate the virtues necessary to commit to promises when the sexual activity one engages in culminates in pornographic consumption. In iconoclastic sex, one cannot consume others. That being said, inside the reality of covenantal love, there is room for partners to make sexual content for one another. For example, the covenantal partner takes intimate photos of themselves as a means to feel their empowerment and significance as well as a gift to one's partner to cultivate affection, desire, and appreciation for themselves and the beloved participating within the covenantal bond. The point is this: the making of content is not the issue, but the virtue it cultivates, the purpose of the content, and the love it encourages.

In sum, sex work and pornography beg the question of whether the consumption and production of sex can fit within the rubric of iconoclastic sex. The discussion offered above illustrates the complexities of both realities. The approach to sex workers cannot be mere condemnation with no responsibility to the bodies that actions impact or considering the agency of the sex workers both must be honored, but there is another insight buried in the background of traditional approaches to sex workers. Individuals pursue sex work and pornography, either through OnlyFans or other means, due to the lack of grace in many circles around the topic of sex. The argument for good sex proposed above illustrates that good sex shows the significance of another. This significance is the place to enter into the world of the one who seeks sex work as a means of empowerment. Those who see sex as that which brings confidence and affirms their humanity as God intended often move outside the church. People use OnlyFans because they see how sex recognizes the value and significance of one's sacred character. To be clear, God does intend sex to affirm the dignity of another. However, the approach offered in my account of sexual ethics and the one who pursues sex work will differ dramatically; each shares this foundational claim. Only when we see that those who engage in sex work do not lack sexual ethics and attempt to affirm the goodness of another in their way, do we find an entry point into a conversation. The error that the sex worker, expressing free choice, makes is that they overcorrect and move sexual ethics to individual attainment, much like the principles of codes and purity. In their quest for liberation, the culture becomes blind to the structural inequality that it creates. Diving more deeply inside the circle of economics is not empowerment.

Trafficking and Purity: Can Sex Be Bought and Sold?

The move to a more sex-positive account of sexuality in Christianity is necessary. Christians must know that sex is a good thing. However, this sex positivity must also be open to the fact that sex is not liberating or a happy occasion for everyone. The one who experience violence and shame as a direct result of the sale of sex must be considered. We can look at Tracy, a survivor of trafficking, who spent years on the streets performing sex for sale. She stated,

> Yeah, you know, and then like and then it got to the point where in my relationships and, you know, the shit that happened to me on the streets, whether . . . I was a willing party for money or not . . . I got a really messed up outlook on sex for a long time like. I had a really messed up outlook on men in general for a while where I felt like I've never been a thief more . . . But there came a point where I started robbing some of those guys like not hurting them just taking [from] them and running. Because I felt like anytime I let you touch me for money, you take something from me I that can't ever get back. So I'm gonna take everything I can from you . . .

In Tracy's words we find a kernel of Kate Ward's claim that work is not inherently dignified. Elevating sex work to work would not do away with these pains and formations. Again, Tracy does not give license to the position that anyone who works in sex work becomes a thief, but rather she articulates a pain emerging from the continual traumas of this work. Sex work as exchange is a code just like purity, it merely shifts what commodity and what kinds of capital one permits. To clarify again, the answer is not rearranging the structure. As a people, humans must learn to live in an entirely new way, one free of the kinds of false liberation found within all code-making schemes. Instead, we need new peoplehood on the far side of code exploitation. Here, we find a God who goes about in the dust of shared humanity even to the point of death to usher a pilgrim people into a new life.

PART III: RELATIONSHIPS BEYOND SEXUAL CAPITAL

Though not every person will find themselves in the web of trafficking and the structural problems of sex work, all people find themselves confronted with human relationships. Relationships are not the primary reason for trafficking, but they nonetheless provide the context for social exclusion in many circumstances. How the communities of faith and those outside such communities structure their romantic lives possesses profound consequences for the surrounding world. For instance, when one particular form of relationships codes into moral, civil, and economic law, it creates the conditions around specific impenetrable social networks that exist and leaves some in precarious vulnerability. The goal is not to cease relationships but rather to cultivate virtuous relationships that are in open, porous communities. The receptive community recognizes that its relationships do not exist in a state of privilege but must humbly remain open to receive the other. The virtues practiced in specific preferential relationships must transfer to neighbors in unique and empowering ways. In short, preferential and romantic relationships must become ways to thicken our accounts of justice, love, humility, and truthfulness while not losing the witnesses of those beyond.

To this end, I discuss what one would find in most books on sexual ethics, namely a discussion on family, marriage, and children without departing from primary concern for survivors of trafficking and those in purity culture. If the previous section detailed the role purity plays in preventing our reception of the sex worker, then this section challenges privilege that argues for personal rights against the needs of the other. To be clear, when I use privilege in this context, I refer to the Kantian privilege detailed in chapter 1, namely that a structure of moral thought arises from the dominant male perspective centered on personal responsibility. I seek to offer a different imagination on how to structure relationships, not according to code, but the virtues and testimonies that arise from the indicative of God's command. I argue that our relationships form the most practical way to resist trafficking. The very practice of raising children, for example, can impact the reality of trafficking. Thus, the preceding reflection first examines the *Haustaflen* as the traditional means by which the privileged position occurs through the historical formation of a sexual and relational hierarchy, wherein women, children, and enslaved people are "available" to men as a means of convenience to the male perspective.

Haustafeln (The Household Codes): Weeding through Problematic Relations

For the Christian tradition, the group of writings in letters attributed to Pauline and Petrine authorship referred to as the Household Codes (*Haustafeln*) influences sexual relationships to this day.[50] The main issues are the strictly Pauline apologetics for the place of Christianity within the fold of the already existing social order of the Roman Empire.[51] The New Testament attempts to show how Christian community does not wish to upset the social order of the Roman Empire. Despite this fact, there are distinctive theological features that Paul does offer to make it a matter of Christian moral responsibility.

Though modern readers of the text might bristle against the *haustafeln*, readers of the Bible must have clear interpretations of this text as a means to resist domestic violence so prevalent in trafficking. Richard Hays shows that four distinctive features help us understand the theological import of the *haustafeln* for moral reflection.[52] Hays's reflection centers on Ephesians, but we can see the import of other passages and weaknesses of other passages. First, in the letters, a general prescription "be subject to one another out of reverence for Christ" (Eph 5:21).[53] Second, "the formal structure of the code is unusual in its pattern of addressing the subordinate persons in the social order (wives, children, and slaves) as moral agents who must *choose*

---

50. The Household Codes include Colossians 3: 18–4:1, Ephesians 5:21–6:9, 1 Peter 2:18–3:7, 1 Timothy 2:8–15, 5:1–2, 6:1–2, and Titus 2:1–10, 3:1.

51. Meeks, *First Urban Christians*, 76.

52. Hays, *Moral Vision of the New Testament*, 64–65.

53. Hays, *Moral Vision of the New Testament*, 65.

to 'be subject.'"[54] Christ's presence is abnormal for ancient *haustafeln* that only addressed the "holders of power" and instructed them on how to treat those under them. Third, the *haustafeln* in the New Testament "is notable for its reciprocity. It does not merely call upon the less powerful to submit (as does, e.g., Titus 2:9–10); it equally charges the more powerful (husbands, fathers, and masters) to act with gentleness toward and concern for those over whom they hold authority."[55] Briefly, this notion seems to collapse back on Hays's second point, fulfilling the primary role of *haustafeln* to inform the powerful. Fourth, "the commandments in this code are given an explicitly theological elaboration that seeks to show how these norms are warranted by the gospel."[56] For better or worse, this last point is the chief achievement of the Pauline and Petrine texts of the *haustafeln*. It gives a theological reading of current social norms to keep them in place. As has been said, the *haustafeln* is an apology for the fledgling Christian community to the Roman Empire. However, Hays does show that there is a subversive purpose, no matter how slight, that illustrates a social defiance.

In order to bring the conversation forward, contemporary readers of the text should read liberative critiques alongside these texts. One such critique that helps us understand the issues at stake in the reading of the *haustafeln* is Clarice Martin's reading. Turning Hays on his head, Martin presents the *haustafeln* as Christians upholding the social structures of domination and giving it a christological depth, thus using Christianity to legitimize specific orders of the world.[57] So it is fitting that women and children were in their subordinated state (Col 2:18; Eph 5:22–4).[58] Martin shows that readings of the text that reify domination cannot be the moral instructions of the text for today on the far side of slavery, colonialism, child abuse, sexism, and racism. Interpreters of Scripture must resist the temptation to present the *haustafeln* to the world in patriarchal terms and instead learn to read them in liberating terms, following the paradigm offered to readers in Paul's baptismal formula in Galatians 3:28–29. This hermeneutic should be privileged over the *haustafeln*, and any texts that do not appeal to this paradigm are false moral readings of the text. For we are not in the image of God in a hierarchical, male-dominated society, but each in their agency (male, female, and child), and all share the gospel's promise.

---

54. Hays, *Moral Vision of the New Testament*, 65.
55. Hays, *Moral Vision of the New Testament*, 65.
56. Hays, *Moral Vision of the New Testament*, 65.
57. Martin, "Haustafeln," 210.
58. Martin, "Haustafeln," 210.

Another helpful critique lies with feminist biblical scholar Elizabeth Schüssler Fiorenza. In her landmark work, *In Memory of Her*, Schüssler Fiorenza seeks a reconstruction of the forgotten women in the text. The inspiration for the title of her book comes from Mark 14: 3–9, of the woman who anoints Jesus' feet and proclaims, "And truly I say to you, wherever the gospel is preached in the whole world, what she has done will be told in memory of her" (Mark 14:9, NRSV). This type of reconstruction unveils those suppressed in the text outside the *haustafeln*. Schüsser Fiorenza's response to the *haustafeln* then is not just a reading of the various passages through Galatians 3:28, as does Martin, but rather a "Subversive Remembering." She draws attention to the patriarchal orders "in order to unmask them," and to recover a "'dangerous memory' that reclaims our foremothers' and foresisters' suffering and struggles through the subversive power of the critically remembered past."[59] Memory is not dismissive but reconstructive. She first recognizes the Bible as a prototype rather than an archetype. She writes,

> Both archetype and prototype denote original models. However, an archetype is an ideal form that establishes a regular timeless pattern, whereas a prototype is not a binding timeless pattern or principle. A prototype, therefore, is critically open to the possibility of its transformation.[60]

Therefore, we bring the conversation forward for moral instruction "to extrapolate new social-ecclesial structures, while preserving the liberating biblical vision by engendering new structural formations that belong to that vision."[61] The memory gives us the approximate *telos* of suffering women in the Bible and then searches its prototypical source for visions of this redemption of social order.

The redemption of the social order through creative, redemptive reconstructions of the *haustafeln* can be read through the text, as Schüssler Fiorenza suggests. For example, moral instruction arises from the larger frameworks of Paul's apocalyptic theology. As J. Christiaan Beker writes, the apocalyptic message of Paul is that "the righteousness of God that has dawned with the death and resurrection of Christ [that] must be conveyed to all people as God's liberating act for his creation."[62] This is the message Schüssler Fiorenza believes is possible in the prototypical understanding of

---

59. Schüssler Fiorenza, *Bread Not Stone*, 86, quoted in Hays, *Moral Vision of the New Testament*, 276.

60. Schüssler Fiorenza, *In Memory of Her*, 33.

61. Schüssler Fiorenza, *In Memory of Her*, 34.

62. Beker, *Paul the Apostle*, 7.

the text because it tells of this message of God. However, it is E. Elizabeth Johnson who helps us bring Paul's apocalyptic gospel to bear in light of the *haustafeln*. As she notes, Paul upholds traditional family roles within the state, as argued by Richard Hays and Clarice Martin. However, Johnson writes,

> The "not-enough" of conventional Greco-Roman family honor required hierarchical and rigidly defined household structure to maintain itself. Everyone's well-being depended on his or her protecting the honor of the *paterfamilias*. Paul, however, speaks of an over-abundance of grace, and the revelation of God's saving power—of God's redemptive wrath and justice—[and] inevitably calls into question the self-preserving, anxiety-inducing preoccupation with status maintenance. The invasion of God's new age both disorients the prevailing values of the old world and reorients believers to live in the new. The reversal of values so familiar from other apocalyptic literature of the day appears in Paul largely as a reversal of status . . . The members of the household of faith (Gal 6:10) are not only an alternative household; they are the new creation (v.15)![63]

The apocalyptic reading of the *haustafeln* upends its social conventions through the radical, disorienting Christ-event. One sees this clearly through a parallel reading between the *haustafeln* in Paul's letters. For example, one must read the word "be subject" (τάσσω) in the various texts of the *haustafeln* under the eschatological passage in 1 Corinthians 15:27. Here, Paul uses the same root to argue for God's subjection of everything to Christ. Paul writes, "God has put all things in *subjection* (ὑπο-τάσσω) under his feet" (NRSV). Paul argues that God puts "every ruler and every authority and power" (15:24) under Christ's feet. One must read the patriarchal and abusive orders of the *haustafeln* with the powers and rulers of the age. Therefore, reading Paul against the *haustafeln* provides a prototypical reading of the text wherein the fallen orders apocalyptically find their defeat in the Christ-event. Jesus is truly the first fruit in that he brings to life, and where Christ shall reign, namely in the church, these orders are already defeated. Our possibilities for moral autonomy, apart from systemic orders that lead to abuse and subjugation, come from Christ's victory over the fallen orders of sin. This victory lives in the community where we are not subject to fallen orders like the *haustaflen*, but rather, as Paul exhorts, "Do not be conformed to this world, but be transformed by the renewing of your minds, so that

---

63. Johnson, "Apocalyptic Family Values," 43.

you may discern what is the will of God—what is good and acceptable and perfect" (Rom 12:2, NRSV).

As such, Paul's account of eschatological victory helps reorient the various relationships central to the *haustafeln*. In this study, one finds that trafficking occurs due to bad relationships: domestic abuse, child abuse, neglect, and even parents trafficking their children for money. The *haustafeln* addresses these relationships precisely, and the more normative reading utilizes them as justification for coercive male headship. In such a reading, Eve is available to Adam. In such a system, male headship is a central feature of a well-formed household and society. Utilizing the upending eschatological logic of Paul and the iconoclastic sexual ethics presented in this chapter, I explore two elements of the *haustafeln* to envision different relationships.

Men and Women

Only certain *kinds* of relationships exist within the *haustafeln*, namely wives to husbands, children to parents, and slaves to masters. Though many relationships remain to be discussed, one relationship emerging from the *haustafeln* requires attention, namely man to woman. The history of patriarchal domination is at the heart of the ethics between man and woman, which bears out in our study of trafficking and purity culture. All women interviewed from groups of trafficking reported male abuse, and the majority in the purity culture group also reported this occurrence. The connection between abuse, secrecy, and male domination cultivates such a posture toward women that a shift to a feminist perspective will address. Patriarchy must be challenged and experience iconoclasm of literalized desire, for male headship limits openness. Though the *haustafeln* talks specifically about marriage, it also provides an entire social logic that gives ontological priority to men over women. Therefore, I argue that the image of man as head must be defunded iconoclastically to motivate the possibility of positive relations between men and women, thus resisting the violence that leads to trafficking. I focus on this account here to defame the violence cultivated in this headship language that, when mobilized socially, can result in the violence of trafficking.

Although criticized for his stance on men and women, Karl Barth provides the possibility of the moral vision of their relations where one does not lord over the other, and each peruse good ends in God. Here we utilize the positive relationship between Jesus Christ and the Old Testament witness. Covenant is central to Barth's theology of creation, and even the creation of man and woman both as a marriage relationship and individually.[64] Barth outright rejects that the male mirrors God in the covenant with creation.[65] Instead, Barth summons God's relationship with Israel to show a new possibility for human marriage that does not originate in people. Because God creates, reconciles, and redeems humanity, there is a unique possibility for humans in relationships.[66]

Barth's emphasis introduces a third party, namely Christ. Therefore, man and woman are no longer reducible to an I-Thou relationship organized under the headship language of husband and wife, and therefore an analogy for social humanity's relationship to God. In short, Barth removes the idea that one can read the husband ontologically as God and humanity as the wife, in a manner that might cultivate male privilege on the ground. Instead, marriage is this relationship of mutuality that includes the life of God as its core.[67]

Barth is often unclear about how this works out; though he is a great resource, he can be unclear. For example, Eugene Rogers names this in his work on sexuality and marriage. He writes, "The I-Thou phenomenology tends to reduce co-humanity to co-individuality."[68] To summon this logic, even to rework it, carries with it this danger. So even when we use it to deconstruct domestic violence, the language can haunt our discussions of man and woman. However, Barth's chief insight remains that all relations must run through a christological mediation, not because Christ is a man, but because Christ is the source of *shared* humanity. Barth writes, "The man Jesus is Himself the revealing Word of God, He is the source of our knowledge of the nature of [humanity] as created by God."[69]

Traditionally, the gendered understanding of humanity codes certain assumptions about qualitative differences in gender as a mapping of the divine onto humanity. A significant portion of the social exclusion model of sexual ethics relies on this coding. Multitude confronting the history of Christianity possesses significant examples of a theology of sex, body, and sexual difference coded within doctrines of the Trinity, which code specific models of gendered hierarchies into the very fabric of the life of the triune God and thus reflected back onto gender. Such hierarchies exist within purity code realism wherein a women's sexuality is available to men. Linn

---

64. Barth, *Church Dogmatics III.1*, 315.
65. Barth, *Church Dogmatics III.1*, 318.
66. Barth, *Church Dogmatics III.1*, 318.
67. Barth, *Church Dogmatics III.1*, 318.
68. Rogers Jr., *Sexuality and the Christian Body*, 184.
69. Barth, *Church Dogmatics III.2*, 3.

Tonstad writes that these theologies "insert an over-againstness between the Father and the Son that ultimately subordinates the Son to the Father and betrays the biblical insight that who has seen Jesus has seen the Father."[70] The transmutation of subordination in the life of the Trinity merely justifies certain elements of finitude into the life of God and the social structures associated with them. Divine subordination, even relationally, justifies power social metaphors such as the subordination of women to men.[71] Mapping such sinful realities into the very life of God codes a specific social order predicated on a "dubious axiom" that grounds human relations in the life of God.[72] Tonstad recognizes that such mapping only exists through available social metaphors that we seek to justify according to sacred life.

Tonstad undoes these harmful elements of trinitarian theology by employing an orthodox interpretation of the Trinity. As Tonstad argues, theologians need "the transformative work of a God who is not subjected to the same antinomies as humankind."[73] The antinomies of sexual difference appear in the coding of the language of sexual difference as a difference between males and females. While appearing innocuous on the surface, this trinitarian resource utilizes the language of Eve's procession from Adam to smuggle a kind of natural theology of sexual hierarchy into the Trinity.[74] Eve proceeds from Adam in this comparison and, though maintaining equality in difference, still submits to a fundamental priority and origin.[75] Adam "makes room" for Eve as a means to assert her equality with him, but the originate motion remains in the background as lesser to the more remarkable, subordinate to the subordinator. Eve and Adam temper, functionally, the Father's relation to the Son as one of origin, not ontologically, but as the begetter to the begotten. Thus, Eve and Adam, like Eve to Mary, code an antinomy into the very life of God.

Tonstad uses a different metaphor to resist the antinomies of human relationships that code submission, namely light. This metaphor does not change the personhood of the members of the Trinity but rather gestures to a word the theologian must say but not understand concerning the

70. Tonstad, *God and Difference*, 14.

71. In the space here, I cannot adequately summarize the nuance of Tonstad's argument other than reference her excellent analysis of the theologians and arguments that undergird this analysis. Particularly, Tonstad critiques three prominent theologians who write about sexed and sexual relations in the triune life. See Tonstad, *God and Difference*, 27–132.

72. Tonstad, *God and Difference*, 14.

73. Tonstad, *God and Difference*, 17.

74. Tonstad, *God and Difference*, 204–5.

75. Tonstad, *God and Difference*, 204.

articulation of the triune life. Light, contrarily, is a biblical language to speak about God. It is, as Tonstad argues, the image of "the communion God establishes, in which human beings live together with God and each other in a glorious city situated in a renewed and recreated earth."[76] The image here is radiant light that does not have an origin or source.[77] Furthermore, light exists in the same space without having to make room for other rays of light. Each person of the Trinity possesses what belongs to one another. As Tonstad writes, "Each person has an irreversible relationship to the others but where relationships are not relations of origin but of intensification or gift."[78] This ordered circle gives and receives simultaneously; each member receives only what they are given eternally but shapes the gift according to their unique personhood.[79] The persons of the Trinity do not compete for glorification in the cross but mutually share the space to enjoy one another.

Tonstad's description of the noncompetitive triune fellowship creates a saving action for humanity in the cross and resurrection. Therefore, the triune Lord does not merely exist and authorize certain relations but saves humanity for renewed fellowship and intimacy with God and related life.[80] God, in short, reconciles and empowers humanity to have relationships where an order of relation need not be and exists only by grace. By sharing in God's triune life, creation can live in mutually existing space without competition as the rays of light in communion.

That the impersonal nature of this description of the Trinity that does not map human relations into it should not alarm. To state that the Trinity lacks a foundation in human gendered relations suggests that God's freedom is above human freedom, not literalized. Thus, a move to a less anthropomorphic vision of God motivates human communion by removing the foundational relations as a key to communion. In short, the saving event opens and blasphemes human relations as an *a priori* of human social networks. The Trinity does not prescribe but ignites all human relationships. To borrow from Robert Jenson, "God is a great *fugue*."[81] As a fugue, the triune Lord bathes humanity in its overabundant melody. Yet, as Tonstad suggests, light is the proper language to account for the non-anthropomorphic language. Deepening this language, theologian Katherine Sonderegger argues

---

76. Tonstad, *God and Difference*, 228.
77. Tonstad, *God and Difference*, 228.
78. Tonstad, *God and Difference*, 228.
79. Tonstad, *God and Difference*, 229.
80. Tonstad, *God and Difference*, 238.
81. Jenson, *Systematic Theology*, 236.

that not only is God in Trinity abundant light but also a fire that sets ablaze.[82] God thus sets fire to all creation, vivifying it with divine life so it might teem with life. In this way, God "intends" creation by welcoming creation with divine vitality and freedom.[83]

Remaining with Sonderegger, such divine fire also reorients holiness and purity in God's life. I do not plan to recover purity as a helpful concept when discussing sexuality, but God's purity blasphemes the social exclusion of purity culture. God's light is impure in the standards of purity set forth by human code-making. One sees this impurity even in the language of Nicea that blasphemes all structures of being and knowing available to humans. Sonderegger envisions the holiness from this enlivening divine life as healing, not exclusionary. She writes, "It cleans and purifies; it contains fathomless 'energy' and it burns, cauterizes, scars."[84] In short, God's holiness is such that it cleans, heals, and leaves its mark. God's fire destroys even as it heals. However, to say that God "cleans" is not a reification of the purity system but rather its end or, as Sonderegger argues, its undoing.[85] Standing before a holy God in this is to witness a "living shape" for the Christian life, namely one that "is self-giving, the pouring out of a life as gift, and it is receiving, welcoming, taking up, and taking home the offering as one's own very life."[86] No longer can a self-emptying for the sake of the originate define the triune fellowship, but only a giving that is also receiving, holiness in the form of welcoming and home bounding. Refusing to privilege relations to Trinity and instead privilege this divine shape heals the wounds of social exclusion and ushers creation back into intimacy, fellowship, and grace.

Utilizing Tonstad and Sonderegger illustrates that the triune Lord does not authorize purity, patriarchy, or social exclusion. Instead, purity in God's holy radiance draws life into God. As Sonderegger writes, to "know this God, the Living Lord, is to hunger and delight and hunger once more. Theology should pant after its God, the love that is better than wine, for God is beautiful, truly lovely, the one whose Eyes are like doves. Eat, friends—all theology should ring out with this invitation—drink and be drunk with love."[87] As with Peter in Acts 10, God sets the heart of our hunger and desire ablaze.[88] God moves our desire, as with Peter, outside the boundaries of

---

82. Sonderegger, *Systematic Theology Volume 1*, 317.
83. Sonderegger, *Systematic Theology Volume 1*, 318.
84. Sonderegger, *Systematic Theology Volume 2*, 358.
85. Sonderegger, *Systematic Theology Volume 2*, 359.
86. Sonderegger, *Systematic Theology Volume 2*, 478.
87. Sonderegger, *Systematic Theology Volume 2*, 472.
88. Jennings, *Acts*, 106–7.

cultural and religious purity that stores up goodness and holiness for the self alone as a possession. God blasphemes all social exclusion at the site of this desire for possession by remaining with the excluded, and all theology must learn to speak from the outside. As Tonstad argues, to "speak theologically from outside intelligibility does not mean the cessation of theological speech; it means that such speech stands under the sign of judgment and cannot pretend to ultimacy or finality."[89] In short, Tonstad argues for a theology "that cannot close its borders for fear of shutting Christ out."[90] This kind of theological speech is iconoclastic, a holy blasphemy that pulls the idols of social exclusion to the ground.

Such sexual ethics emerges from the triune life as an iconoclasm of fidelity. It witnesses to a sexual ethic between people that exists within the same space without competition. An iconoclasm of the coded structures of gender opens humanity up to welcome and brings home all who hunger and thirst for belonging. Sex, thus, is not a metric by which the community can code its neighbors as either pure or impure, but instead forms relations that speak deeply from the place of hunger for belonging.

Tonstad illustrates the misplaced language of headship and submission as a coded, anthropomorphized depiction for God that only allows for patriarchal interpretations of gender. Such divine authorization for submission exacerbates the *haustafeln*, yielding cultures of abuse even in ecclesial communities. For men this is an especially pressing issue. Sexual ethics must shift to an understanding of gender that does not contain violence. Barth anticipated this in his more extensive anthropological reflections. As with the *imago Dei*, Barth does not envision dormant accounts of humanity and human subjectivity to be claimed as possession. Instead, Barth positions humanity under an eschatological light. In Barth's first dogmatic cycle, entitled the *Göttingen Dogmatics*, he provocatively defines humanity as on a pilgrimage.[91] It is difficult to grasp here if one does not read it along with his eschatological treatise, *The Resurrection of the Dead*. One is not identical to what they will yet be. Barth writes in the *Göttingen Dogmatics*, "[humanity's] home is with God."[92] However, the fact is that humanity is not yet home. Thus, Barth's pilgrimage language collectively illustrates the journey not of individuals but humanity. As Barth indicates, there is a contradiction between their fallen state and their true home. The contradiction is one that humanity cannot overcome, and there is no synthesis between

---

89. Tonstad, *God and Difference*, 276.
90. Tonstad, *God and Difference*, 276.
91. Barth, *Göttingen Dogmatics*, 72–83.
92. Barth, *Göttingen Dogmatics*, 73.

this contradiction.[93] Furthermore, there is no way to settle the question of humanity but in God.[94] If humanity is more properly understood as a pilgrimage, then humanity is not a list of universal predicates divided into neat categories. Rather, humanity is a question asked ever anew in each age that cannot be immediately perceived or anticipated. Thus, humanity is a dynamic portrait always needing correction, considering the paradoxes that come along with the contradiction in each age. The universal aspect of humanity, if it can be called this, is its relation to God, which decenters humanity from itself and, thus, ceases to privilege certain forms over and against others. It does not literalize any one picture of humanity but opens humanity to continual transformation through iconoclasm. Humanity only finds itself through its encounter with God and has no final city here on earth and no privileged status. Barth does not then assume a Kantian agency with a particular person with a specific agency but leaves humanity open-ended for necessary correction. A continual need to blaspheme the predicates that become idols must continue in relationship to our theological anthropology. In short, no gender privilege exists in the contradiction; each can stand equally before God.

Trafficking and Purity: Men and Women

Though more relationships *must* be considered as sites of resistance against the code fetish formation, specific attention must be named here between men and women. The attention and focus on men and women does not diminish the need to speak about other genders and other relationships. However, it does take seriously the need to deal with one of the largest factors at the heart of trafficking and purity culture, namely patriarchy. There is a presumption in the stories of the women surveyed that their bodies belonged to another for the sake of sexual pleasure. Many experienced grotesque sexual abuse or manipulation at a young age from a man. For survivors, primarily men treated their bodies as property purchased by them and for those in purity culture, and, as already indicated by Terry, their bodies belong to their future husband. The presumption, as stated at the outset of this section, of women's bodies belonging to men must experience the most radical shift. This relationship, more than most, indicates a contributing factor in trafficking and it strongly influences purity culture. Thus, a place of divinely sanctioned headship and privilege meets an iconoclasm of fidelity in pilgrimage where human subjectivity is decentered from itself

93. Barth, *Göttingen Dogmatics*, 78.
94. Barth, *Göttingen Dogmatics*, 80–84, 86.

and recentered into God's divine command. The universal in the human is not a set of predicates about humanity such as the predicates that make up a universal account of gender. The command that calls to love, as in Barth's theology, arising from reconciliation, is a question put to humanity. This question is the universal that continually challenges our relation to God and one another. Thus, it is not about locating specific intrinsic universal understanding of gender, but how God interrogates our embodiment in order to call it to the Good.

Marriage

Though other relationships remain to be explored, marriage is a central concern for our study of purity and trafficking. For in marriage is the center of purity concern and that metric by which many exclude those who experience trafficking. In culture, marriage can prevent just relations through how culture captures and idolizes it. The purpose of iconoclastic sex is to deconstruct the centrality that certain idols play in sexual ethics, especially the relational violence that can occur according to specific structures. If marriage serves as a balm to the violence, sexual objectification, and sinful marriage accounts, then a positive, constructive alternative must arise while maintaining virtuous reception. To this end, I utilize David Matzko McCarthy's understanding of marriage as a "grace-filled friendship within the fellowship of the Church" to locate marriage as a possible expression of iconoclastic sex.[95]

As the beginning of romantic societal structuring, marriage mobilizes an entire economy of romance that funds everything from dating applications to prime-time television. Thus, love becomes a romantic sentiment packaged to perpetuate certain kinds of subjects and relationships. As Hauerwas and Verhey indicate, romanticism's "basic assumption is that love is a necessary (and sufficient) condition for sex and marriage."[96] The result is that romance is a pre-moral requisite for sex, which short circuits moral reasoning, thus preventing real engagement with sexual ethics. Sex, then, satisfies a longing for adventure and excitement. Marriage, in the commodified romantic model, arises from a neoliberal fantasy that directs individual agency into purchasing power. The industry around romance makes this love and adventure a commodity one can buy and sell. Therefore, it is neither loving nor adventurous though it does produce a character. Sex, in the romantic mindset, is about passion and moments, which themselves can be

---

95. McCarthy, "Becoming One Flesh," 317.
96. Hauerwas and Verhey, "From Conduct to Character," 13.

profound. As such, the romantic mindset cultivates a character and set of practices.

To recall, the shift to covenant is not a prescription only for purity codes. There is no condition or idol required. Instead, the goal is to give marriage a larger theological context that disrupts marriage's neoliberal, cultural fantasy. Marriage in the context of covenant centers on commitment as the expression of the marital bond. Like the romance model, it does serve the needs and interests of the individual measure, but in covenant, the interests of the whole community emerge. Covenant and mutuality locates one's sexual life as an aspect of communal concern. Sex includes others, thus it is a social concern even if performed alone. Who we are as people does cultivate a specific community. Even those who claim sex is a purely private act neglect that the subject's relationships always cultivate virtues that manifest in public arenas. Those relationships that cultivate abuse, for example, impact the individuals in the relationship and its permissiveness to others. The vows one makes in covenant are not only for the honoring of another agency and the development of mutuality but a reflexive promise from and to the community. In short, as McCarthy argues, marriage participates in communal discipleship.[97]

Centering marriage according to commitments internal to the couple and the community forms the community around a shared sense of fellowship. The value of this fellowship does not lie in a mechanism of control but common life in Christ. This shift requires a tightrope approach that must resist too much or too little life together. Too much and the church dominates; too little and the church submits itself to the will of families as its source of life. Instead, the common life emerges within an understanding of mutuality that cultivates intimacy and reconciliation. Marriage requires a broader account of reciprocity in which preferential love can find an external, complementary fulfillment. The practices of covenant as promise-keeping and making cannot serve only the couple but also the community to the couple and the couple to it. As McCarthy writes, "Christians profess [their] marriage vows before God and the Church in the hope that our promises will be made complete. In faith, we hope that our loves will be lifted up and fulfilled through God's grace and love as it radiates through our lives and the whole life of the church."[98] The marriage of two can be transformed by its life in the community and its relationship to God. This is a blessing because the couple does not need to bear the full weight of love, as evident in the romantic marriage model. The community's presence cultivates even greater equity

---

97. McCarthy, "Becoming One Flesh," 321.
98. McCarthy, "Becoming One Flesh," 322–23.

between the couple as they locate their love within the church's practices.[99] Articulating the ecclesiological character of marriage means placing it alongside sacramental practices like the Eucharist, in which the sharing of God's sustaining love is not a private possession but shared. Married couples are not alone at the table and thus are not alone in their marriage. McCarthy identifies a central image of the kingdom of God as the wedding feast, which "is the occasion for gracious hospitality of the host and the gathering of uninvited guests."[100] Covenant within the community known as the church creates a tie that binds the promises and vows made before one another and occurs before the body. Thus, locating marriage within a covenant broadens the promises and practices of marriage to a larger community to cultivate practices in which the couple can flourish and thrive.

The practices of care within marriage, such as preparing, eating, and cleaning up after a home-cooked meal, represent an opportunity to fulfill promises that participate in the larger, more important elements of marriage. As ethicist Brent Waters argues, marriage "directs our attention toward the mundane, and that focus, in turn, helps us identify, solidify, and cherish what is truly most satisfying and worthwhile, what best promotes human flourishing."[101] Grace as celebrating the significance of another finds expression in the mundane to cherish that significance in another and ourselves—furthermore, the mundane tempers our practices within smaller gestures of grace. Sexual ethics requires the broadness of this appreciative kindness to shape sexuality according to the matrix of grace that names the significance of another. Marriage is not exclusively about self-fulfillment but the graciousness to enter the ordinary day-to-day with another.

Marriage, grounded in the mundane, allows the couple to practice justice to those outside their preferential relationships. The spouse is a particular friend capable of accountability and shared participation in the good. To engage in marriage, as Margret Farley writes, one surrenders to a "life marked by mutuality, equality, and fruitfulness" that will spill into other sectors of their life.[102] As Farley writes, marriage leads to an "embodied and inspired union, companionship, communion, fruitfulness, caring and being cared for, opening to the world of others, and lives made sacred in faithfulness to one another and to God."[103] The persons we become in marriage should, if practiced in justice and virtue, lead to the formation of more just

---

99. McCarthy, "Becoming One Flesh," 323.
100. McCarthy, "Becoming One Flesh," 322.
101. Waters, *Common Callings and Ordinary Virtues*, 115.
102. Farley, *Just Love*, 263.
103. Farley, *Just Love*, 268.

communities. In other words, by becoming more attentive and loving to this one in marriage, the individual becomes more attentive and loving in virtue. Properly exercised virtue moves into the entirety of the individual's life. Justice as the careful attention to a concrete person motivates the central convictions of marriage. To fail at this attention risks a foul in marriage.

This attention, though, is couched in mutuality to recall. One cannot expect to give attention to another without reciprocal attention returned. Justice, thus, is reciprocity offered as a gift of care to others who do not flourish. As Farley argues, marriage must bear fruit, but that fruit must be justice and virtue, not merely the bearing of children. Thus, the language of procreation must include all the ways marital fidelity can bring life.

Though bearing children is extraordinary, it is also quite mundane. This fact arises from the simple day-to-day attention and affirmations afforded in marriage to affirm the preferential relationship between spouses. Thus, marriage teaches how to live in the virtues in the mundane and the extraordinary moments of life. For the marriage to take shape in this mundane way, it must be well acquainted with the truth. Truthfulness, furthermore, is a central feature of marriage because, without it, one could not make and keep promises. Marriage is a truthful story sustained throughout a life. Truth generally binds people together in the community and specifically in marriage vows. Marriage cultivates the ability to speak and expect the truth.

Furthermore, this cultivation of the truth is a risk. To name truthfulness, and love, for that matter, as a risk honors the person as unique and different. Truthfulness never takes the other for granted but honors the other as one who can reject it. Sharing the truth of ourselves with another leaves us open to rejection. If the individual must embrace the other, then truth-telling and promise-making are meaningless. Furthermore, truthfulness is the participation in the triune Lord who forms us in truth so that we might be shaped "*by* love and *for* love."[104] Thus, truth fulfills the marital vows, namely that we can always be embraced even in difficult times. The acceptance of the truth is not required but embraced in love.

Love as the attention to the concrete needs of another arises from the truth. To know the concrete reality of another requires truth, but love is the affectionate response to that truth. Relational bonds of any kind are fragile; love is fragile because it is subject to the fragility of humanity, which is why covenantal love expressed in marital love requires what Waters terms "cleaving."[105] Love can be broken because spouses "see each other at their best and worst, in some instances strengthening their covenant while in

---

104. Waters, *Common Callings and Ordinary Virtues*, 109.
105. Waters, *Common Callings and Ordinary Virtues*, 106–10.

others weakening or destroying it."[106] The truth in any given moment requires an honest assessment of who and what we are in relationship to another. As Waters states, cleaving is the best means to describe love "for it depicts love rather vividly, both as a power that binds and as a fragile gift that requires mutual attention and care."[107] In short, it is unselfing for a unique kind of mutuality.

A word must be added about divorce at this point. Divorce is a tragic reality, no matter the time or occasion. The risk of marriage, as already stated, always comes with the possibility of rejection. As such, divorce is never something to be taken lightly or half-heartedly. Due to the covenantal, mutual nature of marriage and sexuality, divorce is not the ideal means to mitigate conflict in a relationship. However, it is to this end that we remember the connection between marriage and covenant. The former only finds meaning in the latter. Therefore, one cannot idealize marriage as an end in itself. Rather, marriages possess the capability to break the covenant in harmful ways. Though not authorized in every sense, divorce can protect individuals from realities such as abuse and domestic violence. To recall the report of the SBC, the failure of a community to truly recognize the pain and suffering caused by another to protect an ideal image of purity causes irreparable damage. Furthermore, the rejection of divorce for women suffering domestic violence creates simultaneous permission for violence to exist within the community. The vigorous rejection of domestic violence must be greater than the purity cultivation in anti-divorce advocacy. To be clear, this is not permission for any divorce. Marriage must maintain a commitment to lifelong covenantal fidelity, but it is not an idol. The teaching on divorce in Scripture is neither consistent nor final on this account, but the tenor of the God revealed in Scripture does not align with the violent treatment of humans. Thus, if a marriage is no longer gracious in its affirmation of significance in another, justly attentive to the flourishing of the bodily integrity of another, and breaks the covenants that cleave fragile people together, then the marriage is no longer fulfilling its theological purpose. Furthermore, if the marriage does not promote the virtues of justice, love, humility, and truthfulness either internally or externally, then it is no longer moral.

In sum, marriage is a unique covenantal bond and one of its highest expressions. It is never more or less than humanity fully bound in its sacredness as the site of divine love. Those in the marriage bond knows that love is not easy, but there is no love without risk. The harm and violence potential in human relationships require strong covenantal and mutual

---

106. Waters, *Common Callings and Ordinary Virtues*, 107.
107. Waters, *Common Callings and Ordinary Virtues*, 107.

bonds that honor the humanity that can be damaged by abuse. The reason for the couching of marriage in covenant and mutuality notes that marriage itself is not a safeguard against abuse. Rather, it too requires covenantal promises, mutuality, justice, truth, and love as the virtuous expressions of its vows. Humility allows humans to see that their relationships, no matter the persons involved, are always subject to failure and risk. Nevertheless, the hope is that Christian sexual ethics presents a base theological conviction in God's commanding and sustaining presence empowers humans to cleave to one another.

Trafficking and Purity: Marriage

In trafficking, the inability to keep and make promises cultivates the grounds for abuse, violence, and commodification. The relationships forged in marriage as a church-centered fidelity cultivates the ability to love one's spouse and others because, as the presence of the community articulates, spouses are not alone. The marriage fidelity must be open to receive others into their love and to make and keep promises to those outside as well. Thus, the virtuous marriage does not see those with differing sexual experiences as threats to their marriage nor does it understand itself as a purity sought for goodness's sake. Instead, each person one meets merely turns marriage vows outward to a just and loving community. The purpose of marriage is not, as purity culture would teach, sex. Rather, the purpose is to develop the virtues necessary to be human, which is also true of those who choose singleness. Therefore, the marriage pairing must resist the temptation to seek privilege or purity for itself, which would betray its communal orientation or see others as a threat to purity. Rather, if the marriage covenant expands to include children, then it must also carry these insights into relationships with neighbors.

Children

Though not an essential aspect of family, children can deepen and foster an account of home and family. As with the ethics of man and woman, children represent one of the areas most pertinent to the discussion of trafficking. A theological account of children must also consider the history and theology of the *haustafeln*. In short, one must not conceive of children as available to men like women and enslaved people in the *haustafeln*. In Paul's writings, the union between individuals in marriage, and subsequently the bearing of children, is not the primary vocation of the church. However, we are charged with the care and attention of our community's children. Therefore, they represent an important area of exploration for our study of ethics in the family.

Two things must be stipulated and prohibited in our study of children in Christian sexual ethics. First, if romantic narratives distort the ethics of marriage, then narratives of fulfillment distort our understanding of children. The pressure families place on children as the fulfillment of their lives is perverse because it directly contradicts human relationship to God. Second, raising children is not the Christian vocation of growing the church. Though, if children are born in the church, a need exists to raise them, including discipleship. Rather, it means that we understand that the Christian faith grows not by birth but by conversion.

Bearing children must avoid the narrative that children are a natural "right." Margret Farley writes, "[a] billion-dollar industry has arisen to insure genetically related offspring. I make this observation not to critique reproductive technologies, but as a way to provoke reflection on how it is we want to reproduce ourselves as humans."[108] Farley asks Christians to consider the relative necessity of natural-born children in our midst. A healthy marriage and family need not include birthing natural-born children.

However, regardless of origin, children must be welcomed in the community. The church has always understood that when children join the community, the entire church must care for them. One sees this well in the stories of Darla and Bobo. Refusing to see all children as members of the body cultivates a church of selective child fidelity. The result leads to certain postures toward what Amy Laura Hall calls the clean versus unclean family. One must recognize the purity language within this rejection of certain children over the natural-born children privileged in certain communities. She writes, "Selling the clean family depends on shaming the dirty family, and linking the latter to unhappiness, poverty, irresponsibility, and illness."[109] This optic is a trap that tempts parents to view their children as reflections of themselves and more positively than others. To this end, the Christian community must see that all children have a place of blessing. Therefore, it is not just the parent's responsibility to raise the children but the entire community's responsibility.[110] Like marriage, it orients the community to mundane tasks in the moral life.[111] Bearing and raising children is a life

---

108. Farley, *Just Love*, 270.
109. Hall, *Conceiving Parenthood*, 9.
110. Mangina, "Bearing Fruit," 512.
111. Mangina, "Bearing Fruit," 513.

of the mundane (e.g., dirty diapers, feeding, doctor visits). Thus, children require simple mundane grace.

In addition to the parental attention to the well-being of all children as a central task of ethics, the parents must cultivate proper environments to raise their children. Considering this as a central task of sexual ethics, it requires that children live and grow in an environment where they can be children without negotiating the value of their bodies through exchanging sex for goods, which is true of purity and trafficking. This protection of childhood is what theologian Rowan Williams calls latency, namely, "the time before certain determinations and decisions have to be made."[112] Children should be afforded, for lack of a better term, a genuine childhood. This space means that periods of play and fantasy without the pressures of being adjudicated as an adult. This is a central moral conviction. A fantasy, for Williams, is best expressed by the children's authors that narrate whole worlds the child can inhabit.[113] The moral purpose is that the "child learns to look with a curious, even skeptical, eye at the everyday; ready to ask what are its non-negotiable bits, what are matters of conventions or even distortion."[114] This type of mentality that questions why we do certain actions versus others is valuable to the continual moral health of the church.[115] It helps us revisit basic questions of morality that undergird our choices. The ability for children to play and fantasize helps adults not to recycle generational vices among their children. Fantasies allow children to act within a world that does not have consequences but also does not require them to commit to them so that "identities can be abandoned without emotional shipwreck."[116] Again, the value of this is that children can try out a variety of roles necessary for informed moral formation without asking them to commit in the neoliberal consumer sense. In short, children do not need to bear the pressures of adulthood.

Creating an atmosphere free of consumer ideology unburdens children from making choices as an economic subject and allows them to find other forms of moral reasoning.[117] The failure to cultivate this space means that the child and the child's body are subject to a competitive marketing ideology curating them as a sexual, social, and economic commodity. The problem here cannot be overstated as the result of such commodification

---

112. Williams, *Lost Icons*, 11.
113. Williams, *Lost Icons*, 15–17.
114. Williams, *Lost Icons*, 18.
115. Williams, *Lost Icons*, 18–19.
116. Williams, *Lost Icons*, 20–21.
117. Williams, *Lost Icons*, 23.

of the children's body does not differentiate enough the difference between the child and the adult.[118] In the Christian community, this ambiguity of the difference between the adult and child's body cannot be maintained. Rather, it must be that the child is, again, allowed to be a child and latency encouraged.

Latency also encourages testimony as an expressed engagement with the command of God. If play aids the cultivation of moral maturity, the church's resources can serve as an imaginative exercise for the child to enter the life of God. Testimony is a necessary feature of ecclesial life but is an essential aspect of the development of children.[119] Allowing children the space to engage allows their testimony to provide iconoclasms of fidelity to resist the images that captivate various adults and gives the child a chance to exercise free response. Thus, a great summary of just Christian ethics of child-raising remains the ability to cultivate spaces for encounters and testimony.

Before leaving children, two further aspects of children must be engaged. First, taking Williams as a point of departure, the child who must experience play and be free from the concerns of marketing and adulthood must also fall outside the realm of sexual objectification. It is deeply unjust to submit children and adolescents to a calculus of sexual desire. They must be protected and allowed to grow into maturity. The child cannot be mutual as they must depend upon adults for care and necessities. This need must be honored as an implicit demand by the child's presence that they are tended to and cared for. Children cannot return authentic mutuality in the way an adult can.

An essential feature of iconoclastic sex is covenant, so that that sex might be practiced for the right time. Children, as Williams states, are those who still play in order to be formed in justice and love. As Farley argues, it is unclear whether children and adolescents cannot exercise justice in response to the formation they receive from the culture around them.[120] However, as Williams argues, they can develop a sense of virtue through play. Thus, they must be allowed to cultivate these virtues and grow into maturity in order to engage in iconoclastic sex.

Second, a new language of procreation must emerge here. As Farley already argued, sex must be fruitful.[121] Traditionally, this means sex must bear

---

118. Williams, *Lost Icons*, 28–29.

119. This is the argument of Amanda Hontz Drury's *Saying Is Believing: The Necessity of Testimony in Adolescent Spiritual Development*.

120. Farley, *Just Love*, 235.

121. Farley, *Just Love*, 268.

children. However, this is not the path laid out by iconoclastic sex. Instead, sex is not merely about the production of children but the affirmation of life and sacredness in the personhood of the beloved. Thus, sex cultivates life. Contrasted with the sex in abuse or violence experienced by so many in the web of trafficking that seeks to destroy the sacredness in another, iconoclastic sex motivates this liveliness in another person. Sexual ethics, then, must be procreative, but it must also broaden its parameters to include a non-childbearing procreation that creates life out of death. In short, it must encourage us to see the humanity at the heart of each person.

Trafficking and Purity: Home

The inclusion of children in marriage requires an ever deeper concept of the family. In the US domestic context, the family traditionally indicates the nuclear family. Though there are many positive features of the Christian family, the family also presents a severe danger. The family becomes an idol when it becomes an end to itself, becoming a kind of *voluntas incurvatus* oriented to perpetuating its future. As such, it is theologically its own *telos*. The family turned toward itself is most properly recognized in the neoconservative construct of "family values," which is the family as the ideal subject to intensify *state* empowerment, moral superiority, and economic advantage. The rise of the nuclear family and family values occurs with the undoing of welfare policies and the rise of free-market alternatives. As Melinda Cooper argues, this shift only happens inside the historical preference for the welfare of families over the individual.[122] Beginning in the 1930s, as the rise of the New Deal emerged, families became a central concern for society.[123] Family values would find chief expression in the Aid to Families with Dependent Children welfare program that provided an implicit preference for specific family structures and thus stigmatized other parts of the population.[124] Therefore, the rise of family values, like the difference between clean and dirty children, comes with assumptions about the priority of race, sexual practice, orientation, and gender.[125] Combined with the challenge to the traditional family structure during the 1970s and 1980s and the rise of Reaganomics, the battle for the family and its protection is the central concern of a neoliberal order bent on its perpetuation. Legal and economic structures emerged that funneled economic stimulation to white,

---

122. Cooper, *Family Values*.
123. Cooper, *Family Values*, 38–39.
124. Cooper, *Family Values*, 34.
125. Cooper, *Family Values*, 24.

heterosexual families.[126] The purpose was this: to press individuals into certain family structures to gain stable social structures that also contain an economic incentive. The privileging of the nuclear family does not mean that sexuality, gender, and family played no role in the economic, political, and social institutions prior to the 1930s. Rather, it merely reasserts "the reproductive institutions of race, family, and nation as a way of ensuring the unequal distribution of wealth and income across time."[127] However, the interests of those who privilege the family treat the survivor and those who break the purity code as enemies of family. In describing marriage and family, a new sense of home must emerge from those who get married and have kids.

The family is not an isolated cell, as trafficking indicates, within a society of equally isolated cells; rather, it must possess an outward focus that emerges from the inward grace. As McCarthy argues, the "social role of family is sustained internally so that its outward vocation can be detached, if need be, from the dominant political order and materialist conceptions of economic life."[128] The moral actions that one exercises in relation to one's family turn outward to the world, for better or worse. The virtue theologically enriched by testimony encourages that the grace shared in one's preferential relationships helps locate how one treats others for the better. Though love is not the same in preferential as it is in non-preferential relationships, one's preferential relationships shape the disciple-agent to receive a special commission. "Family," as McCarthy writes, "is called to hospitality, a preferential option for the poor, and stewardship of the human good; it is called to protect the dignity of human life from economic abuse of laborers and from cultural inhospitality to the elderly and young."[129] The family receives this commission from the church, meaning it must break open to receive the others. Family cannot be literalized but must receive from beyond itself. It is a specific kind of discipleship that forms neighborhoods that "will contribute to the social mission of the church in particular ways."[130] The family, as such, must think from the place of those outside themselves. The family is broken open by its relationship to the church, which precedes all other social commitments to orient it away from its role in social exclusion and toward the command of God. Though the church is by no means a perfect institution, the church is the community that must be broken open by the

---

126. Cooper, *Family Values*, 197.
127. Cooper, *Family Values*, 16.
128. McCarthy, *Sex & Love in the Home*, 122.
129. McCarthy, *Sex & Love in the Home*, 124.
130. McCarthy, *Sex & Love in the Home*, 124.

command of God and the one that hears the testimonies of its witnesses. This is far from the privilege and purity model of many churches that actively perpetuate social exclusion. The church must find its mission in being broken open for the world and the family in the church. Theologically, then, the family exists in service to the world on behalf of the church.

One final word must be said about the family. To place the family as an order of love transformed by the church might reinscribe the neoliberal structure of the family, which begs the question, is there any use for the family in the moral community? I argue that there must be. As much as I argue that singleness is the central hermeneutic of sex, I recognize that loneliness remains an epidemic for those who do not fit in traditional family structures. Thus, family and home are relational concepts that help humans understand themselves. As noted by our study of trafficking, a contributing factor to the reality of trafficking is a lack of durable networks. Family provides the possibility for home, which, as theologian Natalia Marandiuc argues, is not a spatial but a relational term.[131] Marandiuc helpfully locates home in the broader eschatological journey of all creatures. To name home as an eschatological, relational reality turns our longing for belonging and contentment into our desire to be with one another. Utilizing Augustine's account of the far country home to which each pilgrim must return, the pilgrim must differentiate between enjoyment (*frui*) and use (*uti*). Though Augustine acknowledges that only God can be enjoyed, Marandiuc notes how this distinction can collapse back into harmful instrumentalization of other people on a path to love God.

Nevertheless, Marandiuc, utilizing the work of Oliver O'Donovan, unsettles this claim. She writes that there is "a certain kind of love for the neighbor: we can enjoy one another here on earth, but only in God. That is because the neighbor is, after all, not merely an earthly creature, but also one who belongs to the very destiny of divine enjoyment that is our ultimate end."[132] To recall, God is the ultimate excellence in which the actions of our lives must culminate. Thus, the virtues formed in response to the encounter with God shape humanity, and it is in this reality that we recognize our belonging. Home, even in its eschatological and relational posture, sets humans on a pilgrimage where one must crave the presence of others and walk with them into the far country. In short, home is the relational posture of family, and it embraces a broad group of others to love them into this eschatological belonging.

---

131. Marandiuc, *Goodness of Home*, 5.
132. Marandiuc, *Goodness of Home*, 10–11.

PART IV: RECOGNIZING IMPLICATION AND TOXIC GOODNESS

The final piece of iconoclastic sex as a project in sexual ethics must face the complex history of Christian sexual ethics. Truthfulness is difficult because it must admit one's participation in social evil. Toxic goodness is precisely the failure to recognize that implication. Thus, to fully practice truthfulness, one must look brutally at how Christian sexual ethics can cause great harm in its pursuit of goodness. First, sexual ethics does not normally, especially among white theologians, consider racism as an essential theme in sexual ethics. However, systems of racism and sexual violence in slavery leave brutal scars. Second, in recent decades, arguments over sexual orientation and gender expression polarized faith communities beyond recognition. Many faith communities find themselves fracturing along these fault lines, unable to consider other elements of the church's mission, such as evangelism. One's orthodoxy and qualifications for participation in the church come down to questions surrounding orientation and gender expression, no matter what side of the issue one falls. The climate of sexuality does not diminish the importance of the conversation on human sexuality. However, it merely identifies how sex is a zero-sum game in many moral and political perspectives in the US domestic and global context. The problem I raise by naming this tension is merely how sexual ethics, through such hyper-fixation on sexual ethics as the singular marker of one's relationship to Christ and the church, creates a lot of social exclusion and insecurity. In both cases, naming these realities will aid the church in addressing how it expresses its moral commitments.

Racism

One of the barriers to working in trafficking lies in the failure to account for issues of race and racism at the core of trafficking relief. Due to films like *Taken* and the "white slavery" narratives that drastically change journalism, many assume that trafficking is primarily an issue of the abduction of white women for slavery. As the literature above indicates, however, this is largely fiction, whereas the majority face of the person caught in the web is non-white and caught in a web of bad relationships (social capital) and lacking resources. The exploration of racial conditions of trafficking has largely not been explored, but it is an undeniable feature.[133] As Cheryl Butler, professor of law at UCLA, argues, "The modern-day commercial sex industry

---

133. See Bell, "Race and Human Trafficking in the U.S."

perpetuates a long and bitter history of sexual exploitation and racial subordination with respect to people of color."[134] As Butler indicates, a root cause of trafficking lies in the history of the slave trade, Jim Crow laws, and the colonization and fetishizing of black and brown bodies. These historical factors lead to system injustices that perpetuate the reality of trafficking.

Emerging from the histories of colonialism, the North Atlantic slave trade, and Jim Crow were certain caricatures that frame the sexual exploitation of black and brown bodies. Few examples connect the history of slavery, Jim Crow, sexuality, and oppression better than Jezebel's. Readers of the Hebrew Scriptures will recognize Jezebel as the wife of the Israelite King Ahab. She introduced, through the persuasion of her husband, the worship of foreign deities. In Christian New Testament, Jezebel reemerged in revelation as the one who leads the prophets and saints of God away into sexual immorality (Rev 2:20–23). She is a caricature that represents not only sexual immorality and impurity (like Eve) but also one who embodies unfaithfulness (also like Eve). This caricature powerfully reemerges in the antebellum period; ethicist theologian Emile Townes writes, "Jezebel was depicted as licentious and dangerous for White men. This stereotype fortified the perception that Black women were sexually loose and liked sex more than their White counterparts."[135] This image, in both slavery and the Jim Crow period, served to frame black women in such a way, as Cheryl Butler argues, "to justify the pervasive rape, sexual assault, and abuse of Black women during slavery."[136] The image of Black women as possessing an insatiable appetite for sex excused white men from their immoral activity, which is an essential aspect of racist systems.

In addition to the permission of the image, Jezebel also served an economic purpose. Jezebel was a guiding image in which individuals are commodified and codified into an economy of purchase and exchange. The slave trade served as a means to buy and sell bodies based on fetishized features to perpetuate exploitation. As Townes defines, this creates a fantastic, hegemonic imagination wherein a dominant group deploys images and concepts "in a society to secure the consent of subordinates to abide by their rule."[137] Townes continues, "This breeds a kind of false consciousness ... that creates societal values and moralities such that there is *one* coherent and accurate viewpoint on the world."[138] The morals created, as indicated, an entire he-

---

134. Butler, "Racial Roots of Human Trafficking," 1468.
135. Townes, *Womanist Ethics*, 171n6.
136. Butler, "Racial Roots of Human Trafficking," 1470.
137. Townes, *Womanist Ethics*, 20.
138. Townes, *Womanist Ethics*, 20.

gemony of power relations centered on supply and demand. In short, the erotic picture of the insatiable, racial other coded a market principle to take root at the intersections of race, sex, and oppression.

The coding of Black bodies arises from the coding of sexual ethics in general as white.[139] The images of Jezebel offered moral sexuality as embodied in white women.[140] As Cheryl Butler argues, womanhood was "white, pious, chaste, and domestic."[141] The internal logic of Eve and Mary map themselves onto this space as well. Largely ethics considers the space of the pure and uses the impure bodies as a threat and boundary to ethics. The permissibility to violence, danger, and impurity of black and brown bodies creates the conditions of trafficking.

Black and brown bodies make up a vast majority of cases of trafficking, composing roughly 358 cases out of 460 cases between 2008 and 2010.[142] The racial stereotypes, such as the Jezebel, serve as a continuing license for sexual exploitation in trafficking, similar to the exploitation of slavery and Jim Crow.[143] With the disproportionate number of females being Black (roughly 36 percent of women ages 10–19 who experienced trafficking were Black among a general population of which Black women composed 14.5 percent), the tropes and stereotypes continue to hold sway.[144] Combined with media portrayal, these statistics serve little more than buttress the assumption that black and brown bodies trapped in a web of trafficking desire sexual exploitation.

The stereotypes circulate images that enable exploitation but disguise the structural inequality, leading to much of the previously offered statistics. As Butler rightly recognizes, the context for much of the discrepancy in sexual intercourse lies in the lack of resources afforded to people of color. Specifically reflecting on children, Butler notes that the high numbers of minority groups in systems of trafficking remain evidence of historical structural inequalities that make people of color targets for exploitation. She writes,

> Studies show that African American girls become trafficked at younger ages than their racial counterparts. They are more likely to experience poverty, and consequently more likely to be

---

139. Adkins, *Virgin Territory*, 285.
140. Butler, "Racial Roots of Human Trafficking," 1471.
141. Butler, "Racial Roots of Human Trafficking," 1471.
142. "Characteristics of Suspected Human Trafficking Incidents."
143. Butler, "Racial Roots of Human Trafficking," 1483.
144. Mitchell et al., *Crimes against Children Research Center, Sex Trafficking Cases Against Minors*.

disconnected from schools and other community supports. African American girls experience physical and sex abuse at young ages and witness multiple forms of violence at higher rates than their white peers. In 2013, 26 percent of children in the foster care system were African Americans.[145]

Poverty and social capital emerge as a significant history that impacts people of color. Needing to find access to durable networks due to a lack of resources arising from systemic economic injustice due to slavery and Jim Crow, the tendency toward survival sex becomes greater.[146] As such, though poverty and social capital are overarching categories for all people who experience trafficking, it is particularly significant for people of color who are subjected to fetishized stereotypes that serve to ignore and even encourage oppression.

In sum, racism is another important aspect of the moral web of trafficking, in addition to moral injury and luck. Those who live in systems of trafficking suffer from a lack of resources and the perpetuation of stereotypes, but people of color experience these categories to a degree greater than white people. The reason for this lies in the historical stereotypes that fetishize and license the oppression of specific bodies. Coupled with economic hardships imposed generationally from the fallout of slavery, colonialism, and Jim Crow histories, black and brown bodies find themselves disproportionately bound in the web of trafficking. Thus, Christian sexual ethics must decolonize and promote anti-racism efforts as a fundamental feature of its work.

LGBTQ+

In addition to the racism contributing to trafficking, another community that disproportionately finds itself caught in the web lies in members of the LGBTQ+ community. Sexual ethics largely think from the perspective of cisgender, heterosexual positions. A side effect of this condition is that the consequences of such teaching rarely catch the attention of the theologians and ethicists who write most of the literature. Coupled with a pure posture that exercises its moral actions as a means of expulsion, the consequences result in a great deal of exclusion and insecurity. This theological assessment bears out; statistically, roughly 46 percent of LGBTQ+ adolescents find themselves without a home due to familial rejection, members of the

---

145. Butler, "Racial Roots of Human Trafficking," 1489.

146. For a critical, trenchant engagement of systemic racism in housing, see Taylor, *Race for Profit*.

LGBTQ+ community are 7.4 times more likely to experience some kind of violence than heterosexual and cisgender youth, and they are three to seven times more likely to engage in survival sex to meet basic needs.[147] As a result, members of the LGBTQ+ community suffer the consequences of poverty, moral luck, and moral injury all at once, thus, suffering more frequently from the conditions of trafficking.

The reason for this difficult situation has deep ties to religious faith. The family's religious convictions are a possible factor that perpetuates homelessness among LGBTQ+ youth.[148] The social exclusion model presents itself through these statistics, noting that how one expresses their ethics gravely impacts people's lives. Members of the LGBTQ+ community are not by nature more susceptible to trafficking nor are they morally impaired, but the systems around them often result in this experience. Lack of resources for members of the LGBTQ+ community, as with youth from racial minority communities, means the LGBTQ+ community faces greater risks of engaging in survival sex as a means to meet basic needs.[149] This example further illustrates that ethics in general and Christian sexual ethics, in particular, can perpetuate, unwittingly or not, systems of injustice. Questions of sexual and gender orientation flood the market of sexual ethics today, and the stakes have never been higher than right now.[150] Considering that evangelical Christians have a serious concern for ending trafficking, this fact is deeply troubling.[151] Those who will expel LGBTQ+ adolescents and those who passionately seek the end of sex trafficking act inside a particular moral activity that perpetuates trafficking.

147. Polaris Project, "Sex Trafficking and LGBTQ Youth."

148. For information about the cause of homelessness among the LGBTQ community, see Choi, Wilson, Shelton, and Gates, *Serving Our Youth 2015*.

For information on the vulnerability of LGBTQIA+ adolescents and trafficking, see Polaris Project, "Sex Trafficking and LGBTQ+ Youth."

In order to see the evangelical connection to this trend, see the advice given by the evangelical organization Focus on the Family: Focus on the Family, "Responding to a 'Gay Christian' in the Family."

149. For information on the rise of religious connections with homelessness and religious convictions, see Morris, "Forsaken." See also Polaris Project, "Sex Trafficking and LGBTQ Youth."

150. For now, it is merely enough to reference the many denominations in turmoil over the issue of sexual orientation and gender identity. One only needs to cite the current crisis in the United Methodist Church that faces a fracture due to differing ethical teachings on sexual orientation. By naming this reality, I am not yet determining an ethical posture but merely stating that right now, sexual ethics is a zero-sum game that determines the entire value of a person's ministry, work, and vocation.

151. For a brief history of the rise of sex trafficking as a concern for evangelical Christians, see Graham, "How Sex Trafficking Became a Christian Cause Celebre."

The high number of LGBTQ+ youth caught in the web should not escape the imagination of those who explore such issues. To state that they suffer is merely an exercise in explaining the full spectrum of issues that perpetuate trafficking. As stated in the introduction to this chapter, one cannot fully grasp the myriad of choices inherent in trafficking without this information.[152] In short, the realities of moral teaching and the responses articulated therein must remain at the forefront of this work. As indicated in the tension between Eve and Mary, the language of purity creates the conditions for expulsion.

One more element must be stated that considers the statistics above while also naming a different problem, namely privilege. Privilege, again, does not mean evil. It indicates to those who, as Rey Chow already argued, that some stand in the place of narration and others do not. However, when privilege combines with toxic goodness, it exercises moral posture through punishment. Central to this argument, as expressed in Christian history, is that the defending of the privilege takes shape as exclusion. Beyond just cultivating trafficking, this can result in other systemic issues for members of the LGBTQ+ community.

According to the The Trevor Project, an organization dedicated "[to ending] suicide among lesbian, gay, bisexual, transgender, queer & questioning young people," members of the LGBTQ+ community face a higher risk of suicide and self-harm.[153] According to recent studies by researchers independent of The Trevor Project, suicide is already the second leading cause among young people ages ten to twenty-four, and LGBTQ+ youth are more than four times more likely to attempt suicide than their peers.[154]

---

152. Readers need to proceed with caution here. I am aware that merely mentioning LGBTQ+ will cause many to immediately write off this work and the constructive ethics therein. However, the findings offered in this section are merely facts about the demographics of trafficking. If the reader finds themselves angered by the inclusion of this information, I offer a quote from John Adams: "Facts are stubborn things; and whatever may be our wishes, our inclinations, or the dictates of our passion, they cannot alter the state of facts and evidence." (Adams, *Works of John Adams 1*, 113.) This is not to patronize, but merely to know that this inclusion is for the sake of a full account of trafficking, which is necessary before any constructive ethical response can emerge.

153. The mission statement for The Trevor Project can be found at The Trevor Project, "Our Mission." The statistics on LGBTQ+ suicide can be found in The Trevor Project, "Facts About LGBTQ Youth Suicide."

154. For general statistics on suicide among youth, see Hedegaard, Curtin, and Warner, "Suicide mortality in the United States."

For statistics on suicide among LGBTQ+ youth, see Johns et al., "Transgender identity and experiences of violence victimization."

See also Johns et al., "Trends in violence victimization and suicide risk by sexual identity among high school students."

Furthermore, more than 1.8 million LGBTQ youth consider suicide every year, and roughly 45 percent of LGBTQ+ youth consider suicide, with more than half of all transgender and nonbinary youth also considering it. While not all of this can fall at the feet of the religious community, its roots connect to a social exclusion of social identity in which Christianity plays a part. For example, conversion therapy, which first emerged in Europe, is a major factor in LGBTQ+ youth suicide, with a national survey indicating that those who experience it are 2.5 times more likely to attempt suicide multiple times.[155] The prominence of conversion therapy in the mid- to late-twentieth century arose from interest among certain Christian groups in the United States.[156] Christian organizations donated liberally during this period to advertise and promote conversion therapy.[157] Conversion therapy in some cases problematically tortures, utilizing electrocution to change one's sexual desire, and in other cases subjects would be psychologically abused. Without belaboring the point, the issue is that the ones who promoted conversion therapy did not endure it. Nevertheless, they subjected others to it, which caused great harm. Thus, privilege is the ability not to be negatively impacted without personally bearing the consequences. Sexual ethics must consider the weight it casts and who is responsible for it.

In sum, the traditional teaching on sexuality and gender can produce intended and unintended ill effects, especially when coupled with toxic goodness. Ethics is not an exercise in maintaining ethics for oneself as a form of purity, but rather only exists by and for the neighbor. There is no ethics but social ethics. The challenge is to remember that our ethical posture does not arise from self-enclosed individualism but rather other-regard and responsibility. As with holiness, Christian sexual ethics must find its work as it is sanctified in the life of another.

CONCLUSION: FAITH, HOPE, AND LOVE

In conclusion, iconoclastic ethics must be provisional while wrestling with the deep truths of the gospel that include its openness to receiving others. It cannot avoid acting but must lose possessiveness. Though they are provisional, the ethics articulated in this chapter serve the ends of the women surveyed in this book. However, the shift from the code ethics of the social exclusion model to testimony and the accompanying virtues aid the discernment of Christian ethics. The meaning must be considered first in

155. The Trevor Project, "Facts About LGBTQ Youth Suicide."
156. See Merritt, "How Christians Turned Against Gay Conversion Therapy."
157. Merritt, "How Christians Turned Against Gay Conversion Therapy."

sexual ethics, then the relationships that most fulfill that purpose. The ethics I present above cultivate a community capable of resisting trafficking. It sees each as significant and discerns the best sexual practices and relationships that fulfill that significance. It is no longer possessed by false images and creates a community of promises. Lastly, it recognizes its implicatedness in the world around it. I believe the most important aspect of iconoclastic ethics is the internal critique that provides a means for self-correction. Eschatology provides the means to evaluate when the ways that sexual ethics becomes implicated in a system of injustice (i.e., trafficking, purity culture) and need to be redirected to eschatological ends. Iconoclastic sex calls for all sexual ethics to be less confident in its pronouncements to make room for grace.

To conclude this chapter, and as a segue to the end of this work, I return to themes of faith, hope, and love presented in chapter 4. Barth argues that virtues appear through the response to the creating, reconciling, and redeeming God who commands freedom. Virtues emerge as the creaturely possibility for freedom as permission rather than absolute. Christian ethics often forget that it too requires faith in order to proceed. In faith, the disciple-agent proceeds to the moral life, knowing God commands their life to uphold it. Ethics emerges as the freedom to live.

Nevertheless, as this chapter illustrates, it also requires hope. Ironically, hope emerges in the face of God's promise. David Bentley Hart would agree with Barth that hope serves as a necessary cleaving to the promise and an openness to that which one cannot control but gives more than we could imagine. However, the final virtue is love; in the end, the former two will melt away for love to abide. The difference between the three is, as Hart describes, the former "two are destined to fall away when they reach their fulfillment in immediate knowledge; only when love alone abides will we know even as we are known."[158] Love must again be our guide in this world where bodies are bought and sold. We will see rightly when love is set free from the idols of power and death. Love is the way one thinks from another place and, as Paul writes, "love never fails" (1 Cor 13:8).

---

158. Hart, *Tradition and Apocalypse*, 168.

Conclusion

Eschatology and Sexual Ethics

INTRODUCTION: LOOKING BACK, THINKING FORWARD

THIS BOOK AROSE FROM an attempt to think clearly about the problems that perpetuate trafficking and those caused by trafficking. I know many other scholars write and will continue to write on this issue, and I hope that my account of trafficking represents the urgency of its demands, if nothing else. The shifts recorded here represent an attempt to bring the best of the Christian tradition to bear on human trafficking, specifically in the women interviewed in this study. As such, I argue that the end of social exclusion through its various code fetishes must occur, especially regarding the teaching of purity code realism in the Christian tradition. Instead, the indicative of God's reconciliation opens moral energy for the new hearing of God's command. The theological essence of the command, arising from the Christian tradition, finds its best expression through the testimonies of grace, iconoclasm, and covenant, while also vivifying virtues such as justice, love, humility, and truthfulness. I argue that this shift helps orient sex to proper ends in God and the corresponding relationships, at least provisionally, in light of the eschatological posture required for correction. Thus, iconoclastic sex shifts from codes to a new practical reason formed by our continual, relational, eschatological encounter with the command of God.

Before concluding, I desire to address two reflections that linger in the background of this study. This work constantly gestures to the eschatological. For Christian ethics to speak with any seriousness, it must connect to eschatology. Human understanding of creation and, thus, ethics remains provisional until the eschaton. As Barth illustrated, even as important as ethics is to creation, it is still a creation and must reach for ends that exist ever beyond it. Thus, I propose an eschatological posture to postulate the orientation of iconoclastic sex.

APPROACHING THE END: ESCHATOLOGY AND ETHICS

Due to the provisional nature of creation, ethics must temper its speech in light of this lack of final knowledge. Christian hope recognizes that it looks to a future and cannot predict when every wrong will be righted and every wound healed. Thus, with hope comes the humility that human knowledge and ethics are imperfect. Instead, we need the constant realignment to inhabit the eschatological judgments offered in the world to come. This helps us envision our sexual ethics and the complicatedness on the way to a new practical reason not bound by code fetishes.

At the outset of chapter 5 I argued that the ethics proposed in this book are provisional. As already noted, the provisional status of ethics is due to the need for an encounter with God and the eschatological world that breaks in upon humanity. Humanity will not fully see itself until that eschatological morning and only in faith do we see through the mirror dimly. Thus, ethics must proceed with the virtues of faith and hope as much as love. Ethics, thus, must reawaken its attention to the eschatological as an opening to the proper ends of ethics. These ends are surprising yet fitting for our humanity as we exist in the tension of creation and redemption. Barth's ethics of command illustrates the means to stand in the tension, namely through the presence of the indicative, Christ. From Christ's very presence, a reality emerges to which humanity must attune. However, Christ's presence to the world is not a static presence but an eschatological relation in the Holy Spirit. As Barth writes, "[if] Christianity be not altogether thoroughgoing eschatology, there remains in it no relationship whatever with Christ. Spirit which does not at every moment point from death to the new life is not the Holy Spirit."[1] The challenge for ethics is the continued allowance for the disturbance of its thought so that it may continually be confronted by the divine indicative and command. Nevertheless, ethics often looks exclusively inward to preserve an internal structure against literalizing its desires. How can Christian sexual ethics continue to provide provisional ethics yet be tied to the eternal truth of the one God?

A recent argument put forward by theologian David Bentley Hart on the relationship of tradition to eschatology is a helpful companion to our

---

1. Barth, *Epistle to the Romans*, 314.

work on ethics. As Hart argues, tradition in its present usage is incoherent and obscure.[2] Tradition is not merely the passing down of certain ideas into the present, but is "the dynamic and progressive disclosure of an ever wider and deeper and more inexhaustible reservoir of truth, one that it can only ever partially embody."[3] After exploring a few theologians central to the development of tradition as a theological concept, Hart returns to the rudimental understanding of doctrine to critique its coherence. Though Hart primarily envisions and critiques Catholic and Orthodox traditionalists who hold to certain presuppositions of doctrinal claims, he also includes evangelical fundamentalists. The commonality lies in creating certain, pure presuppositions that help each position be most certain.[4] Hart challenges fundamentalism's doctrinal incoherence. The inerrancy of Scripture as a durable, repeatable code is an impossibility that requires one to ignore the exact text it claims as its foundation. This is because the fundamentalists subvert their claimed fidelity to the text through the rigid adoption of the presuppositions they must claim before reading the text. Thus, Hart challenges a certain "fideism" to the possession of truth.

To this end, Hart motivates an understanding of tradition not bound to possession. The fundamentalist and the traditionalist believe they have the fullness of truth that leads directly to God. Faith is, according to Hart, not a certainty to possess the fullness of truth but an openness to receive. It is crucial, according to Hart, that "faith . . . look first to the very failure of a perfect resolution between the history and the dogma of the church as itself indicative of the true nature of a living tradition," which also means that "[faith] must begin from the supposition that the inadequacy of even the most necessary and inevitable formulations of doctrine is proof of the reality of the 'essential' truth to which the tradition bears witness."[5] This kind of faith is "far less frantic."[6] Hart argues that tradition is a posture in faith rather than a set of doctrinal statements to possess. "Apocalyptic expectation—an eager certainty of the imminence of the full and final revelation of God's truth in a restored and glorified cosmos," according to Hart, "and not dogmatic purity was the very essence of faithfulness to the Gospel."[7] The implications of this shift are staggering because instead, it presents tradition

---

2. Hart, *Tradition and Apocalypse*, 1.
3. Hart, *Tradition and Apocalypse*, 12.
4. Hart, *Tradition and Apocalypse*, 179.
5. Hart, *Tradition and Apocalypse*, 101.
6. Hart, *Tradition and Apocalypse*, 179.
7. Hart, *Tradition and Apocalypse*, 134.

as "fidelity to a promise."[8] To be clear, Hart argues that the findings of the historical councils, Scripture, and the theological voices from the past must continue as an essential grammar for theology, but the faithful adherent to tradition will know that one must be faithful "to the future discloser of the full meaning of what little one already knows."[9]

Ethics must also adopt faith's posture as the openness to a new horizon that breaks in on humanity. The apocalyptic expectation of the Christian faith is that God will finally reveal in such a way as to set all things to right and correct all ignorance. The approach of the social exclusion model that rests on specific modes of purity and privilege proposes the same kind of fideism against which Hart warns his readers. Thus, resisting this fideism must require a similar posture of openness to the apocalyptic expectation even as it pertains to sexual ethics. To be clear, as with tradition, this does not mean adopting a hopeless relativism in sexual ethics. There are still recognizable, rational theologies, practices, and relationships that contribute to our flourishing. Christian sexual ethics must, with Barth, think eschatologically about our bodies as not yet identical with what will be. The precarious nature of sexual life and the problematic parts that lead to trafficking need a constant reminder that humans are not final. The provisional state of our current bodies should yield a different expectation beyond our careful ethical instruction about our bodies. In short, there will be more to know even in the resurrection of the dead. Our sexual ethics may be faithful to that reality breaking into the cosmos, but we must recognize that it is not identical. Thus, Christian sexual ethics must take a posture wherein it remains open to a newness not yet present within its historical forms, that promises "to liberate history from its failures, just as it promises to liberate creation from the reign of death."[10]

Only in considering this posture does Christian sexual ethics possess the ability to address the web of trafficking. Like the Israelites bound in the desert in exile, so too must Christian ethics unlearn its reliance on other idols. Traveling to a far country requires an eschatological posture that reminds humanity that they have not seen that treasured land. However, the vision required to lay eyes on it cannot treat the land as a possession but only receive it as a gift. In other words, hope remains that the best is yet to come. Christian sexual ethics must resist the fideism of the social exclusion model in favor of the fidelity to the promise that indeed all will be well. This is true for the one caught in the web, the survivor, and all who find

---

8. Hart, *Tradition and Apocalypse*, 179.
9. Hart, *Tradition and Apocalypse*, 104.
10. Hart, *Tradition and Apocalypse*, 172.

themselves pondering the complexities of sexuality in their mortal form. The good news is this: the ends of our bodies do not find their limit in our sexual lives but, in this reality, are promised. Therefore, humans can hope that the precarity of sex will not diminish this truth, and their bodies will be made new.

To illustrate the importance of this openness, I turn to Gregory of Nyssa's brief tract *On the Soul and the Resurrection*.[11] Gregory learned much of his theology from his elder sister St. Macrina. In this work, Gregory presents a conversation between himself and St. Macrina over the nature of the resurrected body. Working against accounts of the resurrection that do not include the body, Macrina argues that though the body now and then will be different, their similarities still matter. Macrina does not disparage any of the things humans participate in now, but rather only names that the continuity will not be these things. The value and security in these things will be stripped away and, in their place, will be the one life of God. This heavenly virtue is not escapist but one that sits in Hart's eschatological posture of faith that locates one's life firmly in that will be. The moral life requires a just use of the material things that define and limit our bodies now. The provisional nature of these things does not reject the material but helps humans locate the importance relative to the eschatological, heavenly virtue.

Macrina urges Gregory to see this material connection. Again, it would be wrong, although tempting, to interpret Gregory and Macrina as escapists. However, Macrina's theology of the resurrection merely highlights the goodness of the body and the material. The challenge here must be to see how the material comes with its value and meanings that, when overemphasized, not only mistreat the body but fail to recognize its importance. In a certain sense, the body, in the heavenly virtue, is a mean between material and heavenly in a way finally realized in the resurrection. These material things like food, water, and clothing are significant and good according to their place in creation. However, when creation takes the role of assigning idolatrous meaning to other aspects of creation, it is misused. Sex, in the same way, must align with the loveliness of the body revealed in the resurrection. Sex, like all material things, can reveal this sacred character of the body, but when emphasized, it can be used to diminish the body. Such diminishment occurs when the disciple-agent makes too much or too little of sex. The eschatological end envisioned by Gregory and Macrina heals the image of the body whose value is determined by the absence of sex or by the excess of sex through its use for pleasure. Openness to the eschatological, as Gregory and Macrina present, allows for the final determination of the body

---

11. Gregory of Nyssa, *On the Soul and the Resurrection*.

to exist outside of the misused instrumental use of the body in trafficking and purity codes.

The eschatological posture then cracks open moral thought from merely code-making to an aesthetic register. The disciple-agent must be capable, as in Gregory and Macrina, of the ability to renegotiate complex moral decisions in light of the final fulfillment of the cosmos in the resurrection of the dead. The aesthetic involves an encounter with the beautiful and a resulting testimony that cultivates. This is the moral imagination and eschatological faith that does not collapse the work of ethics into a code. In testimony, one often finds themselves liberated from something and to something as one encounters the living God. The living God witnessed in testimony causes rapture, elation, terror, and fear. In any case, what one testifies to in its witness is the living God's judgment on reality. However, this experience captivates the believer in such a way as to set them on a new course. Therefore, beauty and glory serve as better guiding patterns for moral discernment than does the Kantian paradigm's privilege. As Hart recognizes, "the Beautiful has the power to recommend itself to any soul open to its advent, and to evoke from that soul a spontaneous movement of love."[12] There is no privilege in the experience of the glory of the Lord. Thus, as Hart argues, the Kantian paradigm limits the approach to ethics that should captivate our thinking and limits the conditions of moral reasoning and the ability of humanity to draw from "the simplicity of an ontological source beyond the finite."[13] The eschatological, thus, requires humanity to make room for the multitude of moral imagination as it confronts and is confronted by the beautiful.

The power of beauty and glory as the vivifying impetus for the moral life is that it lacks privilege. All can encounter its presence, and one cannot restrict it. When one testifies, it is to this reality of God's beauty that one attests. Furthermore, the ecclesial community cannot restrict God's access to creation, and God is perfectly free to entice. Furthermore, it is the enticing presence of God that attracts humanity to God and thus the content of the seen (i.e., the indicative) into action reflexively. The movement of the beautiful moves from a witness into action. Thus, testimony is not without moral content. Furthermore, the scope of seeing and witnessing translates into a new lens through which all reality is glimpsed. In short, as Hart states, "the experience of beauty is necessarily also the experience of judgment: not

---

12. David Bentley Hart, *You Are Gods*, 45.
13. Hart, *You Are Gods*, 37.

the judgment we pass on whatever beautiful object we might encounter, but the judgment it passes on us."[14]

The opportunity in testimony to switch to judgment and beauty will be how to articulate the moral insight offered. If beauty presents humans with a judgment by which they are judged, then ethics is more about taste than moral codes.[15] In order to free ethical thinking from the privileged posture of the Kantian paradigm, one must resist the "subtle but persistent requirement that certify one's ethical deeds by invigilating them for any trace of 'impure' motives."[16] The beautiful helps move humans past this paradigm because "it is never reducible to mere moral purpose, or to any purpose beyond itself; it is instead the very splendor of purpose, the fulfillment that makes the good the ultimate repose of the will and mind, in perfect concord."[17] Every moment of judgment is a judgment on our ability to judge the beautiful. Hart provides an example of eschatological judgment in Matthew 25:44–46, where the believer finds a threat in their failure to see Christ in the poor, marginalized, infirmed, and imprisoned.[18] In this way, testimony offers not only a judgment on the person testifying but a judgment on the community and its ability to "recognize or fail to recognize an urgent truth that is directly confronting us."[19] God judges Christ in the poor. Humans, to inhabit the good, must receive this judgment in testimony. Presumably, this is a judgment that exists prior to articulation, but it is undoubtedly expressed here. The ability of the congregation and world to bear witness to this testimony results in a judgment upon them. By refusing to hear the testimonies of others or neglecting the poor, the infirmed, or the imprisoned, the church community runs the risk of excluding Christ. Therefore, testimony is a judgment by which the community is judged.

In sum, it is from this place of beauty and testimony that new moral reasoning can take place. It is not code, but goodness itself propelled by God's beauty that confronts humanity and removes privilege. The activities arise from not the perfect adherence to code but the "sentimental education."[20] Again, ethics is a matter of good taste. As Hart continues, taste "indicates how we are disposed to take reality in, how we are likely to recognize what is truly valuable or venerable and what is not, and how

---

14. Hart, *You Are Gods*, 45.
15. On this notion of taste in moral reasoning, see Hart, "Sense of Style."
16. Hart, "Sense of Style," 241.
17. Hart, "Sense of Style," 241.
18. Hart, *You Are Gods*, 41–44.
19. Hart, *You Are Gods*, 42.
20. Hart, "Sense of Style," 244.

our desires are ordered or disordered."[21] Specifically, the ability to see the weak, vulnerable, violated, marginalized, infirmed, and those in need is the measure of the moral community. The community's visibility must proclaim certain iconoclasms of fidelity in its joining to Christ and his actions. What would it look like for testimony to elicit a more robust commitment to the margins? As Hart concludes,

> perhaps the story of the adulterous woman says it all. It enunciates no exact principles or laws, but it compellingly, beguilingly invites us to adopt the style pervading Christ's actions as, so to speak, the most exquisite imaginable . . . In dispersing the woman's accusers with a cool irony that leaves them haplessly silent, and in then granting her forgiveness wholly unencumbered by any ponderous expressions of disapproving decency or piety, and without even any prescribed penance, Christ demonstrates how a single graceful gesture, performed with sufficient moral and aesthetic skill, can express all the dimensions of the beauty of charity. It may seem somewhat perverse.[22]

The challenge of testimony is to witness the eternal beauty that confronts humanity in the command "to do justice and to love kindness and to walk humbly with your God" (Mic 6:8, NRSVue). The command exposes a judgment of grace on the world that calls the community to stand more faithfully in the world. The church must stand for the right things and with the right people lest it be judged. Testimony gives witness and voice to these realities.

The immediacy of testimony also opens Christian ethics to another posture, namely possibility. A posture of possibility opens humanity to a newness and vivified hope for redemption. There is a true openness eschatologically to the human future and the ends of the moral life. The moral life embeds itself within the resurrected body that prioritizes the resurrected body as the form of bodily life to which human life will be accountable before God. Pauline eschatology, for example, describes the resurrected body as a human *incompletion* in the love of God that creates the conditions for correct neighbor-love through the final defeat and removal of the powers. Such incompletion will enable humans to see face-to-face (1 Cor 13:12) and finally speak truth to one another free from sin.[23]

This shift to possibility leaves room for redemption of even the trafficker. If forgiveness begets a new eschatological sociality, then the truth of humanity appears in the light of God's eternal presence. For when all people,

21. Hart, "Sense of Style," 245.
22. Hart, "Sense of Style," 249.
23. Sonderegger, "Towards a Doctrine of Resurrection," 123.

as Sergius Bulgakov states, see the face of God, they must confront the truth of who they are in all of their wrongdoing.[24] Bulgakov's dogmatic clarification of Paul's eschatology gestures to a resurrected body free from sin that enables the possibility for the distinct process of social healing immediately proceeding after truth-telling, bodily healing, and restoration. The ability to see and state the truth and embody its possibility through resurrected life creates the conditions of forgiveness. As interpreted by Sonderegger, the spiritual body reality will manifest "everlasting forgiveness" where God will "drive all sin away . . . all sin and its effects."[25] As such, humanity will finally enjoy "the full, fruitful, and unimpaired relationships that earthly life injured and left for dead, the ones we passed by on the other side."[26] I recall James Alison's trafficker, who himself was sexually assaulted, exposed to horrors, and violated beyond measure. Such violence does not excuse his crime, but it illustrates that he too is a victim. Sonderegger's interpretation of Paul yields a poignant picture of distinct practices that envisions his healing. Communal discernment and restoration of those who have died leads to the healing of sinful flesh, but forgiveness of wrongdoing creates a new communal relationship within a universal piece of God's defeat of death.

In sum, the posture of possibility is simultaneously the hope that our actions are finally open to God's eschatological future and also that a new kind of sociality might emerge in the resurrection of the dead. Beauty, then, plays an essential role to the moral imagination as the disciple-agent craves the life of Christ and the resurrection of the dead rather than exclusion. Iconoclastic sex requires precisely this kind of posture lest we collapse back into our idols. This posture will allow humanity to commit their actions to truly good ends. Only through a continual orientation to God's future can humanity find rest through their actions instead of place the full measure of meaning on them in order to continually seek God for the source of moral life. Ethics is not about codes, social exclusion, or purity. Rather, it is about the excellence of God enacted in our lives.

CONCLUSION: TOUCHING THE IDOLS

I conclude this book with one final reflection. Sex and sexual ethics concern, for many, the perpetuation of power. Iconoclastic sex, as I have described it, seeks to defame those images of power that hold humanity captive and prevent the presence of God from transforming humanity. As such, to say

---

24. Bulgakov, *Bride of the Lamb*, 456.
25. Sonderegger, "Towards a Doctrine of Resurrection," 128.
26. Sonderegger, "Towards a Doctrine of Resurrection," 128.

anything about sexual ethics risks touching the idols, as Jon Sobrino describes.[27] Sobrino uses this phrase to describe the vitriolic reaction many make in response to critiques of the mechanisms of power. Sex and sexuality, for all human history, weave through the heart of the powerful. However, this book speaks about sexual ethics iconoclastically and it not only touches idols but tries to pull them down. For the sake of future generations, the idols that prevent sexual ethics from finally ending slavery must be torn down.

History tells the stories of trafficking so it may be a fool's errand to defame this idol. However, history also tells the story of many who stood by and watched trafficking occur, so the roots are not merely passively in the world but cut into each human heart. The Christian must see Christ in the poor and marginalized and not pass by on the other side. Though many would be incredulous at this claim that they participate through passivity, it is a central theme of this book that humans are implicated in this world. As such, the seemingly small formations one experiences daily arise from the world's structure as it stands. In short, participating in a world of social exclusion and coding can only implicate one in systems of trafficking. However, there is hope—the message of the gospel presses on the enclaves from the place of a crucified and risen Messiah. The incarnation is God's means of implicating Godself in a sinful world. God goes to the place of the forsaken and excluded to expose the violence of the code fetishes that strangle life from the lowly. This should chill our humanity to the core. The crucifixion of Jesus occurred not at the hands of criminals but at the hands of the morally righteous—and he died *with* criminals. From this place, moral thinking must find its base and the site of resistance. This book argues that sexual ethics does not merely determine when one has sex or does not, but the way that sex allows access to the community for some and leads to separation for others. The small counter-formations experienced in the light of the crucified Messiah can motivate the rejection of codes and the prizing of care to those outside.

However, this is a book for those determined unclean and who exist outside the walls of purity. For those outsiders, it means knowing that Christ stands with you, the Judge judged in *your* place. It also means knowing that you are so deeply loved that God stands in that place with you in order to show you that you belong regardless of past. Your body is not dirty, your heart is not evil, and your soul is not ugly. You are radiantly beautiful in the light of God's love. You have agency and light just as precious as anyone in God's creation, and your witness matters too.

27. Sobrino, "Touching the Idols," 22–23.

The vision of iconoclastic sex might be too much to bear. It requires a new kind of formation and valuing new priorities not based on certainty but hope. It requires salvation not based on sexual ethics but faith. It certainly requires a community not based on purity but love. These are the burdens of the gospel, but it too has been rejected. This is the hope of the excluded: along with the gospel they are rejected. Those that reject the gospel will only see it as a threat to power, order, and purity. However, for those who still seek an encounter with the living God the gospel is the bread of life and the possibility of the future.

Bibliography

Adams, John. *The Works of John Adams*. Vol. 1. Edited by Charles Adams. Cambridge: Harvard University Press, 1856.
Adkins, Amey Victoria. "Virgin Territory: Theology, Purity, and the Rise of the Global Sex Trade." PhD diss., Duke University, 2016.
Alison, James. "The Place of Shame and the Giving of the Spirit." In *Undergoing God: Dispatches from the Scene of a Break-In*, 199–219. New York: Continuum, 2006.
Allison, Emily Joy. *#ChurchToo: How Purity Culture Upholds Abuse and How to Find Healing*. Minneapolis: Broadleaf, 2021.
Aquinas, Thomas. *Summa Theologica*. Vol. 4. Translated by Fathers of the English Dominican Province. Westminster, MD: Christian Classics, 1981.
Ashton, Sarah, Karalyn McDonald, Maggie Kirkman. "What does 'pornography' mean in the digital age? Revisiting a definition for social science researchers." *Porn Studies* 6:2 (2019) 144–68.
Austin, J. L. *How to Do Things with Words*. Cambridge: Harvard University Press, 1962.
Bachelard, Sarah. *Resurrection and Moral Imagination*. New York: Ashgate, 2014.
Baker, Steven, dir. *OnlyFans: Selling Sexy*. San Bernardino, CA: ABC Originals Studios, 2021.
Bales, Kevin, and Ron Soodalter. *The Slave Next Door: Human Trafficking and Slavery in America Today*. Berkeley: University of California Press, 2009.
Balthasar, Hans Urs von. *The Glory of the Lord: A Theological Aesthetics. Vol. I: Seeing the Form*. Translated by Erasmo Levia-Merikakis, edited by Joseph Fessio and John Riches. San Francisco: Ignatius, 1982.
———. *The Glory of the Lord: A Theological Aesthetics. Vol. VII: Theology: The New Covenant*. Translated by Brian McNeil, edited John Riches. San Francisco: Ignatius, 1982.
Barth, Karl. *The Christian Life*. Trans. Geoffrey Bromiley. New York: T. & T. Clark, 2017.
———. *Church Dogmatics. Study Edition in 31 vols*. Translated by Geoffrey Bromiley. New York: T. & T. Clark, 2009.
———. "Criminals With Him." In *Deliverance to the Captives*, translated by John Marsh, 76–81. Eugene, OR: Wipf & Stock, 1978.
———. *The Epistle to the Romans*. 6th ed. Translated by Edwyn C. Hoskyns. New York: Oxford University Press, 1965.
———. *Ethics*. Edited by Dietrich Braun, translated by Geoffrey W. Bromiley. New York: Seabury, 1981.
———. *Göttingen Dogmatics: Instruction in the Christian Religion*. Translated by Geoffrey Bromiley. Grand Rapids: Eerdmans, 1990.

———. *The Resurrection of the Dead*. Translated by H. J. Stenning. Eugene, OR: Wipf & Stock, 2003.

———. *Zwei Vorträge, Theologische Existenz heute* NF 3. Munich: Chr Kaiser Verlag, 1946.

Bauer, Jill, and Ronna Gradus, dirs. *Hot Girls Wanted*. Braunfels, TX: Two to Tangle Productions, 2015.

Beck, Richard. *Unclean: Meditations on Purity, Hospitality, and Mortality*. Eugene, OR: Cascade, 2011.

Beker, J. Christiaan. *Paul the Apostle: The Triumph of God in Life and Thought*. Minneapolis: Fortress, 1980

Bell, Jamaal. "Race and Human Trafficking in the U.S.: Unclear and Undeniable." *Huffington Post*, May 10, 2010. http://www.huffingtonpost.com/jamaal-bell/race-and-human-traffickin_b_569795.

Bernstein, Elizabeth. *Brokered Subjects: Sex, Trafficking, the Politics of Freedom*. Chicago: University of Chicago Press, 2018.

Bonhoeffer, Dietrich. *Ethics*. Edited by Clifford Green, translated by Reinhard Krauss, Charles West, and Douglas Scott. Minneapolis: Fortress, 2009.

Bourdieu, Pierre. "The Forms of Capital." In *Handbook of theory and research for the sociology of education*, edited by J. Richardson, 241–58. New York: Greenwood, 1986.

Bowler, Kate. *Blessed: A History of the American Prosperity Gospel*. New York: Oxford University Press, 2013.

———. "The Legal Mind of American Christianity." In *Beyond Old and New Perspectives in Paul: Reflections on the Work of Douglas Campbell*, edited by Christ Tilling, 128–29. Eugene, OR: Cascade, 2014.

Boyle, Gregory. *Tattoos on the Heart: The Power of Boundless Compassion*. New York: Free Press, 2010.

Branson, Mark Lau, and Alan Roxburgh. *Leadership, God's Agency, & Disruptions: Confronting Modernity's Wager*. Eugene, OR: Cascade, 2021.

Brown, Alexandra R. *The Cross & Human Transformation: Paul's Apocalyptic Word in 1 Corinthians*. Minneapolis: Fortress, 1995.

Brueggemann, Walter. *Theology of the Old Testament: Testimony, Dispute, Advocacy*. Minneapolis: Fortress, 1997.

Bulgakov, Sergius. *The Bride of the Lamb*. Translated by Boris Jakim. Grand Rapids: Eerdmans, 2002.

Butler, Cheryl. "The Racial Roots of Human Trafficking." *UCLA Law Review* 62 (2015) 1466–1514.

Butler, Judith. "Can One Lead a Good Life in a Bad Life?" *Radical Philosophy* (November/December 2012) 9–18.

Caccamo, Alexandra, Rachel Kachur, and Samantha P. Williams. "Narrative Review: Sexually Transmitted Diseases and Homeless Youth—What Do We Know About Sexually Transmitted Disease Prevalence and Risk?" *Sexually Transmitted Diseases* 44:8 (August 2017) 466–76. doi: https://10.1097/OLQ.0000000000000633.

Campbell, Douglas. *Pauline Dogmatics: The Triumph of God's Love*. Grand Rapids: Eerdmans, 2020.

Carnes, Natalie. *Image and Presence: A Christological Reflection on Iconoclasm and Iconophilia*. Stanford, CA: Stanford University Press, 2018.

Carson, Marion. "The Harlot, the Beast and the Sex Trafficker: Reflections on some Recent Feminist Interpretations of Revelation 17–18." *The Expository Times* 122:5 (2011) 218–27. https://doi.org/10.1177/0014524610389287.

Casassa, K., L. Knight, and C. Mengo. "Trauma Bonding Perspectives From Service Providers and Survivors of Sex Trafficking: A Scoping Review." *Trauma, Violence & Abuse [s. l.]* (2021) 1. DOI 10.1177/1524838020985542.

Carter, J. Kameron. *Race: A Theological Account*. New York: Oxford University Press, 2008.

"Characteristics of Suspected Human Trafficking Incidents." *2008–2010, Bureau of Justice Statistics* (April 2011). http://www.bjs.gov/content/pub/pdf/cshtio810.pdf.

Choi, Soon Kyu, Bianca D. M. Wilson, Jama Shelton, and Gary Gates. *Serving Our Youth 2015: The Needs and Experiences of Lesbian, Gay, Bisexual, Transgender, and Questioning Youth Experiencing Homelessness*. Berkeley: The Williams Institute, 2015. https://williamsinstitute.law.ucla.edu/wp-content/uploads/Serving-Our-Youth-Update-Jun-2015.pdf.

Chow, Rey. *The Protestant Ethnic and the Spirit of Late Capitalism*. New York: Columbia University Press, 2002.

Clingan, Sarah E., Dennis G. Fisher, Grace L. Reynolds, Michael A. Janson, Debra A. Rannalli, Loucine Huckabay, and Hannah-Hanh D. Nguyen. "Survival Sex Trading in Los Angeles County, California, USA." *Journal of Sex Research* 57:7 (September 2020) 943–52. doi:10.1080/00224499.2019.1703885.

Clough, David. *Ethics in Crisis: Interpreting Barth's Ethics*. Burlington, VT: Ashgate, 2005.

Cochran, Jennifer Agnew. *Receptive Human Virtues: A New Reading of Jonathan Edwards's Ethics*. University Park, PA: Pennsylvania State University Press, 2011.

Cone, James. *The Cross and the Lynching Tree*. Maryknoll, NY: Orbis, 2013.

Cooper, Melinda. *Family Values: Between Neoliberalism and the New Social Conservativism*. New York: Zone, 2017.

Cooper, Thia, and Kristian Braekkan. "A Liberation Theological, Marxist Economic, and Global Feminist Analysis of the Sex in the Sex Trade." In *Contemporary Theological Approaches to Sexuality*, edited by Lisa Isherwood and Dirk Von Der Horst, 146–71. New York: Routledge, 2018.

Delay, Tad. *Against: What Does the White Evangelical Want?* Eugene, OR: Cascade, 2019.

DeSilva, David A. *Honor, Patronage, Kinship, & Purity: Unlocking New Testament Culture*. Downers Grove, IL: IVP Academic, 2000.

Douglas, Mary. *Purity and Danger: An Analysis of Concept of Pollution and Taboo*. New York: Routledge, 2002.

Drury, Amanda Hontz. *Saying Is Believing: The Necessity of Testimony in Adolescent Spiritual Development*. Downers Grove, IL: InterVarsity, 2015.

Du Mez, Kristin Kobes. *Jesus and John Wayne: How White Evangelicals Corrupted a Faith and Fractured a Nation*. New York: Liveright, 2020.

Edwards, Jonathan. *Ethical Writings: The Works of Jonathan Edwards Volume 8*. Edited by Paul Ramsey. New Haven: Yale University Press, 1989

———. *A Treatise Concerning Religious Affections: The Works of Jonathan Edwards Volume 2*. Edited by John Smith. New Haven: Yale University Press, 1959.

Ellis, Dirk. *Holy Fire Fell: A History of Worship, Revivals, and Feasts in the Church of the Nazarene*. Eugene, OR: Wipf & Stock, 2016.

Ellul, Jacques. *To Will & To Do: An Introduction to Christian Ethics. Volume I.* Translated by Jacob Marques Rollison. Eugene, OR: Cascade, 2020.

———. *To Will & To Do: An Introduction to Christian Ethics. Volume II.* Translated by Jacob Marques Rollison. Eugene, OR: Cascade, 2021.

Farley, Margaret. "Forgiveness in Service of Justice and Love." In *Changing the Questions: Explorations in Christian Ethics,* edited by Jamie Manson, 319–42. Maryknoll, NY: Orbis, 2015.

———. *Just Love: A Framework for Christian Sexual Ethics.* New York: Continuum, 2006.

Fausset, Richard, Nicholas Bogel-Burroughs, and Marie Fazio. "8 Dead in Atlanta Shootings, with Fears of Anti-Asian Bias." *New York Times,* March 26, 2021. https://www.nytimes.com/live/2021/03/17/us/shooting-atlanta-acworth.

Florence, Anna Carter. *Preaching as Testimony.* Louisville: Westminster John Knox, 2007.

Focus on the Family. "Responding to a 'Gay Christian' in the Family." https://www.focusonthefamily.com/family-qa/responding-to-a-gay-christian-in-the-family/.

Fonseca, Esperanza. "The Problem with the Phrase 'Sex Work is Work.'" *Proletarian Feminist,* September 8, 2020. https://proletarianfeminist.medium.com/?p=bdac613eb2f0.

Foucault, Michel. *Discipline and Punish: The Birth of the Prison.* Translated by Alan Sheridan. New York: Vintage, 1977.

———. *The History of Sexuality. Vol. 1: An Introduction.* Translated by Robert Hurley. New York: Vintage, 1990.

Frehse, Rob. "Sarah Lawrence Father Trafficking Case." *CNN,* April 6, 2022. https://www.cnn.com/2022/04/06/us/sarah-lawrence-college-father-trafficking-case/index.html.

Gilligan, Carol. "A Different Voice in Moral Decisions." In *From Christ to the World: Introductory Readings in Christian Ethics.* Edited by Wayne Boulton et al., 172–76. Grand Rapids: Eerdmans, 1994.

Glancy, Jennifer and Stephen Moore, "How Typical a Roman Prostitute Is Revelation's 'Great Whore'?" *Journal of Biblical Literature* 130:3 (2011) 551–69.

Graham, Ruth. "How Sex Trafficking Became a Christian Cause Celebre." *Slate,* March 5, 2015. https://slate.com/human-interest/2015/03/christians-and-sex-trafficking-how-evangelicals-made-it-a-cause-celebre.html.

Grant, Melissa. *Playing the Whore: The Work of Sex Work.* Brooklyn: Verso, 2014.

Greene, J. M., S. T. Ennett, and C. L. Ringwalt. "Prevalence and Correlates of Survival Sex Among Runaway and Homeless Youth." *American Journal of Public Health* 89 (1999) 1406–9. https://doi.org/10.2105/AJPH.89.9.1406.

Gregory of Nyssa. *On the Soul and the Resurrection.* Popular Patristic Series 12. Translated by Catharine P. Roth. Crestwood, NY: St. Vladimir's Seminary Press, 1993.

Gushee, David. *Introducing Christian Ethics: Core Convictions for Christians Today.* Canton, MI: Front Edge, 2022.

Hall, Amy Laura. *Conceiving Parenthood: American Protestantism and the Spirit of Reproduction.* Grand Rapids: Eerdmans, 2008.

Hart, David Bentley. "A Sense of Style: Beauty and the Christian Moral Life." *Journal of the Society of Christian Ethics* 39:2 (2019) 237–50.

———. *Tradition and Apocalypse: An Essay on the Future of Christian Belief*. Grand Rapids: Baker Academic, 2022.
———. *You Are Gods: On Nature and Supernature*. Notre Dame: University of Notre Dame Press, 2022.
Hauerwas, Stanley. *A Community of Character: Toward a Constructive Christian Social Ethic*. Notre Dame: Notre Dame University Press, 1981.
Hauerwas, Stanley, and Allen Verhey. "From Conduct to Character: A Guide to Sexual Adventure." *The Reformed Journal*, November 1986, 12–16.
Hays, Richard. *The Moral Vision of the New Testament: A Contemporary Introduction to New Testament Ethics*. San Francisco: HarperCollins, 1996.
Hedegaard, H., S. C. Curtin, and M. Warner. "Suicide mortality in the United States." *National Center for Health Statistics Data Brief (2018)*. Hyattsville, MD: National Center for Health Statistics, 1999–2017.
Heidegger, Martin. *Introduction to Phenomenological Research*. Translated by Daniel O. Dahlstrom. Bloomington: University of Indiana Press, 1994.
Heyrman, Christine. *Southern Cross: The Beginnings of the Bible Belt*. Chapel Hill: University of North Carolina Press, 1998.
Hovey, Craig. *Exploring Christian Ethics: An Introduction to Key Methods and Debates*. Eugene, OR: Cascade, 2018.
Hurtado, Larry. *Destroyer of the gods: Early Christian Distinctiveness in the Roman World*. Waco, TX: Baylor University Press, 2017.
Jennings, Willie James. *Acts*. Belief: A Theological Commentary on the Bible. Louisville: Westminster John Knox, 2017.
———. "Another Knowledge of God is Possible: Barth Among Post-Colonial Epistemologists." Annual Karl Barth Conference 2018. July 3, 2018.
———. *The Christian Imagination: Theology and the Origins and Race*. New Haven: Yale University Press, 2010.
Jenson, Robert W. *Systematic Theology Volume 1: The Triune God*. New York: Oxford University Press, 1997.
Johns, M. M., et al. "Transgender identity and experiences of violence victimization, substance use, suicide risk, and sexual risk behaviors among high school student—19 states and large urban school districts." *Morbidity and Mortality Weekly Report* 68:3 (2019) 65–71.
Johns, M. M., et al. "Trends in violence victimization and suicide risk by sexual identity among high school students—Youth Risk Behavior Survey, United States, 2015–2019." *Morbidity and Mortality Weekly Report* 69, Suppl-1 (2020) 19–27.
Johnson, E. Elizabeth. "Apocalyptic Family Values." *Interpretation* 56:1 (2002) 34–44. https://doi.org/10.1177/002096430005600104.
Johnson, Jessica. *Biblical Porn: Affect Labor and Pastor Mark Driscoll's Evangelical Empire*. Durham, NC: Duke University Press, 2018.
Kant, Immanuel. *Grounding of a Metaphysics of Morals*. In *Practical Philosophy: The Cambridge Edition of the Works of Immanuel Kant*, translated by Mary Gregor, 37–108. New York: Cambridge University Press, 2008.
———. *Observations on the Feeling of the Beautiful and Sublime*. Translated by John T. Goldthwait. Berkeley: University of California Press, 1960.
Kara, Siddarth. *Sex Trafficking: Inside the Business of Modern Slavery*. New York: Columbia University Press, 2009.

Kelleher, Susan. "Teen Missing After Testimony Against Pimp." *The Seattle Times,* December 20, 2010. https://www.seattletimes.com/seattle-news/teen-missing-after-testimony-against-pimp/.

Keenan, James. "Virtue Ethics and Sexual Ethics." *Louvain Studies* 30:3 (Fall 2005) 180–97. 10.2143/LS.30.3.2005019.

Kierkegaard, Søren. *Works of Love.* Translated by Howard Hong and Edna Hong. Princeton: Princeton University Press, 1995.

Klein, Linda Kay. *Pure: Inside the Evangelical Movement That Shamed a Generation of Young Women and How I Broke Free.* New York: Touchstone, 2018.

Kristof, Nicholas. "The Children of Pornhub." *New York Times,* December 4, 2020. https://www.nytimes.com/2020/12/04/opinion/sunday/pornhub-rape-trafficking.html.

Kroeker, P. Travis. *Messianic Political Theology and Diaspora Ethics: Essays in Exile.* Eugene, OR: Cascade. 2017.

Lee, Hak Joon. *Christian Ethics: A New Covenant Model.* Grand Rapids: Eerdmans, 2021.

Long, Julia. "Pornography is more than sexual fantasy. It's cultural violence." *The Washington Post,* May 27, 2016. https://www.washingtonpost.com/news/in-theory/wp/2016/05/27/pornography-is-more-than-just-sexual-fantasy-its-cultural-violence/.

Lorde, Audre. *The Master's Tools Will Never Dismantle the Master's House.* New York: Penguin Random House, 2018.

MacIntyre, Alasdair. *After Virtue: A Study in Moral Theory.* 3rd ed. Notre Dame: University of Notre Dame Press, 2007.

MacKinnon, Catharine A. "Pornography as trafficking." *Mich. J. Int'l L.* 26 (2004) 993–1011.

Mangina, Joseph. "Bearing Fruit: Conception, Children, and the Family." In *The Blackwell Companion to Christian Ethics,* edited by Stanley Hauerwas and Samuel Wells, 506–18. Malden, MA: Blackwell, 2011.

Marandiuc, Natalia. *The Goodness of Home: Human and Divine Love and the Making of the Self.* New York: Oxford University Press, 2018.

Marcus, Ezra, and James Walsh. "The Stolen Kids of Sarah Lawrence." *The Cut,* April 6, 2022. https://www.thecut.com/2022/04/larry-ray-sarah-lawrence-students.html.

Martin, Clarice J. "The *Haustafeln* (Household Codes) in African American Biblical Interpretation: 'Free Slaves' and 'Subordinate Women.'" In *Stony the Road We Trod: African American Biblical Interpretation,* edited by Cain Felder, 206–31. Minneapolis: Fortress. 1991.

McCarthy, David Matzko. "Becoming One Flesh: Marriage, Remarriage, and Sex." In *Blackwell Companion to Christian Ethics,* 2nd ed., edited by Stanley Hauerwas and Samuel Wells, 316–28. Malden, MA: Blackwell, 2011.

———. *Sex & Love in the Home: A Theology of the Household.* 2nd ed. Eugene, OR: Wipf & Stock, 2004.

Meeks, Wayne A. *The First Urban Christians: The Social World of the Apostle Paul.* New Haven: Yale University Press, 1983.

Mehlman-Orozco, Kimberly. *Hidden in Plain Sight: America's Slaves of the New Millennium.* Santa Barbara, CA: Praeger, 2017.

Merritt, Jonathan. "How Christians Turned Against Gay Conversion Therapy." *The Atlantic*, April 15, 2015. https://www.theatlantic.com/politics/archive/2015/04/how-christians-turned-against-gay-conversion-therapy/390570/.

Michael, R. T. "Sexual Capital: An Extension of Grossman's Concept of Health Capital." *Journal of Health Economics* 23 (2004) 643–52.

Milgrom, Jacob. *Leviticus 17–22: A New Translation with Introduction and Commentary. The Anchor Bible*. Edited by William F. Albright and David Freedman. New York: Doubleday, 2000.

Mitchell, Kimberly, et al. *Crimes against Children Research Center, Sex Trafficking Cases Against Minors* 1 (2013). http://www.unh.edu/ccrc/pdf/CV313_Final_Sex_Trafficking_Minors_Nov_2013_rev.pdf.

Monk-Turner, E., and H. C. Purcell. "Sexual violence in pornography: How prevalent is it?" *Gend. Issues* 17 (1999) 58–67.

Morris, Alex. "The Forsaken: A Rising Number of Homeless Gay Teens Are Being Cast Out by Religious Families." *Rolling Stone*, September 3, 2014. https://www.rollingstone.com/culture/culture-news/the-forsaken-a-rising-number-of-homeless-gay-teens-are-being-cast-out-by-religious-families-46746/.

Murdoch, Iris. *The Sovereignty of the Good*. New York: Routledge, 1970.

Noll, Mark A. *The Rise of Evangelicalism: The Age of Edwards, Whitefield, and the Wesleys*. Downers Grove, IL: InterVarsity, 2003.

Perry, Samuel L. *Addicted to Lust: Pornography in the Lives of Conservative Protestants*. New York: Oxford University Press, 2019.

Peterson-Iyer, Karen. *Reenvisioning Sexual Ethics: A Feminist Christian Account*. Washington, DC: Georgetown University Press, 2022.

Pew Research Center. "Religious Landscape Study." Washington, DC, 2014. https://www.pewforum.org/religious-landscape-study/.

Pieper, Josef. *The Four Cardinal Virtues: Prudence, Justice, Fortitude, Temperance*. Notre Dame: University of Notre Dame Press, 2010.

Plato, *Euthyphro*. (10a) *The Dialogues of Plato Volume 1: Euthyphro, Apology, Crito, Meno, Gorgias, Menexenus*. Translated by R. E. Allen. New Haven: Yale University Press, 1984.

———. *The Republic*. Translated by C. D. C. Reeve. Indianapolis: Hackett, 2004.

Polaris Project. "Human Trafficking and the Opioid Crisis." https://polarisproject.org/wp-content/uploads/2019/10/Human-Trafficking-and-the-Opioid-Crisis.pdf.

———. "Sex Trafficking and LGBTQ Youth." May 1, 2016. https://polarisproject.org/wp-content/uploads/2019/09/LGBTQ-Sex-Trafficking.pdf.

Porter, Jean. "Chastity as Virtue." *Scottish Journal of Theology* 58:3 (2005) 285–301.

Ramsey, Paul. *Basic Christian Ethics*. Louisville: Westminster John Knox, 1950.

Ratajkowski, Emily. *My Body*. New York: Metropolitan, 2022.

Roe-Sepowitz, Dominique, Kristine Hickle, Jaime Dahlstedt, and James Gallagher. "Victim or Whore: The Similarities and Differences between Victim's Experiences of Domestic Violence and Sex Trafficking." *Journal of Human Behavior in the Social Environment* 24, 883–98. 10.1080/10911359.2013.840552.

Rogers, Eugene F., Jr. *Sexuality and the Christian Body: Their Way into the Triune God*. Malden, MA: Blackwell, 1999.

Rosen, R. C. "Prevalence and Risk Factors of Sexual Dysfunction in Men and Women." *Current Psychiatry Rep*. 2:3 (June 2000) 189–95. https://pubmed.ncbi.nlm.nih.gov/11122954/#:~:text=Abstract,of%20medical%20and%20psychologic%20causes.

Rowland, Tracy C. "Revelation." *The New Interpreters Bible Commentary*. Edited by Leander Keck. Nashville: Abingdon, 2015.

Sanders, Cheryl. *Empowerment Ethics for a Liberated People: A Path to African Social Transformation*. Minneapolis: Fortress, 1995.

Schüssler Fiorenza, Elizabeth. *Bread Not Stone: The Challenge of Feminist Biblical Interpretation*. Boston: Beacon, 1984.

———. *In Memory of Her: A Feminist Theological Reconstruction of Christian Origins*. New York: Crossroads, 1983.

Shor, Eran, and Kimberly Seida. "'Harder and Harder'? Is Mainstream Pornography Becoming Increasingly Violent and Do Viewers Prefer Violent Content?" *J Sex Res*. 56:1 (January 2019) 16–28. doi: 10.1080/00224499.2018.1451476. Epub 2018 Apr 18. PMID: 29669431.

Simpson, James. *Under the Hammer: Iconoclasm in the Anglo-American Tradition*. New York: Oxford University Press. 2010.

Smith, Ted A. *Weird John Brown: Divine Violence and the Limits of Ethics*. Stanford: Stanford University Press, 2015.

Sobrino, Jon. "Touching the Idols." In *Cloud of Witnesses*, rev. ed, edited by Jim Wallis and Joyce Hollyday, 21–28. Maryknoll, NY: Orbis, 2019.

Sonderegger, Katherine. "Barth on Holy Scripture." In *The Wiley-Blackwell Companion to Karl Barth Vol. 1: Barth and Dogmatics*, edited by George Hunsinger and Keith Johnson, 71-81. Hoboken, NJ: Wiley-Blackwell, 2020.

———. *Systematic Theology Volume 1: The Doctrine of God*. Minneapolis: Fortress, 2015.

———. *Systematic Theology Volume 2: The Doctrine of the Holy Trinity: Processions and Persons*. Minneapolis: Fortress, 2020.

———. "Towards a Doctrine of Resurrection." In *Eternal God, Eternal Life: Theological Investigations into the Concept of Immortality*, edited by Philip G. Ziegler, 115–31. New York: Bloomsbury, 2014.

Soderlund, Gretchen. *Sex Trafficking, Scandal, and the Transformation of Journalism, 1885–1917*. Chicago: University of Chicago Press, 2013.

Spaulding, Henry W., II. *Untangling the Sexual Revolution: Rethinking Our Sexual Ethic*. Kansas City, MO: Beacon Hill, 1989.

Spaulding, Henry Walter, III. *The Just and Loving Gaze of God with Us: Paul's Apocalyptic, Political Theology*. 2nd ed. Eugene, OR: Cascade, 2024.

Srinivasan, Amia. *The Right to Sex: Feminism in the Twenty-First Century*. New York: Farrar, Straus and Giroux, 2021.

Taylor, Charles. "Perils of Moralism." In *Dilemmas and Connections: Selected Essays*, 347–66. Cambridge: Belknap Press of Harvard University Press, 2011.

Taylor, Keeanga-Yamahtta. *Race for Profit: How Banks and the Real Estate Industry Undermined Black Homeownership*. Chapel Hill: University of North Carolina Press, 2019

The Trevor Project. "Facts About LGBTQ Youth Suicide." December 21, 2021. https://www.thetrevorproject.org/resources/article/facts-about-lgbtq-youth-suicide/.

———. "Our Mission." https://www.thetrevorproject.org/strategic-plan/.

Thurman, Howard. *Jesus and the Disinherited*. Boston: Beacon, 1996.

Tietz, Christiane. "Standing on the Boundary, Where Now and Yet Then Touch Each Other, Barth on Theodicy and Eschatology." In *The Finality of the Gospel: Karl*

Barth and the Tasks of Eschatology, edited by Kaitlyn Dugan and Philip Ziegler, 158–79. Boston: Brill, 2022.
Tonstad, Linn Marie. *God and Difference: The Trinity, Sexuality, and the Transformation of Finitude*. New York: Routledge, 2016.
Townes, Emilie M. *Womanist Ethics and the Cultural Production of Evil*. New York: Palgrave MacMillan, 2006.
"Trafficking Victims Violence Protection Act of 2000" (TVPA). Pub. L. 106-386, Statutes at Large, 114 (2000) 1464, sec. 103, 8a.
Trocmé, André. *Jesus and the Nonviolent Revolution*. Scottdale, PA: Plough, 2003.
Trzyna, Thomas. *Pornography and Genocide: The War Against Women*. Eugene, OR: Cascade, 2019.
United Nations. *Trafficking in Persons Report*. Washington, DC: United Nations Office on Drug and Crime, 2020. https://www.unodc.org/documents/data-and-analysis/tip/2021/GLOTiP_2020_15jan_web.pdf.
U.S. Department of Justice. *Report to Congress from Attorney General John Ashcroft on U.S. Government Efforts to Combat Trafficking in Persons in Fiscal Year 2003*. Washington, DC: U.S. Department of Justice, 2004.
U.S. Department of State. "The Link Between Prostitution and Sex Trafficking." By Bureau of Public Affairs. Nov. 24, 2004. https://2001-2009.state.gov/r/pa/ei/rls/38790.htm.
U.S. State Department. "The Intersection of Human Trafficking and Addiction 2017–2021." Office to Monitor and Combat Trafficking in Persons. https://2017-2021.state.gov/wp-content/uploads/2020/10/TIP_Factsheet-The-Intersection-of-Human-Trafficking-and-Addiction-1-508.pdf.
Valenti, Jessica. *The Purity Myth: How America's Obsession with Virginity is Hurting Young Women*. Berkeley: Seal, 2010.
Vitale, Alex S. *The End of Policing*. New York: Verso, 2018.
Walls, N. Eugene, and Stephanie Bell. "Correlates of Engaging in Survival Sex among Homeless Youth and Young Adults." *The Journal of Sex Research* 48:5 (2011) 423–36. DOI: 10.1080/00224499.2010.501916.
Ward, Kate. "Human and Alienating Work: What Sex Worker Advocates Can Teach Catholic Social Thought." *Journal of the Society of Christian Ethics* 41:2 (Fall/Winter 2021) 261–78.
———. *Wealth, Virtue, and Moral Luck: Christian Ethics in an Age of Inequality*. Washington, DC: Georgetown University Press, 2021.
Waters, Brent. *Common Callings and Ordinary Virtues: Christian Ethics for Everyday Life*. Grand Rapids: Baker Academic, 2022.
Webster, John. *Barth's Earlier Theology*. New York: T. & T. Clark, 2005
———. *Barth's Ethics of Reconciliation*. New York: Cambridge University Press, 1995.
———. *Holy Scripture: A Dogmatic Sketch*. New York: Cambridge University Press, 2003.
Whyte, James, IV. "Sexual Assertiveness in Low-Income African American Women: Unwanted Sex, Survival, and HIV Risk." *Journal of Community Health Nursing* 23:4 (2006) 235–44. DOI: 10.1207/s15327655jchn2304_4.
Williams, Rowan. "Beyond Goodness: Gilead and the Discovery of the Connections of Grace." In *Balm in Gilead: A Theological Dialogue with Marilynne Robinson*, edited by Timothy Larsen and Keith Johnson. Downers Grove, IL: InterVarsity, 2019.

———. "The Body's Grace." In *Our Selves, Our Souls & Our Bodies: Sexuality and the Household of God*, edited by Charles Hefling, 58–68. Boston: Cowley, 1996.

———. *Lost Icons: Lectures on Cultural Bereavement*. New York: Morehouse, 2000.

Winright, Tobias, and E. Ann Jeschke. "Combat and Confession: Just War and Moral Injury." In *Can War Be Just in the 21st Century? Ethicists Engage the Tradition*, edited by Tobias Winright and Laurie Johnston, 169–87. Maryknoll, NY: Orbis, 2015.

Wittgenstein, Ludwig. *Philosophical Investigations*. 3rd ed. Translated by G. E. M. Anscombe. Malden, MA: Blackwell, 2001.

Ziegler, Philip. "Ethics and the Catastrophe of Grace—Faith's Obedience in the Ruins of Religion." In *Karl Barth's Epistle to the Romans: Retrospect and Prospect*, edited by Christophe Chalamet, Andreas Dettwiler, and Sarah Stewart-Kroeker, 335–48. Berlin: De Gruyter, 2022.

Zimmerman, Yvonne. *Other Dreams of Freedom: Religion, Sex, and Human Trafficking*. New York: Oxford University Press, 2013.

Name/Subject Index

ableism, 157.
agency, 26–29, 75–77.
Acts of the Apostles, 10–12.
Adkins, Amey Victoria, 34–37.
Austin, J.L., 119.

Balthasar, Hans Urs von, 97–98.
Barth, Karl, 87–102, 104–14.
    command ethics, 104–9.
    covenant, 90–93.
    general resurrection, 99–102.
    Jonathan Edwards and, 112–14.
    on identity, 183–84.
    reconciliation, 87–96.
    resurrection of Jesus, 98–99.
    Römerbrief, 109–12.
    testimony, 115–18.
Bernstein, Elizabeth, 20, 30–31.
Boyle, Gregory, 77.
Bulgakov, Sergius, 218.
Bush, George W., 29–30.

Carnes, Natalie, 3–4, 83–87.
children, 195–99.
code ethics, 52–56, 81.
covenant, 129–32.
    promise making, 160–65.
criminal, 31–34.

defaming, 10–13.
disgust, 40.
divorce, 194.

eschatology and ethics, 211–18.
Eve (biblical character), 34–37.

Fallen Woman, The, 34–37.
Farley, Margret, 9, 25–27, 70–71, 80, 137, 139–40, 142, 160, 192–93, 197–98.
feminism, 75–77.
forgiveness, 217–18.
Foucault, Michel, 35.

grace, 81–120, 124–28, 150–53.
Gregory of Nyssa, 214–16.

Hart, David Bentley, 211–14, 216–17.
Haustafeln, 179–83.
home, 199–201.
horcrux, 146.
Hovey, Craig, 160.
humility, 144–47.
    sacredness and, 146–47.

iconoclasm, 2–3, 83–87.
    of fidelity, 84–85.
    of temptation, 85–86.
image(s), 9, 31–40, 57.
indicative, 81–83.

Jennings, Willie James, 10–12, 88–89.
Jenson, Robert W., 186.
justice, 137–39.
    mercy and, 139.

Kant, Immanuel, 26–29, 216.

LGBTQ+, 205–8.
love, 139–42.
    fidelity and, 141–42.

marriage, 190-95.
Mary (biblical character), 34-37.
men and women, 183-90.
moral injury, 24, 70-72.
    trauma bonding, 24-26.
moral luck, 72-74.

Nazarene, Church of the, 122-23.

Peterson-Iyer, Karen, 9, 75-78, 140-41, 146-47, 158, 162, 170.
pleasure, 155, 158.
pornography, 170-77.
    OnlyFans, 173-75.
purity, 8-10, 34-46.
    evangelical purity industrial complex, 46-52.
    testimonies from purity culture, 63-66.
procreation, 157-58, 198-99.

racism, 202-5.
Ratajkowski, Emily, 156.

sexual capital, 13-14.
sexual disfunction, see ableism.
sex work, 166-70.
singleness, 150-52.
Smith, Ted, 81-83, 104.
social capital, 69-70.
social exclusion, 56-57.
solidarity, 77-78.

Sonderegger, Katherine, 186-88.
Spaulding II, Henry W., ix.
Srinivasan, Amia, 148, 163-64, 167-68, 174.
survival sex, 23.

Taken (movie), 4.
testimony, 12, 118-24.
    of covenant, 129-32.
    of grace, 124-28.
    of iconoclasm, 128-29.
    virtue and, 132-33.
Tonstad, Linn, 184-88.
trafficking, 4-8, 19-40.
    definition(s), 20.
    testimonies of survivors, 60-63.
    Trafficking Victims Protection Act, 20.
truthfulness, 142-44, 159.

Valenti, Jessica, 166.
virtue ethics, 112-15, 132-37.
    Jonathan Edwards and Karl Barth on, 112-14.
    and sexual ethics, 133-37.

white slavery, 21.
Whore of Babylon, 37-38.
Wittgenstein, Ludwig, 19.

Zimmerman, Yvonne, 20, 30-31.

www.ingramcontent.com/pod-product-compliance
Lightning Source LLC
Chambersburg PA
CBHW020406230426
43664CB00009B/1208